D1329531

Labor and Capital in the Age of Globalization

Labor and Capital in the Age of Globalization

The Labor Process and the Changing Nature of Work in the Global Economy

EDITED BY
BERCH BERBEROGLU

ROWMAN & LITTLEFIELD PUBLISHERS, INC.
Lanham • Boulder • New York • Oxford

HD
8072.5
.L27
2002

ROWMAN & LITTLEFIELD PUBLISHERS, INC.

Published in the United States of America
by Rowman & Littlefield Publishers, Inc.
4720 Boston Way, Lanham, Maryland 20706
www.rowmanlittlefield.com

12 Hid's Copse Road, Cumnor Hill, Oxford OX2 9JJ, England

Copyright © 2002 by Berch Berberoglu

All rights reserved. No part of this publication may be reproduced, stored
in a retrieval system, or transmitted in any form or by any means, electronic,
mechanical, photocopying, recording, or otherwise, without the prior permission
of the publisher.

British Library Cataloguing in Publication Information Available

Library of Congress Cataloging-in-Publication Data

Labor and capital in the age of globalization : the labor process and the changing nature
of work in the global economy / Berch Berberoglu, [editor].
    p. cm.
  Includes bibliographical references (p.) and index.
  ISBN 0-7425-1660-1 (cloth : alk. paper) — ISBN 0-7425-1661-X (pbk. : alk. paper)
    1. Labor—United States. 2. Labor movement—United States. 3. Working class—United
States. 4. Capitalism—United States. 5. Globalization—Economic aspects—United States.
6. Social conflict—United States. 7. Marxian economics. I. Berberoglu, Berch.

HD8072.5 .L27 2002
331'.0973—dc21

                                          2001045717

Printed in the United States of America

♾™ The paper used in this publication meets the minimum requirements of
American National Standard for Information Sciences—Permanence of Paper
for Printed Library Materials, ANSI/NISO Z39.48-1992.

Contents

Preface

As we enter the twenty-first century, the continued deterioration of life under capitalism in the United States and around the world is posing a challenge to the working class everywhere to forge ahead with a program of action to fulfill the interests and aspirations of workers throughout the world.

The development of capitalism and the capitalist labor process during the twentieth century has resulted in control over labor to assure its continued exploitation and production of ever-higher levels of surplus value, which constitutes the very basis of the accumulation of capital under the capitalist system. This process of control and exploitation of labor had developed and matured during the nineteenth century in line with the growth and development of capitalism in Europe and the United States from its competitive to monopoly stages in all major sectors of industry across the domestic and later the world economy. In this expansive process, the state has come to play a central role to protect and advance the interests of capital against labor in the intense class struggle that has been maturing over the course of the past century. As the globalization of capital accelerates, and its internal logic and contradictions become apparent, the situation is bound to facilitate the further organization and radicalization of labor, while the state becomes less and less able to deal with (let alone "resolve") the contradictions generated by the globalization process.

An examination of the nature and dynamics of the labor process in various sectors of the U.S. and world economy—from auto to steel to agriculture to services—would provide us with the necessary insight to an understanding of the nature of work under capitalism and relations between labor and capital at the point of production. Such relations, which are at base a manifestation of larger, capitalist relations of production (i.e., class relations), become evident in their social form as workers confront capital and capitalist management who extract from them an ever-growing sum of surplus value or profits. It is in this context of the struggle between labor and capital at the point of production that we begin to see the class nature of this struggle—a struggle that in its broader *class* context becomes a *political* struggle involving the state, hence a struggle for state power. The balance of forces in this class struggle beyond point-of-production work relations translates into a struggle for preservation or transformation of the capitalist system itself.

It is for a clear understanding of the labor process and control of labor under advanced capitalist production—a process that explains the structure of work relations within the context of broader class relations at the global level—that this project was conceived and carried out with the collective participation of the contributors to this book. The detailed analyses of the changing nature of work in late-twentieth-century U.S. and world economy is the product of the intellectual work of a dedicated group of progressive academics and activists who, deeply concerned with the condition of labor and its prospects, have expended much time and effort to expose the inner logic of global capitalist production. They hope that an understanding of the underlying contradictions of advanced, global capitalism can be used by those who side with labor to effect change toward the ultimate transformation of capitalist society into a social order based on the power and dynamism of labor throughout the world.

I would like to thank, first and foremost, all the contributors to this book: Jerry Lembcke, David Gartman, Harland Prechel, Marina Adler, John Leggett, Robert Parker, Behzad Yaghmaian, Julia Fox, Cyrus Bina, Chuck Davis, Walda Katz-Fishman, Jerome Scott, and Ife Modupe. Over the years friends and colleagues at the University of Nevada, Reno, and other universities across the United States and the world have made an important contribution to discussions on the labor process, the nature of work, and the relationship among labor, capital, and the state in the global economy. I thank all of them for their crucial role in shaping the ideas that went into the structure and organization of this book.

This book was originally published in the early 1990s under the title *The Labor Process and Control of Labor: The Changing Nature of Work Relations in the Late Twentieth Century*. This special, revised, updated, and expanded edition, under the title *Labor and Capital in the Age of Globalization: The Labor Process and the Changing Nature of Work in the Global Economy*, includes the latest available data and analysis in the light of recent developments in each of the major areas covered in the book. Chapters 3, 4, 6, 8, and 9 have been thoroughly revised and updated with the most recent data. An earlier chapter on the computer industry by Navid Mohseni has been dropped, and a new chapter on globalization and the state by Behzad Yaghmaian is added as a reprint from *Science & Society,* where it first appeared. I thank David Laibman, editor of the journal, for giving permission to reprint the article in this book.

Many of the arguments presented in the various chapters have been reformulated to address the relationship among labor, capital, and the state in a global context. While the ideas presented in these pages remain substantially the same, the changing nature of the global political economy at century's end has brought up new questions and concerns that are addressed here in a fresh, new way.

All in all, the ten chapters that constitute this book offer probing and provocative analyses on the labor process, the nature of work, and the relationship among labor, capital, and the state in the age of global capitalism.

Introduction

The Political Economy of the Labor Process in the Age of Globalization

Berch Berberoglu

As we enter the twenty-first century, the maturing contradictions of late capitalism—which have developed with great speed throughout the twentieth century—are surfacing in a variety of forms and are calling into question the process of capital accumulation that has facilitated the control and exploitation of labor in the United States and other countries for decades.

Although recent developments in the world economy have their roots in earlier decades when the consolidation of U.S. power began to take hold on a world scale, the transformation of the labor process through automation and high technology on the one hand, and the internationalization of capital and the restructuring of the international division of labor on the other, has effected changes in the nature of work at the point of production—changes that are a manifestation of broader social relations of production between labor and capital. In the struggle between the two contending classes that characterize the nature of the production process in capitalist society, the control and exploitation of labor are the dual motive forces of capital accumulation that assure its continued growth and expansion. While the logic of capitalist development during the twentieth century has led to the growth of transnational monopolies and thus effected transformations in the labor force structure, the labor process, and the nature of work at the point of production in various productive settings, the central characteristic of capital during this period has been the further intensification of control and exploitation of labor throughout the world.

Under capitalism, the intensification of the exploitative process at the point of production has meant the continuation of the struggle between labor and capital during its development, but the specific nature and forms of control of labor have varied from one industry or economic sector to

1

another, as well as across national, regional, and international boundaries. Thus, the labor process and forms of labor control have historical and spatial dimensions. While, therefore, an analysis of the historical development of basic industries, such as auto and steel, reveals the methods and tools of control used by management during capitalist development over the past century, an analysis of the labor process today as it develops in the context of the world economy shows us the varied forms of labor control and exploitation of labor on a world scale. In this sense, the internationalization of capital and its social component—the internationalization of capitalist relations of production, involving the exploitation of wage labor throughout the world—has ushered in a process of control, exploitation, and repression of labor across national boundaries that are now global in nature. The labor process under late capitalism must thus be seen within the context of its global dimensions, but it still manifests itself in determinate national settings. Thus, although the development of capitalism through its competitive and monopoly stages results in its expansion from the national to the global level, its contradictions at the higher, late-monopoly stage unfolding on a world scale affect the process of control and exploitation of labor in its own home base in a contradictory way: Expansion abroad translates into contraction at home and, thus, changes in the nature and structure of the labor force; the forms of control; and the nature, rate, and intensity of exploitation in different sectors of the economy.

As the class struggle between labor and capital develops and matures, and as the working class becomes increasingly class conscious and acts on behalf of its own class interests, the central imperative of transformation of the capitalist system demands a careful study of the nature, mechanisms, and processes of control and exploitation of labor in specific industries, sectors, and segments of the economy and the workforce.

The ten chapters in this book address these questions in varied historical, sectoral, spatial, and topical contexts, examining many of the issues central to the labor process, the changing nature of work, and the relationship between labor and capital in the U.S. and global economy in the late twentieth and early twenty-first century.

The opening chapter by Jerry Lembcke examines a number of critical issues that confront labor in the United States. Providing a critical review of U.S. labor studies over the past few decades, Lembcke argues that although the volume of work on the labor process mounted during this period, its effect on the U.S. working class was minimal, as the inability of labor studies to inform the strategy of a revitalized working-class movement was an outcome of the theoretical and methodological choices made by labor process scholars. To the fragmentation currently characteristic of dominant approaches in labor studies, Lembcke's chapter counterposes an alternative analysis based on class as a relational phenomenon—a new, class-capacities approach to labor studies that captures the nature and role of labor in the class structure, an approach that is better able to explain the recent resurgence of the labor movement in the United States. Adopting such an approach, Lembcke opts for an analysis that understands class capacities as having inter- as well as intraclass dimensions, recognizes the historical and spatial dimensions of class power, and comprehends the dialectical relationship between production relations, union organization, and class consciousness.

Addressing the tough questions around which post–World War II labor politics revolved, Lembcke then examines some key issues that have confronted workers in the United States in recent years: plant closings; declining union membership; lower living standards; automation and deskilling; level of class consciousness and political organization; and the role of the family, unions, and other mediating forces in the formation and transformation of labor and the labor process. Lembcke's essay thus sets the stage for more detailed class-based analyses of the nature, dynamics, and contradiction of the labor process in different historical, spatial, and organizational settings in late-twentieth-century global capitalist production.

In chapter 2, David Gartman takes up a study of labor and the labor process in the U.S. auto industry, which at the turn of the century set the stage for mass production of goods that gave a boost to capitalist expansion reaching far beyond the auto industry. Gartman examines the historical origins of a fundamental aspect of the mass-production process—the minute division of labor. Tracing its origins in the all-important U.S. auto industry, he finds that this was not a neutral technique used by capital merely to increase the efficiency of labor. Rather, the fragmentary division of labor introduced by Henry Ford and other capitalists in the mass production of automobiles was part of a larger political agenda of capital to shift the control of the labor process away from skilled craft workers and toward managers.

The early craft process of producing automobiles, Gartman explains, left a great deal of discretion in the hands of skilled assemblers and machinists, who used it to struggle against their own exploitation. This powerful resistance prevented managers from increasing the intensity of labor sufficiently to mass-produce cars. To overcome this class resistance, the management divided the unitary crafts of auto production into a plethora of unskilled fragments. This minute division of labor not only made jobs easier to fill, hence reducing the power of workers in the labor market, but it also reduced the power of workers in the production process by giving managers greater control over the quantity and quality of labor.

The class struggle, however, was not eliminated in the auto industry by this transformation of the labor process, Gartman argues. Although the division of labor and subsequent changes, like the moving assembly line, undermined the individual power of craft workers, they, ironically, increased the collective power of the new industrial labor force. With this new power, auto workers were able to force their employers to recognize their union and bargain collectively. The strength of employers, however, soon confined bargaining to the narrow issues of wages and benefits, leaving the basic structure of the labor process untouched.

Recently, Gartman points out, renewed class struggles and international competition have forced the automobile industry to reassess the benefits of the fragmented division of labor; they have instituted new programs of job enlargement and worker participation that give workers more responsibility in the labor process. A close examination of these programs, however, reveals them to constitute no fundamental threat to the balance of power held by capital on the industrial battlefield. They are but modest attempts to win greater identification of workers with the firm and greater managerial flexibility in the use of labor. In reality, Gartman concludes, these are merely revised tactics to achieve the long-term capitalist objective of greater control over labor and the labor process in the U.S. auto industry.

Shifting the discussion to another level of the labor process and authority structure on the shop floor, Harland Prechel in his chapter on control over the labor process in the U.S. steel industry demonstrates how the application of neo-Fordist control centralizes authority, reduces the decision-making autonomy of lower and middle managers, and makes it possible to eliminate several layers of management. This change in the corporate structure was top management's response to contradictions and inefficiency within the Fordist mode of control that emerged as a crisis of capital accumulation in the early 1980s. Prechel points out that these changes were implemented through the imposition of formal rational controls over various spheres of the labor process. If managers fail to follow the rules governing the manufacturing process, these interrelated controls simultaneously identify the location of the subsequent cost variation and the manager or production worker responsible for that cost.

Prechel argues that the emergence of neo-Fordism has important implications for the distribution of authority. In addition to extending more precise control over production workers, neo-Fordism demands that lower and middle level managers base their decisions on criteria established in decision centers, redefines the responsibilities of lower- and middle-level managers, and reduces their decision-making autonomy. In contrast to Taylorist and Fordist modes of control, which require extensive managerial hierarchies and the allocation of decision-making authority to lower and middle managers, neo-Fordism reduces managerial hierarchies and simultaneously establishes formal controls to ensure that managers adhere to standardized decision-making criteria. The application of formally rational neo-Fordist controls increases mechanization, standardization, and centralization of authority.

Prechel shows that neo-Fordist controls have placed lower and middle managers in the steel industry at a greater distance from the decision-making centers, while providing the organizational capacity to increase surveillance over them. He argues that one-sided corporate strategies based on work teams, cooperative decision making, and participation on the shop floor masks the basic relations of domination and subordination that prevail when centralized controls are implemented. Rather than allocating authority, neo-Fordist controls centralize authority, which reduces autonomy while increasing responsibility and accountability of both traditional production workers and lower and middle management.

Marina Adler's chapter on gender and the labor process explores the position of women in the workplace. She points out that although working women make up nearly 50 percent of the U.S. workforce, they continue to be in a disadvantaged position compared with working men. Both occupational segregation and the traditional gender division of labor are perpetuated by the organization of work in modern capitalism.

One consequence of the interaction of capitalist and patriarchal structures, Adler argues, is the fact that working women are less likely than working men to have control over their labor. Moreover, in addition to the inequalities arising from the labor process, gender and race divide workers into different jobs and activities. This selection process ranks "gendered" tasks by their importance, resources, and remuneration. Because "women's work" has been historically undervalued, working women retain less control over their work environment than working men.

Adler points out that research on gender, occupational segregation, and power reveals a persistent income and authority gap by gender, which stems from the class and occupational structure of society: Women are overrepresented in occupations with lower average incomes than men's. Overall, Adler concludes, although both working men and women have relatively little control over the labor process—in terms of organizational decision making, supervisory activities, and autonomy—working women have significantly less control at work than working men.

Race, nationality, and the division of labor in U.S. agriculture is the topic of chapter 5. Here John Leggett focuses on farm workers in California's San Joaquin, Imperial, and Coachella valleys. Providing an intimate history of the diverse national origins of the workforce in California agriculture from earlier periods to the present, Leggett examines the division of labor in commercial farming in great detail and describes the multilayered relationship between the growers, the farm labor contractors, the crew chiefs, and the farm workers in the fields.

Given the race and national dimensions of farm labor in U.S. agriculture, historically and today, Leggett insists that one cannot comprehend the division of labor, the labor process, and the superexploitation and control of a segment of the working class in today's corporate agriculture, under conditions of globalization, without a clear understanding of the structural underpinnings of racial and national domination that have persisted in California agriculture ever since the expansion of white settlements, which began in the early nineteenth century. Although the racial and national origins of successive generations of local and immigrant labor have changed over the decades, Leggett concludes, the cruel forms of labor control practiced by a small number of wealthy white growers through their intermediaries on the land have been a constant feature of the lives of farm workers who labor under conditions of modern-day servitude that characterizes the division of labor in U.S. agriculture—a sector that is becoming increasingly important in affecting the production and distribution of food in the global economy.

Another issue concerning the changes taking place in the nature of work in the global economy is the problem of part-time work. In the chapter that follows, Robert Parker discusses changes surrounding the employment of contingent workers in the U.S. economy. He discusses the various types of contingent work in the labor force and points out that increasing numbers of workers are becoming a part of the contingent workforce in the United States, which is part of the process of the globalization of capital and the changes in the labor force structure on a world scale. The shift in production from the advanced capitalist centers to the Third World is related to the explosion of part-time, contingent work in the imperial centers. And this is creating a major problem for the structure of the labor force in the United States and other advanced capitalist countries.

In documenting the growth and spread of contingent employment, Parker stresses that the official government statistics that track the number of contingent workers has been modified over the past decade in ways that understate the true number of contingent workers. The key development in this area has been the creation of three separate definitions of contingent work—all of which rely on a narrow, restrictive conception of contingent work. As Parker notes, underemployment is the defining characteristic that these workers share; it is this central characteristic that makes them contingent, and a distinctive part of the U.S. labor force.

In the last section of the chapter, Parker analyzes several trends that may slow down, or even reverse the move toward the conversion of large segments of the workforce to contingent status. Among these factors are the numerous legal and administrative problems that U.S. corporations have been encountering in their drive to convert their workforce into contingent labor. In some cases, as Microsoft has discovered, the fees and taxes involved in violating federal regulations that cover workers such as "independent contractors" can be substantial. But Parker also emphasizes that worker resistance, in many forms, is causing employers to rethink their labor relations strategies. More and more corporate executives, he argues, appear to understand that worker absenteeism, tardiness, sabotage, and strikes are a high cost to pay for the luxury of employing contingent workers.

Next, Behzad Yaghmaian focuses on the role of the state in the global political economy. He argues that the world economy is undergoing a process of restructuring, and that fundamental transformations are taking place in both the structure of the capitalist system and its institutional/regulatory counterparts. Yaghmaian goes on to point out that the underlying causes of some of the institutional changes, and their interrelations with the structural transformations in the world economy, can be revealed by synthesizing the theory of the internationalization of capital and the basic framework of regulation theory. The continuing internationalization of accumulation, he notes, has led to the gradual ascendance of neoliberalism—the regulatory mechanism for global accumulation.

Yaghmaian contends that institutional arrangements and apparatus conducive to the needs of the emerging hegemonic regime of accumulation and its regulation are being developed, and will lead to the formation of a nascent supranational state. However, the debate over whether this state will represent the collective will of the capitalist class across national boundaries and advance the interests of global capital as a whole, or be an extension of the rule of the dominant capitalist class of one or another of the major capitalist powers over the world economy through the traditional nation-state, will continue to rage in the coming years. In this light, Yaghmaian's chapter forces us to confront this issue head-on and sets the stage for another round of discussion and debate on this important question that highlights the crucial relationship between capital and the state in the global political economy.

The internationalization of production and the employment of a low-wage labor force that increases corporate flexibility and profits in the global economy are examined next by Julia Fox. In her chapter on the new international division of labor, Fox attempts to address the strategic question of why Third World working women have been recruited and integrated into the global capital accumulation process. She develops a theoretical framework, that incorporates both the international division of labor as an outgrowth of the exigencies of capital accumulation on a world scale, and a more concrete analysis of work relations at the point of production on a national level. Within this framework, Fox focuses on the labor process in three countries (South Korea, the Philippines, and Mexico) to analyze how the specific conditions of a labor-intensive investment strategy—export processing—require the use of the cheapest and most controlled segments of labor, and hence, at the national level, how four major conditions (patriarchy, bureaucratic control of work, repressive labor policies, and low instances of unionization of women) combine to produce the cheapest and most repressed forms of labor—Third World working women.

Fox argues that although the mediation of the political, cultural, social, and organizational dimensions of control make Third World working women one of the most exploited segments of the international labor pool, the internal contradictions of this exploitation have created the conditions for more militant forms of resistance in which Filipino, South Korean, and Mexican working women are becoming an integral part of the global working-class struggle against transnational capital.

Addressing the political implications of the transnationalization of capital and the emerging global labor process, Cyrus Bina and Chuck Davis raise the level of discussion to the political level in chapter 9. They examine the position and prospects of the international labor movement in response to the globalization of the production process and the proliferation of capitalist relations of production on a world scale.

Bina and Davis show that the transcendence of capitalist social relations beyond the boundaries of nation-states leads to the emergence of the global labor process and contradictions that are historically unique to the present stage of capitalism. They point out that the transnational character of today's production is the product of two simultaneous transformations: (1) the evolution of the labor process in advanced capitalist countries and (2) the spread of capitalist social relations into the less-developed countries at the various stages of economic development. Bina and Davis argue that it is due to these transformations that the current stage of globalization takes on a historical significance.

Bina and Davis further argue that the technological advancements, which have taken several decades to develop in the industrialized countries, have quickly found their way into the remaining part of the global economy during the last three decades. Today, these global technologies lead to fast-paced universal skill redundancy and skill formation (i.e., skills that are invoked by the machine) on the part of the working class everywhere. Bina and Davis conclude that today, given the rising complexity of technology and rising exploitation of the working class globally, the prospects for international working-class solidarity and cooperation are more promising than ever before.

In the final chapter, Walda Katz-Fishman, Jerome Scott, and Ife Modupe focus on the relationship among the changing role of labor in capitalist production, the crisis of capitalism, and the political response of the working class to increased control and exploitation of labor. They argue that a major change in the labor force structure of the United States has taken place during the past several decades, such that traditional machine-based factory production, which constituted the basis of U.S. manufacturing industry for more than a century, is giving way to computer-automated mass production. This development, coupled with the internationalization of U.S. capital since World War II in search of cheap labor, and a more favorable investment climate overseas, has effected a shift toward low-paid service occupations and has led to increased unemployment among a growing segment of the working class—a situation that has become a permanent fixture of contemporary

U.S. capitalism. The resulting decline in purchasing power and the standard of living of workers, who are now consuming less and less of the goods produced in a shrinking market, has plunged the U.S. economy into a structural crisis that has ushered in a period of decline and decay, pushing the country to the edge of depression.

Responding to this deteriorating economic situation, U.S. labor has begun to mobilize and take action to reverse the defeat it has suffered under an increased capitalist assault during this period. Documenting this response, Katz-Fishman, Scott, and Modupe survey the various forms of class struggle waged by workers at the point of production and beyond the shop floor, which are manifested in strikes, demonstrations, and other forms of protest and political action.

Together, the ten chapters of this book make an important contribution to the study of labor, the labor process, and the nature of work in late-twentieth-century global capitalism—processes that are a product of the relationship between labor, capital, and the state on a world scale.

1

Labor and Capital at the Dawn of the Twenty-First Century

Jerry Lembcke

The amount of academic work on labor history and the labor process during the last three decades of the twentieth century was impressive. Less impressive, however, was its impact on the crisis of the labor movement, which deepened during this period. Only in the latter half of the 1990s did labor show signs of resurgence.

In the pages that follow I argue that, although much of the study done on labor between 1970 and 1990 was carried out by radical historians and political economists, their work was based on assumptions consistent with those of neoclassical economics and pluralist sociology that dominated the field during the 1950s and 1960s. It is the failure to break with these assumptions, moreover, that impaired scholars' ability to find a path out of the labor movement's morass.

In this context, I highlight a new trend begun during the late 1980s that holds promise for future studies. Of particular importance is the theoretical work focusing on class capacities, and some recent work that explores the relationships between the temporal and spatial dimensions of working-class formation.

SOCIAL HISTORY AND DEGRADATION OF WORK

In 1970, the editors of *Radical America* heralded the emergence of a new school of historiography.[1] The new trend was characterized by its separation from mainstream "celebrationist" accounts of U.S. history and by its critical posture toward the history of "old left" political practice.

Many of the new radical historians had been or were students of William Appleman Williams at the University of Wisconsin, but it was the British historian E. P. Thompson who had the greatest influence on their development. Thompson's emphasis on the subjective aspects of human history encouraged the framing of historical questions in terms of "shared experiences."[2] The new generation of radical scholars was captivated by the notion that history could be studied as occurring within a cultural context as well as a process that created the symbolic world.

The radicals also challenged the mainstream approach of the time: institutionalism. Institutionalism had arisen early in the twentieth century, when the theories of neoclassical economics, rooted as they were in psychological assumptions about human behavior, appeared to be inadequate to deal with the task of understanding monopoly capitalism. Thorstein Veblen and John R. Commons were among those who accorded increased importance to institutions as determinants of political and economic behavior. Commons and his student Selig Perlman took the institutionalist approach into the field of labor history and, until the 1970s, it was the dominant paradigm.[3]

The radicals attacked institutionalism at two levels. The first was the preoccupation of the institutionalists with trade unions as the sole vehicle through which working-class history unfolded and could thus be studied. The followers of Perlman had narrowed the field to the point where the only relationships being studied were the contractual ones, and the only subjects in their accounts were union functionaries, company negotiators, and government arbitrators.[4] The new left scholars rejected these traditional formulations and endeavored to restore workers to a class-conscious part in their own history.

At another level, the attack on institutionalism became a euphemism for criticism of practices identified with certain political tendencies. It was argued that institutions (unions, political parties, and so on) *per se* were prone to conservatism[5] and that the political movements, such as the Communist Party, which had emphasized the building of unions and party organizations in their work, had retarded the development of the U.S. working class.[6] In their work, the anti-institutionalists emphasized the place of mass movement, general strikes, spontaneous worker rebellions, and the anarcho-syndicalist traditions in the U.S. working-class experience.[7]

The ability of the social history trend to speak meaningfully to the deepening crisis of the U.S. labor movement of the 1970s was thus limited in several ways. First, its approach compelled questions relevant to the specific historical period when U.S. working-class culture was shaped by the influx of large numbers of immigrants and the heyday periods of anarcho-syndicalist movements, such as the International Workers of the World (IWW). Second, it had an additive notion of class power based on the "association" of sovereign individuals in the production process. This notion elevated the role of craft and skilled workers in history, and dovetailed with the assumptions of the "degradation of labor" school of political economy.[8] Third, its disdain for certain political traditions sometimes led to contemptuous treatment of important organizations and to sectarian interpretations of critical turning points in U.S. labor history. Moreover, by equating working-class capacity with control of production, the trend toward deskilling, which accompanied the development of monopoly capitalism in the twentieth century, was difficult for social historians to deal with dialectically; the fact that masses of lesser skilled, industrial workers, not the craft and skilled workers, had been at the forefront of the battles of the 1930s was difficult to interpret. All of these traits made it difficult for radical historians to examine effectively the period most relevant to the needs of contemporary labor activists: the period of the CIO, 1935–1956.

In other words, the shift away from an institutional analysis also shifted attention away from the historical period when institutions were clearly the focus of labor history, and it refocused our attention on time periods leading up to the formation of unions and/or the very early years of organized labor—the late nineteenth and early twentieth centuries. Embedded in the *method* of anti-institutionalism, then, was the political consequence that its adherents were able to avoid confronting head-on the anticommunism of the postwar labor establishment and the anticommunist bias of academic labor historians. In that respect, the new social labor history provided an ideological escape hatch for academics. As the 1980s proceeded and the crisis of the labor movement deepened, labor historians retreated further and further into the nineteenth and eighteenth centuries, endlessly producing case studies having less and less to do with the pressing issues facing the labor movement today.

The shift in focus produced by the anti-institutionalist trend had two other consequences. One was that it elevated the importance of craft and skilled workers, versus twentieth-century industrial workers, as agents of social change under capitalism. Another was that the prominence given to craft and skilled workers by the social historians carried with it implications for our analyses of the objective capacities to make social change. The latter question, about the relative capacity of skilled versus less-skilled workers to make change, was at the center of studies of the labor process done following the publication of Harry Braverman's *Labor and Monopoly Capital.*

Braverman has been credited with reviving the Marxist tradition of labor studies, and establishing the relationship between class relations and the development of technology.[9] His followers produced copious studies attempting to specify the relationships between technological change and job displacement, the labor market, skill level, and world system integration. The empiricism spawned by this "decomposed" research agenda rivals that of the social history trend, whereas its influence on the real world of labor strategy and tactics is equally hard to find.[10]

Contrary to claims that Braverman restored Marxist premises to the study of labor, the deskilling school, like the social history trend, continued within, rather than broke with, the fundamental premises of its predecessors. Braverman wrote at about the same time as the early social historians, when the dominant paradigm in the sociology of labor, based on neoclassical assumptions, was best represented by the work of Seymour Martin Lipset and his associates.[11] In accordance with the methodological empiricism dominant at the time, Lipset et al. defined their variables in ways that were neatly operationalized and quantifiable—occupational characteristics, such as income, skill level, and status, were associated with the voting habits of union members. Workers in lower-status skill and income levels were found to be less democratic in behavior. In this manner, Lipset et al. isolated work-related studies from larger historical and political economic contexts, and reduced the unit of analysis to the level of individuals and individual job characteristics.[12]

Most important, Lipset et al. inverted the relationship Marx identified between development and working-class capacity.[13] For Lipset et al., workers with the least skill were the least capable of what they considered socially efficacious behavior. These findings, of course, supported their hypothesis that only the middle class was capable of democracy, and they conformed to the prevailing Cold War ideology that the proletariat was prone to totalitarianism.

Despite the heavy polemics of radical academics against liberal sociology, much of the radical scholarship of the 1960s and 1970s retained the fundamental premises of liberal pluralism. The unit of analysis continued to be the individual or, as for Braverman, the properties of individual job positions. Working-class power, in these studies, was equated with aggregated individual sovereignty, albeit sovereignty in the workplace rather than in a political process. These studies were characterized by a strongly normative bias holding proletarianization or deskilling to be "bad," and attempts at resisting proletarianization to be virtuous. Finally, these studies located the cutting edge of history at the interface between monopoly and competitive forms of production, and elevated the central importance of the labor aristocracy in the historical process. In sociology, the result has been a virtual preoccupation with the "middle class."

There is no gainsaying the fact that the voluminous empirical contributions of historians and political economists working within the respective schools of social history and degradation of work have advanced the field of labor studies enormously. What is also true is that the paradigmatic flaws they inherited from their predecessors were not corrected for, with the result that they continue to impair the field.

A summary of the problems as they currently manifest themselves in the study of labor is, first, that the working class has been more or less written off the agenda. Work done under the rubric of class analysis has largely been concerned with questions of class boundaries and class identities, and for this purpose, the middle class has been of much greater interest than the working class.[14] State-centered theory has similarly displaced workers from its accounts of the New Deal policy in favor of an autonomous stratum of state managers.[15] Finally, there is a neoinstitutionalist stream that avoids the atomism of neoclassical analyses but only by downgrading the role of human agency.[16]

Second, there is in recent work a postmodernist tendency toward "fragmentation, indeterminacy, and intense distrust of all universal or 'totalizing' discourses."[17] Ira Katznelson and Al Zolberg, for example, conclude their edited volume of European and American working-class studies with the observation that the classical Marxist notion of *a* working class under capitalism is mistaken; each national working class has to be understood on its own terms.[18] The class analysis trend, on the other hand, tends to overly dichotomize class capacities and class consciousness, and uses survey research and voting behavior to infer meaning about class properties from the response of individuals.[19] Also, work degradation studies tend to compartmentalize institutionally the economic aspects of the labor deskilling process from the social institutions through which that process is refracted.[20]

Third, the relationship between the working-class formation and the long-term process of capitalist development is inadequately understood. As I have argued above, the dominant literature holds that the long-term consequence of capitalist development is the erosion of working-class capacity and that the cumulative effect of the class struggle is the progressive *dis*empowerment of the working class. Each successive period of class struggle results in working-class defeat, and each period of history begins with the working class buried deeper in the ruins of the past. The problem in this regard is the basically functionalist bent to the literature that radical scholars of the 1970s and 1980s did not address.[21]

Finally, there are anti-working-class and anticommunist biases running through the field of labor studies. The former has been nearly constant since Lipset et al.'s studies in the 1950s. More recent literature treats workers sympathetically, but its bias causes it to misinterpret important data.[22] Lillian Rubin, for example, sees working-class reluctance to pursue higher education as evidence of victimization, whereas I think it could be read as evidence of class solidarity in the culture.[23] The anticommunist prejudice of work done during the 1950s and 1960s was never challenged by "New Left" scholars. C. Wright Mills added fuel to the fire when he wrote that "communists' rule within unions they control is dictatorial,"[24] and Stanley Aronowitz, whose work was probably the most influential for a new generation of labor activists, reinforced that bias.[25]

NEW BEGINNINGS FOR THE STUDY
OF LABOR AND THE LABOR PROCESS

The task of retheorizing the agenda of our work remains to be done. Retheorizing means, first, getting the problem out of the atomizing neoclassical discourse common to the social history and work degradation paradigms that undergird much of the recent work in labor studies. It means focusing on *class*, rather than individual workers, as the unit of analysis, and it means we try to understand the contradictory, rather than the normative, implications of the proletarianization process. Retheorizing also means getting clear about what it is that needs to be understood, and that, it seems to me, is class capacities.[26]

Retheorizing in Labor Studies

During the late 1980s, a new trend in labor studies emerged that restored the centrality of the working class in labor struggles and portrayed working-class culture in an affirmative way. This new trend does not shy away from the tough ideological questions around which post–World War II labor politics revolved. Its dialectical approach explores the relationships between social consciousness and social organization, understands class capacities as an inter- as well as intraclass phenomenon, and recognizes the historical and spatial dimensions of class power.[27]

We find these characteristics in several recent studies of labor. Rick Fantasia, for example, using studies of recent strike activity, shows that working-class capacity was *not* destroyed by deskilling, bureaucratization, co-optation, and cultural diversification.[28] Howard Kimeldorf begins his work with the observation that the U.S. working class evinces both class-conscious militancy and business union conservatism, and he uses historical-comparative methods to study under what conditions each of those arises and is reproduced.[29] My own recent study combined case histories of CIO unions with organizational analysis to show that proletarianization enhanced working-class capacity but that the unevenness of that process produced a divided working class.[30]

All three of these studies depart from mainstream approaches by the way they treat working-class culture. Within the pluralist tradition, working-class culture is defined by the *absence* of certain personality traits and values.[31] Lacking these personal attributes, pluralist argue, workers have a low level of political efficacy, the result being low working-class capacity.[32] Because the assumptions of pluralist theory are widely accepted, there have not been many attempts to cast working-class traits and values positively as the basis of a collective culture. Those that do, however, make a case for an affirmative concept of working-class culture that is based on collectivity.[33]

The positive treatment of working-class culture in these recent studies is related to the fresh approach they take to the history of Communists in the U.S. labor movement. The power base of Communists within CIO unions was the mass of unskilled workers brought into the union movement by the organizing efforts of Communists themselves. Pluralist sociology during the McCarthyite climate of the 1950s denigrated Communists and constructed the fiction of an authoritarian working-class personality to explain the link between workers, their Communist leaders (a link that was real), and fascism (a link that was not real).

The political culture of the New Left during the 1960s and 1970s was sufficiently ambivalent about Communists in the labor movement that the pluralist interpretation was either reproduced or avoided altogether. Nonconformity with the Cold War code could, in fact, be risky business for academics. When Roger Keeran broke out of that mold and wrote the first scholarly account of the purge of Communists from the United Auto Workers,[34] he lost his job at Cornell. With the exception of Harvey Levenstein, who wrote from an academic position in Canada, there were no other major attempts to challenge the Cold War mythologies until the mid-1980s.[35] By then, Zeitlin and Kimeldorf were able to pull together papers from authors who, in the words of labor historian, Robert Zieger, who commented on the collection, "appear untroubled by association intellectually with a Popular Front world view."[36] Why the Cold War mold for labor studies may have begun to thaw in the midst of the Reagan decade is not clear, but that volume coincided with a renewal of interest in the CIO period.[37]

Dialectical, theoretical, and methodological approaches to labor studies began to emerge during this period with Erik Olin Wright's distinction between relational and gradational definitions of class, and Claus Offe and Helmut Wiesenthal's demonstration that class capacities are class-specific.[38] Goran Therborn has further specified the notion of class capacities by distinguishing between *petty bourgeois* sources of power and *working-class* sources of power: for the petty bourgeoisie, the source of power is the autonomy in the labor process; for the working class, the source of power is its collectivity.[39] Therborn also distinguishes between the *intrinsic capacity* that classes have—the respective power resources available to them—and the *hegemonic capacity* of classes—their ability to deploy their intrinsic capacity against opposing classes. The essence of hegemonic capacity rests on the ability of one class to intervene in the process by which the opposite class generates its own intrinsic capacity. Moreover, Therborn points out, class power is not a zero-sum game, and the power of one class is not necessarily the weakness of its opposite. Rather, the process that increases capitalist class power through capital accumulation simultaneously and contradictorily collectivizes the working class and, thus, empowers it, not in material ways, but in social ways.

The key insight here is that capitalist class success depends on its ability to maintain the accumulation process (and thus continue to generate *its* intrinsic capacity) while blocking the contradictory effects of accumulation by mitigating the collectivization of the working class—that is, to exercise hegemonic capacity.[40] There is an important *spatial* dimension to that process that I think provides one of the missing keys to a fuller understanding of U.S. working-class capacity and labor's current situation. Therborn argues that "the extent to which the public practices of the working class are coextensive with the territorial range of the supreme political power which the class must confront" is a key determinant of which class will hold sway at any historical moment.[41] In other words, there is a sense in which the history of class relations under capitalism can be understood as a series of flanking actions, with the capitalist class first attempting to expand its geographical options and then attempting to block working-class efforts to keep pace.

The class-capacities approach makes a significant methodological break with the dominant approaches to labor studies, because it asks questions at the level of class, *qua* class. It does not reduce analysis of class relations to the level of individuals, and thus, it provides a basis for the criticism of survey research methods in class analysis.[42] It also places labor studies in a time-space matrix that creates possibilities for more dialectical analyses of the labor movement.

TEMPORAL AND SPATIAL DIMENSIONS OF CLASS CAPACITIES

Our attention to the temporal dimension of class capacities has been called by several recent studies. Some authors have noted the tenacity of a working-class culture of collectivity,[43] whereas others suggest that it is even an intergenerational phenomenon.[44]

There are, of course, many impediments to the intergenerational transmission of collective culture,[45] but recent studies also tell us that family and unions play an important role in reproducing working-class culture across generations. The social psychological literature on family and political socialization provides confirmation that, not only are opinions, attitudes, and values on matters such as party identification and social mobility passed from one generation to another,[46] but that, at a deeper level, "what is really transmitted from parents to children is basic personality orientations, some of which . . . have important political consequences."[47]

Unions also play an important role in the transmission of working-class culture. Studying the West Coast longshoremen's community, William Pilcher found, "It is the union and its peculiarly democratic nature that is responsible for the maintenance of the essential features of the longshore subculture. . . . The union serves as the center and focus of the community, welding the longshoremen together into a social group and furnishing them with a very real community of interest. . . . Children are often brought into the hiring hall" where the battles and exploits of the heroic "34 men" are recounted "almost every day."[48]

Family: The Mediator of Workplace Deskilling

The connections between intergenerational transmission of culture and class capacities are made most clearly in the literature that examines the intersections of workplace and family life. In his reexamination of the Braverman skill-degradation thesis, Harold Benenson found that the gender specificity of the industrial changes taking place during this period made the working-class family central to the way the changes played out.[49] The "importance of the family economies," he points out, "is that they encompass in microcosm the skill range of their respective industries. Workplace issues affecting one occupational group had direct bearing on the welfare of family members employed in other job categories. Industrial conflicts, refracted through the family, mobilized working-class communities *en bloc*."[50] In point of fact, the vertical distance between unionized, skilled, male workers and nonunion, unskilled, and female workers in the garment, shoe, and mining industries was often bridged by father–daughter family bonds. In industries like meat packing, the grievances of young, female workers, "commanded support among the better-organized, skilled male butchers" when the workplace relations were mediated by family ties. In addition, there appeared to have been a transmission of values and organizing skills from one generation to another. Newcomers to the world of industrial work—often daughters of male craft or skilled workers—"learned about organizing from their fathers who already belonged to craft unions and mutual aid societies."[51]

There is also a spatial logic to the formation of class capacities that needs to be taken into account. As David Harvey argues, economic development is always regionally specific.[52] Economic periods, and periods when certain kinds of technology and skill levels are dominant, are also regional periods. Thus, using the skill-degradation example, we would expect to find that lower-skilled industrial labor developed not only at a later time than craft-oriented production, but that it also came on line in a different geographic region. Thus, the generation entering the emergent, mass-production, economic sector was typically physically apart from the generation steeped in the experience of an earlier era of economic development. In these instances, the "daughters" (from Benenson's study) employed in the new plants would either have relocated from their family residence, in which case the mediating role of the family would be greatly diminished, or, as was often the case, the new workforce would be immigrant workers whose "inherited beliefs" would be consistent with the preindustrial work experience of their families.[53]

An expanded presentation of the relationship between labor-capital migration and collective culture would allow several important correlative points to be developed. One of those involves the distinction between *social* mobility (i.e., the movement of individuals from one class or social strata to another through change of occupation, income, or education) and *geographic* mobility. When family ties keep upwardly mobile professionals in touch with their working-class roots, they retain a greater commitment to the needs and values of that class. In such cases, academically acquired skills of, say, a lawyer or teacher can in fact enhance the capacity of the working-class community. If upward social mobility occurs simultaneously with geographic mobility, on the other hand, the intergenerational ties may be broken. Also, simultaneity is probably more the rule than the exception. It is the opening of new sectors of the economy that creates new occupational strata, thus enabling individuals to change social location in significant numbers, and the opening of new economic sectors typically occurs through the expansion of economic space, which means that *social* mobility presumes spatial relocation.[54]

The skill-degradation argument, in other words, does identify important aspects of class capacity—deskilling *does* diminish the autonomy of individual workers—and the aggregated result of many deskilled workers would seem to be diminished working-class capacity. If we view the U.S. working-class experience in its most comprehensive dimensions, however, we can see that class capacity has not been diminished by skill degradation, *per se.* Rather, skill degradation created the possibility for capital to own and control, in absentia, through its managers. Being able to control in absentia, employers were, and are, able to move assets while maintaining a relatively stable existence for themselves, as a class.[55] Workers, meanwhile, are pulled hither and yon by the increasing rapidity of capital's mobility, and their capacity to produce, much less *re*produce, a collective culture increasingly diminished in the later stages of capitalist development. It was the control of space, in other words, that was as important as the control of skill.

Is there any inherent advantage to one class or another in being geographically mobile? David Montgomery argues that nineteenth-century craftsmen were "honor bound" to walk out of a shop if the traditional rules of employment were broken; indeed early twentieth-century industrial workers resisted harsh employers by quitting and seeking work in another factory.[56] On the other hand, Barry Bluestone and Bennett Harrison, as well as Richard Peet, have argued that *capital's* mobility in the mid- to late-twentieth-century destroyed unions and weakened working-class communities, thereby diminishing working-class power.[57] In fact, both of these arguments may be viewed as correct. Prior to the era of finance capital (roughly the turn of the twentieth century), capital was largely locally owned and insufficiently concentrated to afford the cost of strategical relocations. Moreover, the separation between ownership and management functions was not yet fully realized, so that if capital moved, capital*ists* would also have had to move. Monopolization and the advent of finance capitalism altered these conditions. Absentee ownership and management through a newly created stratum of professional managers and engineers shifted the cost/benefit ratio of geographical mobility to capital.

Unions: The Mediators of Spatial Fragmentation

Just as the effects of deskilling were refracted through the family, the effects of spatial particularization were refracted through union organizations. The craft unions, most of which were affiliated with the American Federation of Labor (AFL), adopted a protectionist posture toward the new developments and resolutely refused to organize the unskilled immigrant workers or to adapt their forms of organizations to one that followed industrial lines. Moreover, because the AFL was formed in the late nineteenth century when industry was still heavily concentrated in the eastern states, most of its members were located in the East and, as a result, the balance of power within the AFL was skewed toward the eastern states.

In *Capitalist Development and Class Capacities*, I showed that craft unions emerged from the nineteenth century with organizational forms based on business union principles. One of those principles was that control of financial resources for organizing purposes was based on a pecuniary logic— those locals and regions that paid the most had the most say in how and where organizing activities were conducted. Given that the nature of pecuniary organizational forms translated size into power *vis-à-vis* other class segments, it was a historical impossibility for more progressive forms to take root and supplant the pecuniary forms within the same industrial and geographic space. Space unoccupied by previous organizational forms had to be created by the class struggle, and working-class advances could not proceed until that occurred.

In the 1930s, the Congress of Industrial Organizations (CIO) was born out of the AFL craft unions. It represented not so much a destruction of the past as a negation of a sectoral and regionally specific level of organization for one that was more inclusive in both respects. The CIO thus constituted a kind of historical elbow joint between the accumulated capacity of the U.S. working class and the potential that lay in a different sectoral and geographic space.

The potential capacity of the unorganized sector lay, first, in the large number of workers there. Second, the more proletarianized conditions of workers in the industrial sector encouraged collective action. Brought into the union movement, these workers stimulated a kind of unionism that went beyond the workplace and spoke to the needs of the working class in broader *class* terms. The CIO unions took up issues of national politics, foreign policy, civil rights, environmental control, and the welfare of the unemployed. They also brought more collectivist cultural forms, such as theater and group singing, into union institutions. Theoretically speaking, these more collectivist orientations were expressions of a key contradiction within advanced capitalism: namely, that with proletarianization, individualism would break down, workers would begin to think and act as a class, and in so doing lay the groundwork for a Socialist movement. They represented, in other words, a transition from individualized struggle aimed at preserving individual autonomy to collective struggle aimed at class control of economic and social life.

Organizational form was the mechanism linking the *accumulated* capacity of the working class (the AFL unions) and the *potential* for increasing the class's capacity. It was only through organization that the unevenness created by the development process, which capital could endlessly manipulate to its advantage (by fostering competition between fractions of the working class and geographic regions), could be offset or counterbalanced by the unions. The key, in other words, was to mobilize the sectors of the working-class movement that were regionally, sectorally, and politically *over*developed in such a way that those sectors underdeveloped at the time could advance, slingshot fashion, beyond the presently more advanced sectors. This is, in effect, what happened during the growth years of the CIO.

Finally, the link between temporal and spatial dimensions of class formation is made by Stephen Thernstrom, who argues that the *length of time* a group of workers reside *in a particular place* is an essential variable in the formation of class solidarity.[58] This makes immanent sense because, not only does the group have to share a common experience, but the process of reflection through which the group comes to a certain consciousness about its commonalities takes time. Collective identity, in other words, emerges out of a social process that occurs across time. Culture, collective or otherwise, however, is something more than experience. It includes the symbols (language) and an interpretive framework by which the group knows and understands that experience; it is the combination of the "inherited belief" component and the experience itself. The notion of inheritance, moreover, presumes the presence of more than one generation in the process by which a class becomes conscious of itself.

A CLASS-CAPACITY PERSPECTIVE ON LABOR TODAY

The bridge to full working-class consciousness has seldom been crossed, in part, because, by moving, capital has been able to destroy repeatedly working-class community and thereby disrupt the process of long-term, intergenerational class formation. This is the context in which labor's current situation needs to be understood.

The period of expansion that began with World War II ended in about 1970. At that point, corporate managers in basic industry "found themselves confronting an unprecedented profit squeeze" and, in response, they created "an unprecedented wave of total plant shutdowns."[59] The class logic of this sequence is made clear by Richard Peet, who constructed an index of class struggle and ranked all states by this index.[60] He found that capital moved from states and regions that ranked high on the index to locations that ranked low. Similarly, David Jaffee found that "the level of unionization was the best predictor of capital flight, such that in the 1970s corporations tended to move to states without powerful trade unions."[61]

The deindustrialization decade amounted to "a class war on workers"[62] and a war against the communities "where the great worker organizing drives of the 1930s and 1940s were most successful and which also retained their industrial structures virtually intact until recently."[63] It was an exercise of capitalist hegemonic capacity that brought to a close a period of working-class formation that began with the radical working-class movements of the 1930s and continued for about forty years.

The social conflict of the Great Depression formed a political generation with a radical culture and a set of institutions with the potential to transmit that culture to the next generation (e.g., the industrial unions of the CIO, political organization like the Communist Party, and community social centers). The economic stability afforded by unions meant that families were stable, and community institutions, like schools, churches, and social services, made it desirable and feasible for the children of that formative generation to stay in the community. In regions like the Pacific Northwest, where working-class radicalism was widespread among woodworkers and longshoremen during the 1930s, the continuity experienced between the generation of the 1930s and their sons and daughters who still lived in the community was readily apparent well into the 1970s.

The intergenerational links had already begun to weaken, however, from the combined effects of antilabor legislation during the post–World War II years and the Cold War purges of labor leaders, who had broad visions of unionism, that narrowed the scope of union activity in the United States to bargaining for wages, hours, and working conditions. It is the havoc wrought by capital flight and plant closings, however, that all but eliminated the settings in which collective culture might be passed from one generation to another. The union halls that provided the "tribal fires" around which "grizzled warriors" recounted "tales of their exploits"[64] are boarded up, and the voices of the elders are silent. Workers who have stayed in declining regions have generally been pushed to the margins of the economy, whereas those who have moved have broken ties with one or more generations of their families.[65] With some exceptions, children growing up in working-class families have little more exposure to the culture and traditions of their own class's experience than children of other families.

CONCLUSION

The crisis in the U.S. economy and society has changed since the days of massive plant closings and capital flight from the industrial Northeast in the early 1980s. Yet the economic devastation left behind by those years is evident in the boarded-up store fronts and vacant lots that dot the urban landscape. The disparity between rich and poor has reached gaping proportions as a small number of young venture capitalists make billions while millions of wage earners are left with jobs that provide no security or benefits. Adequate health care is but a dream for 40 million Americans, as is the prospect of a public school education that offers any real hope for their children.

During the 1990s, the labor movement began to stir again. Among the hopeful signs was the new leadership of John Sweeney that initiated an aggressive campaign to recruit a cadre of young organizers through programs like Union Summer and the AFL-CIO Organizing Institute. Unlike twenty years ago, when many radical academics and their students were saying "farewell to the working class" and talking about the "false promise" of unions, there is today a new alliance of labor leaders and academics called the Scholars, Artists, and Writers for Social Justice which has attempted with some success to bring progressive intellectuals into a working relationship with organized labor. College students today seek out opportunities to work with local labor organizations and have in fact taken the lead in efforts to combat sweatshop conditions in the garment industry.

It is unclear whether the small trend toward a more class-based approach to labor studies begun in the late 1980s has had an impact on the changes in the labor movement. What I think is evident is that those changes confirm the continuing centrality of the working class to the strategies for social change and validate a class analysis. An analysis that understands class capacity as a relational phenomena with intraclass and interclass dimensions, that is historical, that has spatial dimensions, and that comprehends the dialectical relationship between social relations and class consciousness is what is needed if academic labor studies is going to be relevant for labor leaders and activists working to revitalize the working-class movement.

NOTES

1. Editors of Radical America, "New Left Historians of the 1960s," *Radical America* (November 1970).

2. E. P. Thompson, *The Making of the English Working Class* (New York: Pantheon Books, 1963).

3. John R. Commons et al., *History of the Labor Movement in the United States* (New York: Macmillan, 1918); Selig Perlman, *A Theory of the Labor Movement* (New York: Macmillan, 1928).

4. Philip Taft, "Attempts to 'Radicalize' the Labor Movement," *Industrial and Labor Relations Review* 1 (July 1948), 580–92; Walter Galenson, "Why the American Labor Movement Is Not Socialist," Reprint No. 168, Institute of Industrial Relations (Berkeley: University of California, 1961).

5. Frances Fox Piven and Richard Cloward, *Poor People's Movements* (New York: Pantheon, 1977).

6. Stanley Aronowitz, *False Promises: The Shaping of American Working Class Consciousness* (New York: McGraw-Hill, 1973).

7. Jeremy Brecher, *Strike!* (Greenwich: Fawcet, 1972).

8. Harry Braverman, *Labor and Monopoly Capital: The Degradation of Work in the Twentieth Century* (New York: Monthly Review Press, 1974).

9. Braverman, *Labor and Monopoly Capital.*

10. David Hakken, "Studying New Technology after Braverman: An Anthropological Review," *Anthropology of Work Newsletter* 1, no. 1 (1988).

11. Seymour Martin Lipset, Martin Trow, and James Coleman, *Union Democracy* (New York: Anchor, 1956).

12. Lipset, Trow, and Coleman, *Union Democracy.*

13. For Marx, the problem was not whether technology deskilled, but rather (and how) the capitalist development process empowered the working class. He argues that this process was a contradictory one: As capitalist development occurred, working-class empowerment increased.

14. See Erik Olin Wright, *Classes* (London: Verso, 1985).

15. See Theda Skocpol and K. Finegold, "State Capacity and Economic Intervention in the Early New Deal," *Political Science Quarterly* 97 (1982). A notable exception to the dominance of state-centered theory is Rhonda Levine's attempt to "bring class back in" through a study of labor and the New Deal. See Rhonda Levine, *Class Struggle and the New Deal: Industrial Labor, Industrial Capital, and the State* (Lawrence, Kans.: University Press of Kansas, 1988).

16. Larry J. Griffin, M. Wallace, and B. Rubin, "Capitalist Resistance to the Organization of Labor before the New Deal: Why? How? Success?" *American Sociological Review* 51 (April 1986).

17. David Harvey, *The Condition of Postmodernity: An Inquiry into the Origins of Cultural Change* (Cambridge: Basil Blackwell, 1989), 9. Harvey also describes this tendency as a rejection of "meta-narrative" in favor of what Thomas Eagleton calls "laid-back pluralism." I will generally us the term *pluralism* to describe this tendency, but *reductionism, particularism,* and *structuralism* would also apply. In other words, the tendency I am describing refers both to analyses that resort to psychology-based explanations for sociological phenomena (e.g., pluralist explanations derived from neoclassical assumptions) and to analyses that separate dimensions of social reality that can be fully understood only through their relation to each (i.e., structurally or dialectically). What I call a dialectical approach may be called a "synthetic" approach by others. See Michael Kazin, "Struggling with the Class Struggle: Marxism and the Search for a Synthesis of U.S. Labor History," *Labor History* 28 (Fall 1987).

18. Ira Katznelson and Al Zolberg, eds., *Working-class Formation: Nineteenth-Century Patterns in Western Europe and the United States* (Princeton, N.J.: Princeton University Press, 1986).

19. Wright, *Classes.*

20. The exchange between Harold Benenson, "The Reorganization of U.S. Manufacturing Industry and Workers' Experience, 1880–1920: A Review of 'Bureaucracy and the Labor Process' by Dan Clawson," *The Insurgent Sociologist* 11, no. 3 (1982) and Dan Clawson, "Reply to Benenson," *The Insurgent Sociologist* 11, no. 3 (1982) on this point should be consulted.

21. Mike Davis, "Why the U.S. Working Class Is Different." *New Left Review* 123 (September–October 1980) is probably the best example of this reasoning. M. Gottdiener, *The Social Production of Urban Space* (Austin: University of Texas Press, 1987) and Michael Storper and R. Walker, *The Capitalist Imperative: Territory, Technology, and Industrial Growth* (New York: Basil Blackwell, 1989) are critical of political economic urban studies—for example, William Tabb and Larry Sawers, *Marxism and the Metropolis: New Perspectives in Urban Political Economy* (New York: Oxford University Press, 1984), for its functionalist quality, and John Willoughby, "Is Global Capitalism in Crisis? A Critique of Postwar Crisis Theories." *Rethinking Marxism* 2, no. 2 (1989) raises the same issue about the social structure of accumulation school—for example, David Gordon, R. Edwards, and M. Reich, *Segmented Work, Divided Workers* (Cambridge: Cambridge University Press, 1982).

22. Richard Sennett and J. Cobb, *The Hidden Injuries of Class* (New York: Knopf, 1972).

23. Lillian Rubin, *Worlds of Pain: Life in the Working Class Family* (New York: Basic Books, 1976).

24. C. Wright Mills, *The New Men of Power* (New York: Harcourt, Brace, 1948), 199–200.

25. Aronowitz, *False Promises*, 13–14.

26. Jerry Lembcke, *Capitalist Development and Class Capacities: Marxist Theory and Union Organization* (Westport, Conn.: Greenwood Press, 1988).

27. In this context, capitalist class power is based on its accumulation of capital, whereas working-class power is based on the association of workers. See Claus Offe and Helmut Wiesenthal, "Two Logics of Collective Action: Theoretical Notes on Social Class and Organizational Form" in *Political Power and Social Theory*, vol. 1, ed. Maurice Zeitlin, (Greenwich, Conn.: JAI Press, 1980), 67–115. *Capacity* is used here to mean the capability of the working class to act in its own interests (which is to say, against the interests of the capitalist class) in a way that transforms the basic social relations of capitalism. It refers, in other words, to the means available to the working class to liberate itself from its subordination to the capitalist class.

28. Rick Fantasia, *Culture of Solidarity: Consciousness, Action, and Contemporary American Workers* (Berkeley: University of California Press, 1988).

29. Howard Kimeldorf, *Reds or Rackets? The Making of Radical and Contemporary American Workers* (Berkeley: University of California Press, 1988).

30. Lembcke, *Capitalist Development and Class Capacities*.

31. Lipset et al., *Union Democracy*; Bernard Rosen, "The Achievement Syndrome: A Psychocultural Dimension of Social Stratification." *American Sociological Review* 21, no. 2 (1956), 208.

32. Stanley Renshon, *Psychological Needs and Political Behavior: A Theory of Personality and Political Efficacy* (New York: The Free Press, 1974).

33. See Fantasia, *Cultures of Solidarity;* Kimeldorf, *Reds or Rackets?;* Lembcke, *Capitalist Development and Class Capacities;* Richard Oestreicher, "Urban Working

Class Political Behavior and Theories of American Electoral Politics, 1870–1940," *Journal of American History* 74, no. 4 (1988); Joe Trotter, *Black Milwaukee* (Urbana: University of Illinois Press, 1985).

34. Roger Keeran, *The Communist Party and the Auto Workers' Unions* (Bloomington, Ind.: Indiana University Press, 1980).

35. Harvey Levenstein, *Communism, Anticommunism, and the CIO* (Westport, Conn.: Greenwood Press, 1981).

36. Maurice Zeitlin and H. Kimeldorf, eds., *Political Power and Social Theory* (Greenwich, Conn.: JAI Press, 1984); Robert Zieger, "The Popular Front Rides Again" in *Political Power and Social Theory*, ed. Zeitlin and Kimeldorf, 298.

37. Still, work that pointedly challenges anticommunist interpretations of the CIO period has been slow in coming. In addition to the work already cited and chapters in Zeitlin and Kimeldorf by James Prickett, Frank Emspak, and Ronald Filippelli, there is Jerry Lembcke and W. Tattam, *One Union in Wood: A Political History of the International Woodworkers of America* (New York: International Publishers, 1984); Kimeldorf, *Reds or Rackets*; and Judith Stepan-Norris and Maurice Zeitlin, "Why Gets the Bird? Or, How the Communists Won Power and Trust in America's Unions: The Relative Autonomy of Intraclass Political Struggles," *American Sociological Review* 54 (August 1989).

38. Erik Olin Wright, *Class Structure and Income Determination* (London: Verso, 1979); Claus Offe and Helmut Wiesenthal, "Two Logics of Collective Action," in *Political Power and Social Theory*, eds. Zeitlan and Kimeldorf.

39. Goran Therborn, "Why Some Classes Are More Successful than Others." *New Left Review* 128 (March–April 1983).

40. One way of doing that is for the capitalist class to *displace* collectivizing forms of organization that are intrinsic or indigenous to the working class with organizational forms that are intrinsic to the capitalist class. For example, if the capitalist class can foist on workers the notion that labor union reliance on larger treasuries and high-paid legal experts is more effective than rank-and-file mobilization, the capitalist class will essentially be able to place the class struggle on terms most favorable to it.

41. Therborn, "Why Some Classes Are More Successful than Others," 41.

42. Fantasia, *Cultures of Solidarity*, 8.

43. See David Montgomery, *Workers' Control in America* (Cambridge: Cambridge University Press, 1979); Bruce Nelson, "'Pentecost' on the Pacific: Maritime Workers and Working Class Consciousness in the 1930s" in *Political Power and Social Theory*, ed. Zeitlin and Kimeldorf; Roy Rosenzweig, *Eight Hours for What We Will: Workers and Leisure in an Industrial Community, 1870–1920* (Cambridge: Cambridge University Press, 1983).

44. Fantasia, *Cultures of Solidarity*; Kimeldorf, *Reds or Rackets?*; and David Bensman and R. Lynch, *Rusted Dreams: Hard Times in a Steel Community* (New York: McGraw-Hill, 1987).

45. Throughout the nineteenth and twentieth centuries, the capitalist class gained increasing control over many of the institutions through which working-class culture might have been conveyed. Jean Anyon, "Ideology and United States History Textbooks," *Harvard Educational Review* 49, no. 2 (1979); and Rosenzweig, *Eight Hours for What We Will*.

46. Rosen, "The Achievement Syndrome"; Renshon, *Psychological Needs and Political Behavior*.

47. Renshon, *Psychological Needs and Political Behavior,* 174.

48. William Pilcher, *The Portland Longshoremen: A Dispersed Urban Community* (New York: Holt, Rinehart and Winston, 1973), 84, 116.

49. Harold Benenson, "The Community and Family Bases of U.S. Working Class Protest, 1880–1920" in *Research in Social Movement, Conflicts and Change,* ed. Louis Kriesberg (Greenwich, Conn.: JAI Press, 1985), 112.

50. Benenson, "Community and Family Bases," 118.

51. Benenson, "Community and Family Bases," 128.

52. Harvey, *The Condition of Postmodernity: An Inquiry into the Origin of Cultural Change,* 201–13.

53. Herbert G. Gutman, *Work, Culture, and Society in Industrializing America* (New York: Random House, 1977).

54. See Michael Stroper and R. Walker, *The Capitalist Imperative: Territory, Technology, and Industrial Growth* (New York: Basil Blackwell, 1989), 10.

55. Marvin Dunn, "The Family Office as a Coordinating Mechanism within the Ruling Class" in *The Insurgent Sociologist* (Fall–Winter, 1980).

56. Montgomery, *Workers' Control in America.*

57. See Barry Bluestone and Bennett Harrison, *The Deindustrialization of America: Plant Closings, Community Abandonment and the Dismantling of Basic Industry* (New York: Basic Books, 1982); Richard Peet, ed., *International Capitalism and Industrial Restructuring* (Boston: Allen & Unwin, 1987).

58. Stephen Thernstrom, "Socialism and Social Mobility," in *Failure of Dream? Essays in the History of American Socialism,* ed. J. Laslett and S. M. Lipset (Berkeley: University of California Press, 1984).

59. Bluestone and Harrison, *Deindustrialization,* 34–35.

60. Peet, *International Capitalism,* 50–51.

61. David Jaffee, "The Political Economy of Job Loss in the United States, 1970–1980," *Social Problems* 33 (1986), cited in Carolyn Perrucci et al., *Plant Closings: International Context and Social Costs* (New York: Aldine De Gruyter, 1988), 24.

62. Bluestone and Harrison, *Deindustrialization,* 19.

63. Peet, *International Capitalism,* 51.

64. Pilcher, *The Portland Longshoremen,* 48.

65. Bluestone and Harrison, *Deindustrialization,* 99–104.

2

Labor, Capital, and the Struggle for Control at the Point of Production

David Gartman

In a few short years after Henry Ford revolutionized automobile production with the introduction of mass-production techniques at the beginning of the twentieth century, the tradition of skilled, unitary, intelligent work was dismantled and replaced by a regime of minutely divided, monotonous, mindless labor. Adam Smith, the prophet of this monumental development in industry, set the tragic tone of commentary on the division of labor for centuries to come. He recognized its detrimental effects on detail laborers: "The man whose whole life is spent in performing a few simple operations . . . has no occasion to exert his understanding. . . . He generally becomes as stupid and ignorant as it is possible for a human creature to become."[1] Yet he also saw the division of labor as the necessary foundation for the efficient production that increases the wealth of nations: "But in every improved and civilized society, this is the state into which the laboring poor, that is, the great body of the people, must necessarily fall."[2]

Recently, however, the U.S. automobile industry, which helped pioneer the system of minutely divided labor, has experienced a monumental crisis that has shaken the faith of many in the productive efficiency of this industrial mode. Highly competitive automakers across Europe and in Japan have adopted new techniques of industrial organization, like quality-control circles and autonomous work groups, that recompose previously divided tasks. U.S. manufacturers have slowly begun similar changes. What has motivated this reversal in the direction of the division of labor? Have automobile managers, long noted for their hard-nosed, driving approach to labor, suddenly changed into humanitarian do-gooders, concerned more with people than profits?

To begin to answer these questions, we must first know the original motives of the minute division of automotive labor and the conditions under which they were formulated. The current changes can be understood only in the light of the historical formation of this hitherto unquestioned cornerstone of the auto labor process. In what follows, I will concentrate on the historical roots of the division of labor in the U.S. auto industry, and then offer on this basis a few observations about the current change in this aspect of the labor process.

The process of producing commodities within a capitalist society is not a neutral one, shaped solely by technological imperatives, but an instrument of social domination, shaped by the struggle of opposing classes. The division of capitalist society into those who live by the wage and those who live by profits turns the workplace into a battleground, with capitalists seeking to extract as much surplus labor as possible from the hide of workers who, not surprisingly, resist this hiding. To overcome this worker resistance and exert absolute control over work, capitalists and their managers structure the labor process in a way that strips workers of all power. Work is deskilled and degraded so as to remove from it all discretion on the part of workers, who might use that discretion to resist exploitation.

I will seek to demonstrate in the following analysis that the fragmentation of the original automotive crafts into a plethora of minute tasks was motivated by the employers' drive to overcome the resistance of a powerful skilled labor force. Although my analysis of the labor process under capitalism follows the approach initiated by Harry Braverman,[3] it departs from his specific treatment of the division of labor. I will argue that at least in the U.S. automobile industry, the cheapening of wages was not the main motive behind the fragmentation of work. Rather, the motive was a complex combination of corporate attempts to increase labor productivity and intensity.

THE CRAFT LABOR PROCESS IN THE EARLY AUTO SHOPS

Before work fragmentation and rationalization, autos were produced in small shops dominated by skilled craft workers. The main task of the skilled mechanics was the assembly of parts—chassis, body, engine, transmission, wheels, tires—purchased from other industrial firms. Only craft workers of the highest skills could turn the heap of ill-fitting and incompatible parts into a functioning vehicle. Teams of from two to five such workers labored together at stationary positions on the shop floor to build an entire automobile from the ground up. At each assembly station was a workbench, where workers kept their standard tools and performed various necessary operations. The auto parts necessary for assembly were generally kept in a central storeroom, to which the members of the assembly team journeyed back and forth as they saw fit.

The skilled automobile mechanics largely controlled their own work in these early craft shops. Because of their knowledge and skills, the successful completion of the assembly depended entirely on them. They could not be replaced by specialized workers, for as long as the imperfect parts required fitting and adjustment, work could not be divided but had to remain unitary. Workers had necessarily to keep in mind the peculiarities of each part, and adjust subsequent parts and operations accordingly as they proceeded. The skilled and variable nature of assembly work also gave workers control over their own work pace. It was impossible for the capitalist or his foremen to dictate to workers detailed commands of what was to be done and how fast. These uncertain elements remained necessarily in the discretion of the workers. Further, strict supervision was thwarted by the legitimate absence of workers from their stations. Long and leisurely trips to the parts storeroom were used to get out from under the foreman's watchful eye and thus reduce the intensity of labor.

The integration of parts manufacture into growing auto firms did not alter the nature or control of the labor process, for the production of precision auto parts required highly skilled machinists. The machine tools available at this time for cutting metal—lathes, millers, planers, grinders—left much to be desired in the way of accuracy and precision. Only the careful guidance of highly skilled hands could coax precision parts out of the mechanisms. Further, the small volume of production of these early firms prevented the use of specialized machines, and dictated the use of universal or general-purpose machine tools. The latter could be adapted to a wide variety of auto work, but required skilled machinists to so adapt and operate them.

As in the assembly shops, the nature of work in these machine shops prevented its fragmentation and left it largely in the control of skilled workers. The variable nature of the tasks and materials left great discretion in the hands of machinists. They controlled the details of machine operation to ensure accuracy and precision. The capitalists and their managers could not dictate exact tasks and times for their completion. Further, as in assembly shops, the layout of early machine shops also made for greater worker discretion and control. Machines were generally grouped by the function they performed. If the production of an entire part was assigned to a specific worker, as it often was, he had to move about the shop from machine to machine to perform all the necessary operations. Because this gave workers a great amount of discretionary time and movement, supervision was difficult.

This control of craft workers over the labor process was not particularly problematic for capital as long as automobile production was aimed at a small luxury market. However, early in the industry's history, a few visionaries began to aspire to tap the potentially large U.S. market for cheap transportation through the volume production of simple, low-priced autos. At this point, worker control of the craft process loomed as a major obstacle in the road to the mass-produced car, for the employers found that the "human element" was often recalcitrant and refused to produce in the manner and pace required by capitalist mass production.

The resistance that auto companies aspiring to mass production encountered from skilled workers was *not,* as some have postulated, the *cultural* resistance of a group of workers with preindustrial backgrounds against the strange demands of industrial labor.[4] Those who manned the early auto shops were generally second- and third-generation industrial workers and were perfectly at home in their industrial environment. They had a well-developed sense of industrial time, were largely organized into craft unions, were highly disciplined both individually and collectively, and regarded factory production as natural. Rather, this was the *class* resistance of workers who had developed a sense of class struggle. As David Montgomery has documented in his study of industrial craftsmen of this period, these workers were engaged in a collective and deliberate struggle with their bosses, who were seeking to lower wages and intensify labor in response to the ongoing crisis of competitive capitalism.[5] Under these antagonistic relations of capitalist production, workers' control over production, its pace, and accuracy was one weapon that they used to struggle against their own exploitation. As long as they possessed this power, the mass production of autos was impaired.

Often this class struggle in the early auto shops erupted into overt, organized, conscious struggle, as when union machinists struck Oldsmobile in 1897 and again in 1901 over wages and working conditions. However, such overt struggle was the exception rather than the rule for several reasons. The most important was the smashing of the early craft unions in the auto shops. Seeing unions in general as an obstacle to renewed capital accumulation, U.S. employers launched an aggressive "open shop" campaign in the first few years of the twentieth century. As part of this national campaign, Detroit capitalists formed the Employers' Association of Detroit (EAD) with the avowed purpose of making the city a bastion for the open shop. They very nearly succeeded. Using a variety of methods—lockouts, discharging and blacklisting union workers, wage-fixing, strike-breaking—the EAD had virtually eliminated the craft unions by 1907.[6]

A second factor weakening collective, conscious struggle in the early auto shops was the tight labor market for skilled autoworkers. An extremely short supply of skilled mechanics and machinists led to competition among employers for workers and consequently high rates of labor turnover. As a result, these early autoworkers developed a spirit of individual power and independence. They moved from job to job, enticed by high wages. Also, on the shop floor, they refused to tolerate overbearing foremen pushing for production. Thus, in these early years, much discontent found expression in the individual escape of turnover rather than collective struggle.

Because of these obstacles to organized, collective struggle, early autoworkers' resistance to managerial demands was more often covert, clandestine, and only partly conscious. Because they were aware at some level that it was the owners and not themselves who reaped the main benefits from production, workers were not particularly concerned with working very intensively or sometimes very accurately, for that matter. Evidence of this clandestine struggle is found in a series of reports by a labor spy hired by the Ford Motor Company in 1906 to keep an eye on the workers in the shop. The spy reported that "many of the men neglected their work, malingered, put imperfect parts into cars, and cheated the timekeeper."[7] One trade journalist complained that, as a result of the free mobility of workers in the shops, "time is lost and it is impossible for the department heads to keep in accurate touch with the location of the men and at the same time to check the progress of the work."[8] A series of maxims labeled "Profit Chokers" that appeared in Ford's employee magazine indicated numerous ways in which skilled workers in control of their own labor could thwart capitalist attempts to intensify production. The series included the following: "Chronic strollers and time killers," "Killing time under day-work pay," "Sulkers, grunters, back-talkers, mumblers, knockers," "Employees not doing what they are told," "Antagonism to improved methods," "Employees working 'their' way instead of the 'Company's'," and "Padded pay rolls through tardiness and shirking."[9]

Automobile companies seeking to tap the potentially large market for cheap cars realized that they could ill afford to leave the control of the labor process to the discretion and skills of a class of recalcitrant workers. Within the context of the antagonistic production relations of capitalism, to leave the control of the pace and accuracy of labor in the hands of workers inevitably meant to settle for less than maximum output and accuracy. So capital began to transform the craft process to seize control of work from the workers. The foundation of this transformation of automobile work was the fragmentation of unitary, skilled crafts into a plethora of unskilled detail jobs.

STAGES IN THE DIVISION OF LABOR

The employers first attacked the skilled craft process of assembling cars. About the middle of the first decade of the twentieth century, they began to divide the actual labor of assembly from that of transporting materials by hiring a group of unskilled workers exclusively to carry parts from the stockroom to the assembly stations. By 1907, many of the larger auto companies had begun to assign specialized tasks to the members of the small assembly team. "In place of the jack-of-all-trades who formerly 'did it all,' there were now several assemblers who worked over a particular car side by side, each one responsible for a somewhat limited set of operations."[10]

This initial division of assembly work was made possible by the advent of interchangeable parts, which rendered the various assembly operations independent and invariant. However, this method was limited by the number of specialized assemblers who could crowd around one assembly station. This problem was solved by the invention of a system of rotating, specialized "assembly gangs." At Ford about 1907, for example, about fifty highly specialized gangs of workers rotated around a circle of the same number of cars, doing their fragmentary tasks on each. There were gangs specialized in frame assembly, motor mounting, wheel mounting, fender assembly, body assembly, and so on. As soon as the last gang had finished its work, the complete car was removed, and an uncompleted frame was put in its place.

A similar division of labor in the machine shops of early industry was preceded by a change in the layout of work. As soon as the volume of production reached a level at which it was feasible to devote a machine to a single task, corporate managers began to arrange machines progressively within departments specialized in a single part or product. Instead of grouping machines by the function they performed—milling, turning, boring—all those devoted to one part were grouped together and arranged in order of their work on it. Such an arrangement was known as progressive layout. Although Ransom Olds seems to have been the early leader in progressive layout, Henry Ford was not far behind. In 1906, Ford arranged his engine-machining department progressively. Each machine tool and its operator performed one, and only one, operation on the engine block, after which it was passed to the adjacent machine and its operator, who did likewise.[11]

This progressive layout of machine work was accompanied by a heightened division of labor. No longer was the worker engaged in a variety of tasks on a number of different machines. He was confined to one specific operation on one specific machine in the progressive line, and because he performed the same operation time and time again, day in and day out, there was no need for skill or discretion on his part. In fact, as the labor of machine shops became more and more divided, the remaining operations that required skill and knowledge were split off from the ordinary machine operator and concentrated into specialized occupations. Machine setters adjusted and set up machines; tool grinders sharpened and replaced cutting tools; oilers cleaned, oiled, and performed routine maintenance on machines; and repair workers repaired them.

By 1910, the skilled craft worker was becoming a rare commodity in the rapidly changing automobile factories. A survey of automobile manufacturing occupations in Cleveland revealed that only 11 percent of the work force required more than one year of training, and 44 percent required one month or less.[12] Henry Ford spoke for the entire industry when he stated that the basic principle of his shop organization was "the reduction of the necessity for thought on the part of the worker and the reduction of his movements to a minimum. He does as nearly as possible only one thing with only one movement. . . . Dividing and subdividing operations, keeping the work in motion—those are the keynotes of production."[13]

CAPITAL'S MOTIVES BEHIND THE DIVISION OF LABOR

Some of the motives for minutely dividing labor offered by automobile companies parallel those cited by classical political economists more than a century earlier. In his classic treatment, Adam Smith argued that dividing labor increases its productivity.[14] Following Smith, Karl Marx also endorsed this notion.[15] By being forced to concentrate on one task day in and day out, the detail worker develops a certain dexterity that is lacking in the versatile worker, whose switching from task to task prevents him or her from doing one job long enough to get good at it. Auto managers also recognized this advantage of increased productivity, citing it as a motive behind their push toward a greater division of labor. Henry Ford thus wrote that "it is necessary to establish something in the way of a routine and to make most motions purely repetitive—otherwise the individual will not get enough done to be able to live off his own exertions."[16] Upon examining the division of labor in the Ford shops in 1914, two engineering journalists similarly concluded: "Minute division of operations is effective in labor-cost reducing . . . by making the workman extremely skillful, so that he does his part with no needless motions. . . . Where a workman can perform absolutely similar successions of movement, he very soon gains great skill combined with great rapidity of muscular action."[17]

Recent Marxist critics of the division of labor have raised doubts about this argument endorsed by Marx himself. In *Labor and Monopoly Capital*, Harry Braverman is skeptical about whether dividing labor actually increases its productivity.[18] So is Stephen Marglin, who states that the division of labor increases labor productivity only to the extent that work skills are difficult to acquire and thus improve with experience.[19] He argues, however, that most of the tasks that early industrialists minutely divided were quickly learned and that consequently the potential increase in dexterity afforded by this division was quickly exhausted. The complex skills of automobile assembly and machine-tool operation, however, are the type that are acquired only through long experience and hence benefit from the concentration on one task allowed by the division of labor.[20] So these recent doubts would seem unfounded.

Braverman argues that the main motive behind the division of craft labor is another principle of classical political economy, which he labels the "Babbage Principle."[21] Following Charles Babbage, he holds that the minute division is introduced by capitalists mainly to lower wage rates. Dividing a craft cheapens its parts by allowing employers to hire low-wage labor to perform unskilled tasks and to use high-wage, skilled labor solely on skilled tasks. Although the Babbage Principle may have been a major factor in the division of labor of other industries, there is little evidence of the operation of this motive among automobile managers. General labor market conditions made the lowering of wage rates an impossibility. In the first decade of the century, there were great shortages of labor, skilled and unskilled, to fill the growing auto factories. These shortages empowered worker resistance and struggle, forcing auto employers seeking to attract and hold workers to pay high wages, often above those paid for similar work in other industries. As a result, despite an increasing division of labor during this period, real wages of autoworkers rose steadily.

If auto manufacturers could not use the division of labor to slash wages, they could and did use it to achieve a third economic advantage—overcoming the shortage of skilled workers. The supply of skilled workers available to the burgeoning auto industry was not large enough to meet its growing demand. Although unskilled industrial labor was also relatively scarce, it was more abundant than skilled labor. Hence, auto employers were motivated to divide skilled jobs into myriad unskilled fragments, each of which could be filled by the unskilled immigrants or farm migrants. Henry Ford thus stated, "As the necessity for production increased it became apparent not only that enough [skilled] machinists were not to be had, but also that skilled men were not necessary in production. . . . If every job in our place required skill the place would never have existed."[22] The answer to this problem, Ford continued, was the division of labor, for this "subdivision of industry opens places that can be filled by practically anyone."[23]

If the motives advanced by auto managers for the division of labor are examined closely, however, an entire set of motives qualitatively different from these simple economic arguments emerges. It is clear, especially from their more private communications in trade publications, that employers also fragmented skilled craft jobs to break the power of skilled workers and exert greater control over the labor process.

Control over Labor

Skilled craft workers exercised a great deal of power over their own work because of their knowledge and skills. Also, because of a recalcitrant shop culture of class conflict, they often thwarted attempts by their employers to produce in a manner and pace that maximized output and minimized costs. One way that managers sought to overcome this resistance of workers to greater production and profits was by eliminating their skills and power through dividing labor into unskilled fragments. Their ultimate motive was the same economic one of increasing the production and profitability of their firms. The way this end was achieved, however, was qualitatively different from simply increasing labor productivity and overcoming labor shortages, the other aims of the division of labor. The enhanced managerial control over the process of production that accompanied the division of labor increased the output and profits of mass-production automobile manufacturers solely by overcoming the resistance of workers. Hence, this motive behind the division of automotive labor was necessitated solely by the antagonistic class relations of capitalism. A different set of social relations—one that was more cooperative and less exploitative—would have rendered this control motive unnecessary and superfluous.

The use of the division of labor to overcome shortages of skilled labor was actually motivated as much by attempts to exert greater managerial control over the labor process as it was by the attempt to secure sufficient labor for expansion. The shortage of skilled autoworkers not only made industrial growth difficult; it also enhanced the power of workers on the shop floor. Tight labor market conditions severely attenuated the major sanction used by managers to maintain control of the early labor process—firing. Realizing that their bosses were reluctant to fire them because of the difficulty of finding replacements, skilled workers were strengthened in their struggle with managers on the shop floor. This relationship between worker power and labor shortages was obvious to managers, as evidenced by a trade-journal editorial during World War I, when the industry again suffered tight labor market conditions: "High wages coupled with extraordinary demand [for labor] create a situation where workers may be independent, not only of their jobs, but also of the employer, with a result that includes costly labor turnover, increased accidents, extravagant time demands, exorbitant accident compensation and other evils."[24]

Given such conditions, automobile employers were motivated to divide labor and draw on the more plentiful—but not altogether abundant—supply of unskilled labor to enforce stricter discipline on the shop floor. With skilled jobs shattered into unskilled fragments, managers could fill them with even the "greenest" workers with a minimum of training. As a result, workers in the shops were more reluctant to defy managerial authority because of the fear of losing their jobs to the numerous immigrants and rural migrants.

Not willing merely to create the potential for a greater labor supply by dividing labor, the employers actively sought to expand this supply of unskilled workers with control motives in mind. As one critic of the auto industry observed: "The charge is often made that individually, if not concertedly, the big plants stimulate the coming of workers to Detroit in order to have a sizable labor pool to pick from, to spread the fear of losing your job, and to keep control in their hands."[25]

In Detroit, the vehicle of labor-market manipulation was the Employers' Association of Detroit (EAD). This association worked in a number of ways to control the competition for labor and to expand the labor supply. The EAD sought to persuade U.S. immigration authorities to divert a large part of the incoming stream of immigrants to Detroit. Also, the association financed a nationwide advertising campaign to draw on the internal labor resources of the United States. The EAD's *Labor Barometer,* a weekly bulletin on the

Detroit labor market, was also used to manipulate labor supply. Instead of reporting factually, Detroit employers used inflated reports of employment opportunities in this publication to stimulate the flow of workers to the city. Individual auto companies used similarly erroneous newspaper reports about increased employment to attract the labor supply to their factories.[26]

Until World War I, the auto industry drew mainly on immigrants as its primary source of unskilled labor. The war, however, stopped the flow of immigrants to the rapidly expanding auto shops, forcing manufacturers to turn to alternative sources of labor supply, namely rural workers, blacks, and women. Recruitment from the rural hinterlands, a traditional source of automotive labor, was intensified by offering "farm boys" incentives, like special deals on tractors. Southern black workers were enlisted by labor agents, who often brought them back en masse on trains. By 1930, about 4 percent of all autoworkers were black. Women were also actively courted to fill labor shortages, resulting in auto labor force composed of up to 12 percent women during World War I. While blacks maintained a relatively permanent and growing presence in the auto shops, however, most women were turned out as soon as shortages of male workers were overcome.[27]

That the stimulation of the supply of unskilled labor was a conscious managerial strategy aimed at greater control of workers on the shop floor is evident from an editorial in *Automotive Industries*. After stating that an "oversupply of labor is far from furnishing the ultimate answer to the labor question," the author observed that:

> During the recent labor shortage, some manufacturers looked to the importation of unskilled labor from Europe as the solution to our labor problem. They believed that the solution consisted chiefly in getting so many men for every job that each individual would work harder because he feared losing his job. That situation has come about to some extent at present.[28]

The division of labor had another effect on the struggle for control of the labor process, apart from its effect on the labor market. By replacing skilled with unskilled workers, the division of labor greatly reduced the power that the former exerted over the labor process. Because the craft labor process required workers to use their knowledge to determine the precise nature of work, they had a wide range of discretion with respect to its productivity, intensity, and accuracy. The employers realized that this exercise of discretion lowered the intensity of labor in their shops. Recalcitrant workers could use this power to slow down operations to a human pace and take breaks between tasks. The division of automotive labor centralized the skill and intelligence of work into the hands of capital. By fragmenting the crafts into minute, unskilled jobs, capital eliminated the workers' need to think and, along with it, the pores in the working day. As the two engineering journalists wrote of bench assembly work at Ford: "If the routine of the workman's movements is broken, he must inevitably call his brain into action to find the best means of bridging his troubles, and must lose some time in devising and executing his unusual line of procedure." The minute division of labor "allowed" the worker "to perform his unvaried operation with the least possible expenditure of willpower and hence with the least brain fatigue."[29] In reality, managers were less concerned about workers getting tired brains than their using the discretionary time to decrease the intensity of labor.

The division of automotive labor destroyed one large area of workers' discretionary time by eliminating the necessity of movement about the shop. With specialized "stock chasers" to bring parts to assembly locations, workers no longer had an excuse to take leisurely trips to the stockroom. Assembly could now proceed "without there being any need for the mechanics to walk more than a yard between the stand and the supply."[30] Also, in the machine shop, with workers similarly tied to one position and one machine: "No time is lost by the operator. The parts come to his machine and are removed to the next automatically. His attention is only on his job."[31] His foreman was sure to see to that. With workers confined to specific work positions, their foreman could maintain constant surveillance of their work and thus exercise stricter supervision.

The drastic reduction in skilled workers effected by the division of labor also strengthened capitalist control of the labor process by eliminating the inhibiting traditions of these workers. They had developed through long experience traditional norms governing how work should be done—the speed, feed, and setup of machines; a normal day's work; the quality of output. These traditions quickly proved to be a major obstacle in the path of complete capitalist control of labor. By dividing labor into unskilled fragments, the auto companies sought to eliminate these skilled workers and their traditions, and replace them with unskilled workers who, having no memory of craft traditions, put up little resistance to the absolute control of capital. As one academic spokesman for capital wrote: "The unskilled or semiskilled worker is more apt to be content with the simple and repetitive task. He will perform the work for which he is trained and is not so likely to question the method of doing the job or to fuss over unnecessarily good quality."[32] However, perhaps engineering journalists Horace L. Arnold and Fay L. Faurote best captured this employer disdain for the skilled and preference for the unskilled when they wrote:

> As to machinists, old-time, all-around men, perish the thought! The Ford Company has no use for experience, in the working ranks, anyway. It desires and prefers machine-tool operators who have nothing to unlearn, who have no theories of correct surface speeds for metal finishing, and will simply do what they are told to do, over and over again, from bell-time to bell-time.[33]

Progressive Layout and Intensity of Labor

Similar capitalist motives of greater control over work and consequently greater work intensity were in back of the progressive layout that often accompanied the division of labor. There were, of course, advantages to this spatial arrangement of work that had nothing to do with control. For example, placing successive work operations close to one another cut down on the amount of backbreaking labor necessary in hauling heavy parts from place to place. Further, progressive layout reduced substantially the amounts of resources tied up in stock and inventory. These advantages certainly played a part in motivating capitalists and managers to adopt this new method. However, an examination of the historical record reveals that attempts of employers to exert greater control over the *intensity of labor* formed the *main* motive.

Progressive layout increased capitalist control of the work pace in several ways. First, it made supervision of work closer and easier. With workers crowded together in a small area, foremen could maintain a large force under constant surveillance. Further, one engineering professor noted, "The steady flow of work through the line automatically leads to the quick detection of delays. It also holds operators at their work; on certain lines each worker must be on the job continuously."[34]

Second, progressive layout gave capital greater control over work intensity by allowing "stretch out," the operation of more than one machine by a worker. Because machines were grouped close together, it was possible for the first time for a worker to cover the short distance between them. The stretch out that often accompanied progressive layout was illustrated at the Cadillac plant, where a change in the layout of connecting-rod production forced half the previous number of workers to operate all the machines.[35]

The main way, however, that progressive layout enhanced capitalist control of work intensity was by ensuring a rapid, continuous flow of work past operators. Even though work at this time was simple, passed by hand between operations, this movement exerted a certain "pull" on workers and forced them to work rapidly so as not to fall behind. As the engineering journalists noted of progressive layout in the Ford shops of 1914, "it succeeds in maintaining speed without obtrusive foremanship."[36] Another engineer noted generally that progressive line production produced a "tautness in operating sequence":

> One of the psychological advantages of the line production is the tendency to draw closely upon the work ahead. In most cases there will be but a few parts between operations. Employees will make a constant effort to keep this material from building up ahead of them and to pass the work along promptly to the other workers on succeeding operations. This results in a steady pull from operations down the line which tends to increase production.[37]

Auto companies and their managers were not content, however, to allow the natural "pull" of the line to speed up work. They used other methods to actively control the pace of line work. One was time study.[38] By setting and enforcing job times that allowed no discretionary actions by workers, the companies could control work intensity. Once labor became divided and no longer unified by the individual craft worker, capital imposed itself as the unifier and coordinator of the fragmented labor process. It had to determine the proper timing and manner of all tasks in order to ensure a smooth, un-interrupted flow between them. Furthermore, automobile companies and their managers did not miss the opportunity afforded them by this new role to speed up workers by eliminating their discretionary time. Standard times for jobs were set so as to allow workers little or no time between operations. For example, a Bureau of Labor Statistics (BLS) researcher reported that in one auto body factory that had recently instituted progressive layout and ap-plied time study, "much of the slack between operations was obliterated, and a steady flow of work was secured throughout the establishment, so that an operation on one body would be finished just in time to make way for the next body."[39]

The results of such time study in the auto industry were reported from the workers' point of view in a letter to the *Industrial Worker*, organ of the In-dustrial Workers of the World (IWW):

> Calculations made by the pushers [time-study agents] are based upon what a man could turn out by working the lathe, drill press, milling machine, gear cut-ters, etc., at top speed; cut out the too frequent sharpening of tools, bumming a chew from a fellow worker on the other end of the floor, going after a drink too often, etc. . . . (When the men ran their (?) [editorially inserted question mark] machines at slow speed, they had a chance to sit down and watch while resting, but now the dirt is flying.) . . . No more loafing 'round the grindstone to sharpen drills and tools, no more excursions to the tool crib or stock room and many more scientific schemes of working while a fellow is resting. As a matter of fact, those seeming little time killing tricks are absolutely necessary, for no man can work steady at top speed and not get bughouse and worn out in short order.[40]

The other method of controlling the pace of progressive line production was the use of "pacesetters." These were particularly fast and loyal workers who were placed in strategic points along the line to maintain a rapid work pace. Of one such pacesetter on a progressive milling operation at Ford, a researcher wrote that "when he worked very rapidly he passed the materi-als on to the others at the same rate, and the others had to either keep up or pile up an excess of parts and thus call the attention of the boss to their delay."[41]

An MIT expert on progressive line production summed up its effects on control of work intensity in this way:

> The operator in a production line has less control over his working speed than the job-shop employee. . . . The fact that the pace of work is more directly under management's control in line production is an important one. The power which management is thus given to set the speed of the line is not to be taken lightly. Used wisely, it may maintain production at a high level.[42]

Thus, both the minute division of automotive labor and the progressive layout that accompanied it were motivated in large part by the conscious efforts of capitalists and managers to centralize the control of the labor process out of the hands of skilled craft workers. These measures resulted in higher levels of production and higher profits not mainly because they made work more productive or efficient, but because they overcame the resistance of a recalcitrant workforce to capitalist exploitation. Under different relations of production, in which workers were not alienated from the means of production and thus labored willingly for the social good, these methods would be superfluous.

Yet in the capitalist mode of production, the minute division of labor formed the foundation for the subsequent transformation of the automotive labor process. Once the various tasks were fragmented and laid out progressively in a line, it was only a short leap of the imagination to the idea of continuous, mechanical movement of work in progress—that is, the moving assembly line. The division and specialization of machine-tool work also laid the basis for mechanization and automation. Once a machine was devoted to one task alone, it could be rigidly specialized and automated so as to operate itself virtually without worker intervention. As with the division of labor, each of these innovations had as a major motive the further erosion of worker discretion and centralization of control into the hands of capital.

Workers in the early auto factories did not, however, passively accept these managerial assaults on their power over the labor process. These early stages in the transformation of work were met with an explosion of worker resistance. Most of this took place at the individual level and was unorganized, as when workers quit and stayed away from the transformed factories in droves, sending turnover and absentee rates soaring. Some of this struggle, however, was collective and class-conscious, as when the IWW led a strike against Studebaker in 1913 and the United Automobile, Aircraft, and Vehicle Workers' Union organized a series of strikes and walkouts after World War I. Ironically, the changes originally introduced in the labor process to overcome the resistance of skilled craft workers actually ended up strengthening the collective power of the unskilled industrial workers who replaced them. Not only did the new Fordist methods concentrate a growing mass of discontented workers into large factories and remove the division of skill and wages between them, but they also enhanced the power of autoworkers by rendering production more interdependent and hence vulnerable to disruption.[43]

Realizing that one ironic result of the division of labor was the creation of a homogenized and powerful collective workforce, auto manufacturers sought to reassert their authority by creating artificial divisions within it. This divide-and-conquer strategy took the form of hierarchical job structures. Jobs fundamentally similar in skill were arrayed in steps differentiated by wages and benefits. New workers entered the job ladder at or near the bottom, and progressed up the steps as they demonstrated their reliability and subservience to managers. Such schemes encouraged workers to seek individual advancement in the artificially differentiated promotional ladder and diverted their energies from collective advancement through class struggle.

The divisive effects of these job hierarchies were enhanced by the superimposition on them of racial and gender divisions. The sexist and racist hiring practices of auto manufacturers resulted in blacks and women being occupationally segregated in divisions at or near the bottom of the hierarchy, with little chance for promotion. Women were confined to a narrow range of jobs related to the unpaid labor they performed at home: sewing, fitting fabric, small-parts assembly. Also, blacks were ghettoized in the hottest, hardest, and most dangerous work: painting, sanding, foundry work, manual labor. Although such discrimination by manufacturers does not seem to have been consciously aimed at furthering divisions within the workforce, this was the effect nonetheless. Privileged white male workers found it more difficult to identify and cooperate with workers separated from them not only by wages, but also by deeply rooted racial and gender hatreds and hostilities. Blacks and women at the bottom of the job hierarchies often resented the privilege of white males who monopolized the better jobs as much as they resented the discrimination of managers. Furthermore, auto manufacturers were not reluctant to use the hostilities and divisions fueled by job discrimination to weaken the collective resistance of workers. They played off race against race and gender against gender to speed up workers, cut wages, and break strikes.[44]

By the mid-1930s, however, the contradictions of the labor process, together with the deprivations of the Great Depression, overpowered the divisive efforts of auto manufacturers and produced a burst of militant conflict in the auto industry. Under the leadership of class-conscious Communists, Socialists, and syndicalists, autoworkers launched a wave of sit-down strikes. Some manufacturers tried to manipulate black workers as a strike-breaking force, but close cooperation between some farsighted black leaders and union forces thwarted these efforts, and autoworkers finally forced the employers to recognize their union—the United Auto Workers union. However, adamant managerial resistance to repeated worker demands for increased control over the labor process succeeded in containing this struggle within the bounds of a bureaucratic collective bargaining system focused on wages and benefits. By the early 1950s, workers had completely bargained away any claim to control their own labor within the increasingly automated and fragmented auto factories.[45]

RECENT INNOVATIONS: AN END TO THE DIVISION OF LABOR?

By the early 1970s, these hitherto inviolable assumptions about the production of automobiles were being fundamentally questioned. Experiments began in U.S. factories that enlarged work tasks and, in some cases, gave teams of workers responsibility for organizing their own work. What had come over the auto capitalists and managers? Had they suddenly abandoned a hard-nosed concern for efficiency and profitability to adopt a humanitarian concern for the quality of employees' work experience?

This latter conclusion flows from a naive perspective that sees aspects of work organization as neutral instruments for the achievement of efficiency under all circumstances. Thus, if a neutral technique like the division of labor is rolled back, then it certainly must be at the expense of industrial efficiency. However, the perspective adopted here views techniques as conditioned by social relations of production. The division of labor increases productive output only under specific conditions of class antagonisms. Altering this staid method of production may signal not abandoning profitability as the key criterion of production, but rather an attempt to achieve it under changed conditions of class struggle.

In the mid-1960s, the U.S. system of collective bargaining began to be undermined by class struggles at home and abroad. In the Third World, national liberation struggles challenged U.S. economic hegemony abroad. On the domestic front, workers excluded from the bargaining system demanded a better dispensation, while workers in large industries began to shift their attention to the previously excluded issues of health, safety, and workers' control.[46] The U.S. auto industry was a center of this renewed class struggle. Black workers, who faced discrimination inside and outside of the auto plants, struggled against both with militant new organizations, like the League of Revolutionary Black Workers.[47] Young workers of all races who had never known the harsh discipline of economic scarcity began to question the trade-off of monotonous, degrading work for relatively high wages. Soaring rates of absenteeism, turnover, and work stoppages reflected a rebellion against the nature of Fordist work and authority. As the plant manager of a General Motors assembly plant stated, "It was during this time that the young people in the plant were demanding some kind of change. They didn't want to work in this kind of environment. The union didn't have much control over them, and they certainly were not interested in taking orders from a dictatorial management."[48] This rebellion came to national attention in 1972 with the three-week strike at the GM plant in Lordstown, Ohio, whose central issue was not wages, but working conditions.[49]

Managers responded to this renewed struggle with a shift toward control structures emphasizing responsible autonomy. Although retaining overall control of production, they allowed workers some discretion over the immediate labor process.[50] In the auto industry, managerial programs of job enlargement, worker participation, and quality of work life were initiated to overcome the renewed struggle of workers. As the director of employee research at GM stated: "We know that we have to take action to avoid situations like Lordstown. We've got to learn how to prevent those problems."[51] Regardless of their ostensible motives of enhancing the quality of work life, it is clear that the real managerial motives remain increased output per dollar cost. By making unskilled jobs a little less monotonous and giving workers largely formal decision-making responsibilities, managers hoped to increase job satisfaction and "promote employee identification with [managerial] goals. Such positive identification increases not only workers' motivation to work but also their sense of belonging in the workplace and their pride in the plant's achievement."[52] In a detailed analysis of many such programs that enlarge the previously minute division of labor, one study found that they increased labor productivity in ways unrelated to worker identification and satisfaction—namely, by reducing the labor force, cutting balance delay time between line jobs, and eliminating idle time.[53]

There is another managerial objective behind this rollback in the division of labor that explains its persistence under the more quiescent labor relations emerging in the 1980s and 1990s. This is flexibility, which helps account for the recent popularity of a workplace reorganization system pioneered by the Japanese known as lean production. One drawback of the rigidly and minutely divided Fordist labor process is the obstacle it poses to changing products to respond to fluctuating demand. Narrowly specialized workers and machines make it difficult and costly to change the production process to accommodate new products and new levels of production. Such inflexibility problems became serious only in the 1980s, when international competition and realization problems forced U.S. automakers to shift to new and more diversified product lines and placed a premium on rapid change in the labor process.[54]

To achieve a more flexible labor process in response to a more competitive and volatile marketplace, many U.S. car manufacturers have begun to adopt features of the lean production system practiced by Japanese automakers. This system allows the production of a greater variety of rapidly changing car models through more flexible technology and work organization. Lean production breaks with the rigid occupational division of labor of Fordism and "transfers the maximum number of tasks and responsibility to those workers actually adding value to the car on the line."[55] Line workers are responsible for and must learn the skills of simple machine repair, quality-checking, housekeeping, and materials-ordering. They are also expected to learn all the jobs in their work groups and participate in quality circles or teams to anticipate and solve production problems. Such an organization not only eliminates lots of indirect labor—hence its "leanness"—but also renders workers more flexible and able to adapt to new products introduced regularly. Pay systems are also more flexible, based more on seniority than job, and more determined by enterprise-based bonuses than industrywide formulas.[56]

U.S. automakers are seeking in many ways to reproduce the relations of Japanese lean production. In recent years they have pushed the union, under threat of plant closure, to abandon centralized industry bargaining and work and seniority rules based on narrow job definitions in favor of decentralized enterprise bargaining and broader, more flexible occupational categories. As part of this reorganization, most companies have also introduced programs of participatory teams which give workers greater responsibilities and discretion in their own work.[57]

Critics have rightly challenged the idea that lean production and team work in either U.S. or Japanese plants leads to any significant increase in worker skills. What this really entails is forcing workers to do a number of rather simple, plant-specific jobs that require manual dexterity, stamina, and an ability to follow directions. Although lean production does not reverse the Fordist deskilling dynamic, it does seem to challenge the imperative for managers to centralize all discretion in their hands. Even critics recognize that to achieve flexibility workers are required to be cooperative and voluntarily impose high standards of productivity on themselves. But how, then, do managers ensure that workers use this discretion and initiative to speed production rather than slow it down?[58]

The Japanese solution, which U.S. automakers have tried to emulate, involves team pressure and internal labor markets. Because workers receive part of their pay in bonuses based on plant production and profitability, team members have an interest in pushing each other to work harder. And workers also use their discretion to increase production to obtain promotions in the firm's job hierarchy. This is an especially important incentive in Japan, where strict policies of filling jobs by internal promotion mean chances for advancement are tied closely to the firm. But it has also become increasingly salient in the United States during times of high rates of unemployment that discourage labor market mobility. Also important in making workers in Japan dependent on firms is the lack of social welfare programs that provide nonmarket income. The U.S. industry's attempt to approximate Japanese conditions has not only led to efforts to weaken unions like the

United Auto Workers but also to roll back programs like welfare and unemployment insurance so as to make U.S. workers similarly dependent solely on wages for a livelihood.[59]

Although new conditions of struggle and competition have forced auto companies and their managers to alter somewhat the traditionally minute division of labor in the industry, this in no way signals a change in the basic logic of the labor process under the capitalist mode of production. The capitalist attempt to increase the production of surplus value through exerting absolute control over production and overcoming the resistance of an exploited and recalcitrant working class lies behind both the initial fragmented division of labor and its recent alterations. As long as this capitalist logic based on antagonistic relations of production persists, the substantial increase of worker skills and power will remain an unrealized dream rather than a palpable reality.

NOTES

1. Adam Smith, quoted in Karl Marx, *Capital*, vol. 1 (New York: International Publishers, 1967), 362. First published in 1867.

2. Smith in Marx, *Capital,* 362.

3. Harry Braverman, *Labor and Monopoly Capital: The Degradation of Work in the Twentieth Century* (New York: Monthly Review Press, 1974).

4. Herbert Gutman, *Work, Culture, and Society in Industrializing America* (New York: Knopf, 1976).

5. David Montgomery, *Workers' Control in America* (Cambridge: Cambridge University Press, 1979); and *The Fall of the House of Labor* (Cambridge: Cambridge University Press, 1987).

6. Allan Nevins and Frank Hill, *Ford: The Times, the Man, the Company* (New York: Scribner's, 1954), 376–80; William E. Chalmers, "Labor in the Automobile Industry" (Ph.D. diss., University of Wisconsin, 1932), 188–93.

7. Nevins and Hill, *Ford,* 381.

8. "Mills on All Three Sides," *The Automobile* 29 (1913), 279.

9. Stephen Meyer III, *The Five Dollar Day: Labor Management and Social Control in the Ford Motor Company, 1908–1921* (Albany: State University of New York Press, 1981), 74. On informal and unorganized worker resistance in the early years of the U.S. auto industry, see also Joyce Shaw Peterson, *American Automobile Workers, 1900–1933* (Albany: State University Press, 1987), chap. 7.

10. Keith Sward, *The Legend of Henry Ford* (New York: Rinehart, 1948), 32.

11. Nevins and Hill, *Ford,* 325.

12. R. R. Lutz, *The Metal Trades* (Cleveland: Survey Committee of the Cleveland Foundation, 1916), 97.

13. Henry Ford, *My Life and Work* (London: Heinemann, 1923), 80, 90.

14. Adam Smith, *The Wealth of Nations* (New York: Penguin, 1982), 112–13. First published in 1776.

15. Marx, *Capital*, vol. 1, 519–20.

16. Ford, *My Life and Work*, 103–04.

17. Horace L. Arnold and Fay L. Faurote, *Ford Methods and the Ford Shops* (New York: Arno, 1972), 245, 275. First published in 1915.

18. Braverman, *Labor and Monopoly Capital*, 76–78.

19. Stephen Marglin, "What Do Bosses Do? The Origins and Functions of Hierarchy in Capitalist Production," *Review of Radical Political Economics* 6 (1974), 37–38.

20. Chalmers, "Labor in the Automobile Industry," 72–84.

21. Braverman, *Labor and Monopoly Capital*, 72, 84.

22. Ford, *My Life and Work*, 77–78.

23. Ford, *My Life and Work*, 209.

24. "Industrial Relationship," *Automotive Industries* 37 (1917), 887.

25. Paul U. Kellogg, "When Mass Production Stalls," *Survey* 59 (1928), 726.

26. Chalmers, "Labor in the Automobile Industry," 192, 200–201.

27. August Meier and Elliott Rudwick, *Black Detroit and the Rise of the UAW* (New York: Oxford University Press, 1979); Ruth Milkman, *Gender at Work* (Urbana: University of Illinois Press, 1987); David Gartman, *Auto Slavery: The Labor Process in the American Automobile Industry, 1897–1950* (New Brunswick, N.J.: Rutgers University Press, 1986), 138–41.

28. "The Manufacturer's Opportunity," *Automotive Industries* 43 (1920), 284.

29. Arnold and Faurote, *Ford Methods and the Ford Shops*, 275, 245.

30. W. K. White, "What Some New England Makers Are Doing," *The Automobile* 20 (1909), 434.

31. "Twenty Operations to Make Knight Sleeve," *The Automobile* 29 (1913), 649.

32. Richard Muther, *Production-Line Technique* (New York: McGraw-Hill, 1944), 239.

33. Arnold and Faurote, *Ford Methods and the Ford Shops*, 41–42.

34. Muther, *Production-Line Technique*, 24.

35. Fred H. Colvin and Frank A. Stanley, *Running a Machine Shop* (New York: McGraw-Hill, 1948), 51.

36. Arnold and Faurote, *Ford Methods and the Ford Shops*, 6–8.

37. Muther, *Production-Line Technique*, 22–23.

38. Time study was part of the program of scientific management promoted by Frederick Taylor. However, the first managerial efforts in the auto industry to time and study minutely divided jobs do not seem to have been directly inspired by Taylor. Auto managers independently discovered and applied time study without knowledge of Taylor's work. See Nevins, *Ford*, 468–69. For an insightful treatment of Taylorism in general, see Dan Clawson, *Bureaucracy and the Labor Process: The Transformation of U.S. Industry, 1860–1920* (New York: Monthly Review Press, 1980).

39. Mortier W. La Fever, "Workers, Machinery, and Production in the Automobile Industry," *Monthly Labor Review* 19 (1924), 17.

40. "Scientific Management," *Industrial Worker* 3 (1911), 3.

41. Chalmers, "Labor in the Automobile Industry," 155–56.

42. Muther, *Production-Line Technique*, 233.

43. On the contradictory strengthening of collective struggle by the new Fordist methods, see Richard Edwards, *Contested Terrain: The Transformation of the Work-*

place in the Twentieth Century (New York: Basic Books, 1979), 126–29; David M. Gordon, Richard Edwards, and Michael Reich, *Segmented Work, Divided Workers* (Cambridge: Cambridge University Press, 1982), 162–64; Jerry Lembcke, *Capitalist Development and Class Capacities: Marxist Theory and Union Organization* (Westport, Conn.: Greenwood Press, 1988), 4–9.

44. Gartman, *Auto Slavery*, 233–57.

45. On the rise and decline of militant industrial unionism in the auto industry, see Nelson Lichtenstein, "Auto Worker Militancy and the Structure of Factory Life, 1935–1955," *Journal of American History* 67 (September 1980), 335–53; Roger Keeran, *The Communist Party and the Auto Workers' Unions* (Bloomington: Indiana University Press, 1980); Martin Halperin, *UAW Politics in the Cold War Era* (Albany: State University of New York Press, 1988).

46. See Samuel Bowles, David Gordon, and Thomas Weisskopf, *Beyond the Wasteland* (London: Verso, 1984).

47. Dan Georgakas and Marvin Surkin, *Detroit: I Do Mind Dying* (New York: St. Martin's Press, 1975); James Geschwender, *Class, Race, and Worker Insurgency* (Cambridge: Cambridge University Press, 1977).

48. Quoted in Robert H. Guest, "Quality of Work Life—Learning from Tarrytown," *Harvard Business Review* 57 (July–August 1979), 78.

49. See Stanley Aronowitz, *False Promises: The Shaping of American Working Class Consciousness* (New York: McGraw-Hill, 1973), 21–50; Emma Rothschild, *Paradise Lost: The Decline of the Auto-Industrial Age* (New York: Random House, 1973), 97–119; Barbara Garson, *All the Livelong Day: The Meaning and Demeaning of Routine Work* (New York: Penguin Books, 1975), 86–98. Twenty years later, in 1992, a massive shutdown of the Lordstown plant, which brought most of GM's operations to a halt across the nation, attested to the continuing problems of worker alienation and morale which have not been (and cannot be) fully resolved under capitalist production.

50. Andrew Friedman, *Industry and Labor: Class Struggle at Work and Monopoly Capitalism* (London: Macmillan, 1977).

51. Quoted in David Jenkins, *Job Power: Blue and White Collar Democracy* (New York: Penguin, 1974), 199.

52. Richard E. Walton, "Work Innovation in the United States," *Harvard Business Review* 57 (July–August 1979), 89.

53. John Kelly, *Scientific Management, Job Redesign, and Work Performance* (London: Academic Press, 1982). "Balance delay time" is the idle time of workers whose job cycles along a production line cannot be made equal to the duration of other workers' job cycles. Hence, it is the productive time lost when balancing the various jobs on the line.

54. Friedman, *Industry and Labor*, 106–8; Charles Sabel, *Work and Politics: The Division of Labor in Industry* (Cambridge: Cambridge University Press, 1982), 209–14; Michael Piore and Charles Sabel, *The Second Industrial Divide* (New York: Basic Books, 1984); Stephen Wood and John Kelly, "Taylorism, Responsible Autonomy, and Management Strategy," in *The Degradation of Work? Skill, Deskilling, and the Labor Process*, ed. Stephen Wood (London: Hutchinson, 1982), 74–89.

55. James P. Womack, Daniel T. Jones, and Daniel Roos, *The Machine That Changed the World: The Story of Lean Production* (New York: Harper Perennial, 1990), 99.

56. Womack, Jones, and Roos, *The Machine That Changed the World,* 99.

57. Alan Altshuler, Martin Anderson, Daniel Jones, Daniel Roos, and James Womack, *The Future of the Automobile* (Cambridge, Mass.: MIT Press, 1984); Harry C. Katz, *Shifting Gears: Changing Labor Relations in the U.S. Automobile Industry* (Cambridge, Mass.: MIT Press, 1985).

58. Mike Parker, "Industrial Relations Myth and Shop-Floor Reality: The 'Team Concept' in the Auto Industry," in *Industrial Democracy in America,* ed. Nelson Lichtenstein and Howell John Harris, (New York: Cambridge University Press, 1993), 264–72; Ruth Milkman, *Farewell to the Factory: Auto Workers in the Late Twentieth Century* (Berkeley: University of California Press, 1997), 151–60.

59. Parker, "Industrial Relations"; Francis Fox Piven and Richard Cloward, *The New Class War* (New York: Pantheon, 1982); Barry Bluestone and Bennett Harrison, *The Deindustrialization of America* (New York: Basic Books, 1982).

3

The Labor Process and the Transformation of Corporate Control in the Global Economy

Harland Prechel

Three historically distinct types of scientific management have emerged in response to economic crises that undermined corporations' capacity to accumulate capital during the twentieth century. Until the 1980s, scientific management took the form of Taylorism and Fordism, which focused on production functions, the separation of conception from execution, and managerial control over the labor process.

Capitalists experimented with various forms of scientific management following the accumulation crises near the end of the nineteenth century. By the early twentieth century, capitalists hired consultants such as Frederick Taylor who set up control systems that reduced jobs to their elemental components. Taylorism was the first method to identify discrete manufacturing activities and reunify them into an integrated production system. These control systems then timed and recorded the necessary motions as they were completed. These "time-and-motion" studies were used to define the "one best way" to produce a product and provide management with a standard to evaluate workers. Capitalists relocated this information into centralized engineering and planning offices, where work rules were developed. Then, capitalists hired managers to implement these rules and ensure that workers complied with them. This centralization of control separated conception from execution by removing many of the production decisions previously incorporated into the craft tradition and placed them into the hands of management, which reduce production work to tasks that required fewer skills and less knowledge.[1]

In response to the capital accumulation crisis that resulted in the Great Depression, Fordism gradually replaced Taylorism, but was only fully implemented in the post–World War II era. Fordism continued the trend of centralizing control by transferring workers' knowledge to managers, incorporating workers' "know-how" into the production machinery, and creating taller managerial hierarchies. Fordism also continued to fragment tasks and specialize work activities. A primary characteristic of Fordism was the mechanization of the production process by reincorporating the various tasks into an assembly line. This reorganization of the labor process required several layers of management to supervise the various tasks and specialized work activities.

This chapter analyzes the emergence of neo-Fordism, the third mode of control based on principles of scientific management, in the age of globalization. I will demonstrate how neo-Fordism computerizes information flows to further centralize control, making it possible to eliminate several layers of management and reduce the decision-making authority of lower and middle managers. This analysis has several dimensions: First, I discuss how top management ensured centralized control over the growing number of lower and middle managers within the Fordist mode of control. Second, I analyze the source of contradiction and inefficiency within Fordism. Third, I demonstrate that the corporation's response to the crisis of capital accumulation that followed the recessions in the early 1980s was to overcome the inefficiencies of Fordism. Fourth, I identify three types of control and discuss how each specified more precise control over a distinct sphere of the corporation. The analysis also shows that much of the capital used to restructure corporations was provided by the state, and that this process has been unfolding at full speed in the most recent period under conditions of globalization.

HISTORICAL TRANSITION AND
THE TECHNICAL LIMITS OF FORDISM

Several changes have undermined the capacity of the Fordist mode of control to ensure an acceptable rate of capital accumulation in the late twentieth century. First, the oil crises of 1973 and 1979–1980 raised fuel costs in energy-intensive industries. Second, although quality standards increased in the marketplace, the capacity of Fordism to increase manufacturing quality had reached its technical limits. The cost of "defective" products constituted a considerable proportion of production costs and eventually became an impediment to capital accumulation. Third, the tall managerial hierarchies necessary to enforce the wide range of rules and regulations within the Fordist mode of control represented a significant operating cost. Fourth, bureaucratization within Taylorism and Fordism removed decision making from the point of production, which impeded the decision-making process and reduced manufacturing flexibility. Fifth, in contrast to the immediate post–World War II era when wages steadily increased, earning power declined for blue-collar workers after the mid-1970s. This slowed the rate of increased demand for consumer products, which added to the problem of overproduction in relation to the consumption capacity of society. Sixth, the emergence of Newly Industrializing Countries (NICs) in the global economy and their success at penetrating markets in the United States increased economic competition. In conjunction with the decline in consumer buying power, the penetration of U.S. markets by NICs reduced utilization rates of domestic manufacturing corporations. Seventh, economic competition undermined the capacity of oligopolistic industries (e.g., steel, automobile) to set prices, which was a primary mechanism to ensure an adequate rate of capital accumulation in the post–World War II era; when production costs increased, oligopolistic industries would increase their prices.

Together, changes in the global economy and the technical limits of Fordism have become impediments to capital accumulation in the late twentieth century.[2] To ensure an acceptable rate of accumulation, Fordist task fragmentation, specialization, and mechanization (e.g., assembly-line principles) are being replaced with a neo-Fordist social organization of production.[3]

NEO-FORDIST CONTROLS

By controlling information flows, neo-Fordism attempts to overcome the limits of Fordism where individual reaction time, faculties of perception, and the speed at which individuals can coordinate their actions limit productivity increases. Neo-Fordism includes the application of more precise accounting techniques to organizational control systems to reduce labor, inventory, manufacturing, and managerial costs, while increasing control over the production process to enhance product quality.

Several arguments associate the decentralization of decision-making authority with recent changes in corporate management.[4] For example, managerial theory suggests that decision-making authority has been decentralized to lower levels within the managerial hierarchy throughout the twentieth century,[5] and especially in the 1980s.[6] Even recent critical analyses suggest that automatic production controls and integrated production complexes are based on work teams, cooperative decision making, and participation on the shop floor.[7] If these arguments are correct, decision-making authority should become more equally distributed.

In contrast, I argue that a very different dynamic is occurring in response to recent increases in economic competitiveness. Specifically, my analysis shows that the mode of control is being redefined in such a way that it centralizes authority while decentralizing responsibility for decisions. Contemporary forms of participation and cooperative decision making result in a significant decline in the autonomy of both traditional production workers and lower and middle management.[8]

I selected a corporation in the steel industry for study because the low quality of steel produced in the United States and increased competition in the global economy resulted in a serious capital accumulation crisis in this industry in the early and mid-1980s. For example, the steel industry did not realize a profit between 1982 and 1986. Although the industry reported a 4 percent rate of return in 1987, it reported a net loss again in 1988.[9] Moreover, to avoid bankruptcy, several large steel corporations filed protection under Chapter 11 (e.g., Wheeling-Pittsburgh, LTV). Therefore, if a new mode of control emerged in the late twentieth century, it should be readily observable in the steel industry where an extended capital accumulation crisis existed.

THE LIMITS OF CENTRALIZED CONTROL

This study suggests that in addition to the increased competition, the crisis of accumulation in the 1980s is a consequence of contradictions within the Fordist mode of control. It demonstrates that the particular social organization of Fordism shaped the interest of managers.[10] However, dimensions of Fordist control were opposed to one another because they shaped the interest of middle managers in such a way that their decisions were in opposition to the interest of top management; these oppositions will be considered contradictions.

Contradictions express themselves as crises when they undermine the efficient use of resources and capacity to realize a profit. Two contradictions are of concern here: (1) those that occur between dimensions of the Fordist mode of control and the corporation's capital accumulation goals, and (2) those that occur between the corporation's capital accumulation goals and the economy. A contradiction emerges within the firm when the mode of control generates a course of action that undermines the corporation's goal. Contradictions emerge from the economy when oscillating business cycles create overproduction and underconsumption, which results in a falling rate of profit.[11]

Historically, top management attempted to resolve these contradictions by extracting more labor from workers. Scientific management (e.g., Taylorism, Fordism) was applied to more spheres of the corporation, which created a central role for middle management and steadily removed control from the point of production.[12]

However, there were technical limits to the centralization of decision making within Taylor's "one best way" that stemmed from the complexities of the manufacturing process. In steelmaking, for example, it is often easier to provide general guidelines over production decisions than definitive solutions to specific problems. The manufacturing process itself restricts the effectiveness of identifying, establishing, and incorporating rules into the production process. Steel manufacturing includes numerous variables and countless permutations of these variables for each product. Moreover, large integrated steel corporations make hundreds of products that have unique production specifications. Establishing and implementing a separate set of rules for each product creates a complex managerial system, and restricts the necessary flexibility at the point of production to adjust the manufacturing process to meet product specifications.

Hence, despite top management's efforts to increase control by establishing managerial hierarchies, the technical limits to scientific management resulted in comparatively high skill levels among workers and lower level managers (e.g., foremen), and required some decentralized control over production. Similar to other manufacturing industries, to ensure flexibility many decisions in the steel industry remained at the point of production.[13]

THE PROFIT-MAKING STRATEGY
AND ORGANIZATIONAL CONTROL

When the political-legal institutional arrangements were changed to create the modern corporation in the late nineteenth century, capitalists monitored a wide range of operating and coordinating decisions (e.g., scheduling manufacturing line-ups). This centralized managerial system allowed capitalists and their top managers to oversee cost inputs directly within the various organizational units. However, as the corporation's size and complexity increased in the post–World War II era, its centralized managerial system became an impediment on profit making. As organizational complexity exceeded top management's cognitive capabilities, they were no longer able to make decisions and exercise control over the wide range of day-to-day manufacturing activities.[14] To overcome this problem, top management implemented a decentralized managerial system, which delegated decision-making authority to the managers of the various organizational units.

Once top management relinquished direct control, it implemented bureaucratic controls (e.g., rules, regulations) to specify the limits of middle managerial authority over operating units. However, the complexity of steelmaking, in conjunction with the corporation's wide product line, placed limitations on the degree to which bureaucratic controls could be implemented. On the one hand, bureaucratic controls could not govern coordinating decisions because it is difficult to establish rules governing changes in the linkage of the manufacturing facilities when those linkages frequently change. Similar to other expanding corporations, coordinating the flow of materials (i.e., scheduling, alignment of production units) through the manufacturing process was achieved by personal cooperation among the middle managers. On the other hand, the large number of individual products and the numerous variables in the steelmaking process made it difficult to routinize production. Hence, many decisions remained at the point of production. Knowledge and craft traditions continued to govern many manufacturing activities.

The complexity of steel manufacturing restricted the degree to which Taylorism and Fordism and the concomitant bureaucratic controls could be implemented to: (1) coordinate the various production units and (2) exercise control over the manufacturing process. To retain control over costs, top management established more intensive *financial controls* (i.e., controls based on return on investment) by specifying operating budgets for each organizational unit. However, the financial conception of control only provided managers with information on the return on investment within an operating unit. Financial controls did not provide useful decision-making information on the cost efficiency of individual products or product groups.[15]

ORGANIZATIONAL EXPANSION AND
THE CONTRADICTIONS OF BUDGETARY CONTROLS

During the rapid economic growth of the 1960s and 1970s, the corporation increased its manufacturing capacity by 24 percent. By the late 1960s, the lower and middle segments of the managerial hierarchy expanded to seven levels. Budgetary controls remained top management's primary means to exercise control over the middle managers who had decision-making authority within the organizational units. The primary purpose of these controls was to determine if middle managers remained within their budgets. Budget controls were also the primary criterion to determine if these managers merited a salary increase. However, this incentive structure to keep operating costs low within the organizational units often contradicted the corporation's profitability goal, because it encouraged middle managers to make decisions that frequently undermined product quality. For example, if mill superintendents stopped the manufacturing process to reroll defective steel, their operating cost increased, which reflected poorly on their managerial abilities. Hence, this system of control encouraged production managers to pass flawed products to the next stage in the manufacturing process.

This contradiction undermined capital accumulation by reducing the quality of the final product. In addition, the longer the defective product remained in the manufacturing process, the higher the capital investment (e.g., labor, energy, raw materials) in that product. Moreover, the defective product had to be sold at a lower price, scrapped, or rerolled. Each of these alternatives undermined the corporation's profitability goal. Whereas low-quality steel had to be sold at a lower price, reprocessing the product increased manufacturing cost. Although these decisions were the most rational means to realize the subunit goal to remain within assigned budgets, they undermined the corporation's profitability goal.

Two interrelated issues contributed to this contradiction between the financial conception of control and the corporation's capital accumulation goals. On the one hand, because middle managers were evaluated by their ability to remain within assigned budgets, they often made decisions based solely on how they would affect their budgets. These decisions often undermined product quality. On the other, as steelmaking became more complex and the organizational units expanded (e.g., some units had more than five-hundred employees), middle managers focused increasingly on the day-to-day supervisory responsibilities within their operating units. In both cases, the Fordist mode of control generated interest among managers that resulted in decisions that undermined the profitability goals of the corporation.

The Fordist mode of control did not change because it was cost-effective enough to realize an acceptable rate of capital accumulation in this oligopolistic industry, where the steel corporations set prices. Moreover, the high cost of production was not detected, because as long as middle managers remained within their assigned budgets, they met the technical criteria of success as defined by the budgetary controls.

GLOBAL COMPETITION

Several changes in the economic environment in the early 1980s undermined the corporation's capacity to accumulate capital. Competition intensified because global steel manufacturing capacity exceeded demand, several foreign corporations were dumping steel into U.S. markets,[16] and foreign steelmakers were producing lighter, higher quality steel.

Although these trends had been emerging throughout the late 1970s, they did not result in a crisis until the recessions in the early 1980s, when domestic steel demand dropped from 100 million tons in 1979 to 61.5 million tons in 1982. In 1980, the corporation's utilization rate declined to 67 percent and its rate of return dropped to 2.3 percent. These higher costs restricted capital accumulation even more during the 1981–1982 recession, when the corporation did not realize a profit for the first time since the Great Depression. To regain its competitive position in the marketplace, top management had to reduce cost while improving product quality.

These contradictions undermined efficiency and together with the increased competitiveness in its economic environment restricted the corporation's capacity to accumulate capital. The core dimension of the corporation's strategy to improve its profitability position was to increase efficiency by intensifying control. The first step in this process was to identify cost inputs in more detail. The calculation of detailed input cost was necessary before the corporation could identify where cost could be cut.

CORPORATE POLITICAL BEHAVIOR AND THE STATE

Like many corporations, this steel company experienced an acute capital shortage in the late 1970s and early 1980s. Corporations needed capital to modernize their plants and equipment to become competitive in the global marketplace. When big business is unable to generate capital internally, it pursues external sources. One of the primary external sources of capital is the state. The state is one of the few institutions in modern society that has the authority to transfer capital to corporations. This transfer typically occurs through tax laws by making adjustments in, for example, depreciation allowances and investment tax credits. Corporations are particularly dependent on this form of financing during periods of crisis when they are less capable of generating capital internally. However, because there are competing classes that have different political and economic interests, the state does not automatically transfer capital to corporations.

By the late 1970s, in response to the growing capital accumulation crisis, the industrial capitalist class segment mobilized politically to change the institutional arrangement within which the capital accumulation process occurs.[17] By the early 1980s, this class segment had garnered adequate political support to persuade the Reagan administration to pass the Economic Recovery Tax Act of 1981 (ERTA). This legislation provided industrial corporations with billions of dollars in tax breaks. These tax write-offs were so generous that profits from new investments were often higher after, rather than before, taxes and some corporations could not use all of their tax breaks.[18]

To enable low-profit industries such as steel to take full advantage of the ERTA, a special tax-leasing provision was passed by the federal government that allowed corporations to sell their unused tax deductions to more profitable corporations. Under this provision, corporations were allowed to lease everything from blast furnaces to fork lifts to computers. The tax-leasing arrangements benefited both companies engaged in the transaction. The company that owned the equipment and facilities benefited by obtaining additional capital by leasing them to other companies who used the tax deductions. The company leasing the facility paid less for it than the actual value of the tax deduction. These new institutional arrangements resulted in a massive increase in corporations' cash flows. It is estimated that the steel industry received $400 million between 1982 and 1983 alone from the ERTA.[19] Corporations used this additional capital for many purposes, including setting up systems to control information flows and establish more precise budget, bureaucratic, and technical controls.

THE EXTENSION OF BUDGETARY CONTROL

By 1984, the accounting department had identified and calculated more than 50,000 cost points, which were used to establish more precise controls in two ways. Initially, *managerial accounting* was extended to more decisions: the dimension of accounting that transforms data into decision-making information. Managerial accounting provides production managers with predetermined standard cost data, which can be compared with actual cost inputs. Production managers are responsible for identifying the reasons for any variances located between standard and actual costs. The specification of cost also made it possible to intensify responsibility accounting: cost accounting by area of responsibility. *Responsibility accounting* specified the location in the manufacturing process where cost inputs occurred.

These changes in the accounting system made it possible to identify where specific cost inputs occurred, and evaluate the cost efficiency of specific manufacturing activities.

THE EXTENSION OF BUREAUCRATIC CONTROLS

There were two dimensions of top management's efforts to increase efficiency with more precise bureaucratic controls. Top management created a decision-making center that specified rules governing how to manufacture each product, which extended premise controls over production decisions. *Premise controls* establish guidelines within which a decision can be made. Technical experts in the decision-making center established these premise controls by calculating the most cost-efficient means to manufacture each product and, through a complex computer system, transmitted the rules governing production decisions to the manager on the shop floor. Premise controls established decision-making criteria over dimensions of the decision-making process that previously escaped control. In addition, top management and its administrative staff specified the span of control and lines of authority in more detail. More precise rules identified the manager accountable for each input cost and ensured that every manager was directly accountable to a more senior manager.

Budget and bureaucratic controls together made it possible to hold the lowest level decision makers accountable for input costs by incorporating more spheres of the decision-making process within the formal control system. Whereas budget controls provided the information to determine where the cost inputs occurred, bureaucratic controls identified the production manager responsible for each cost input. These new controls allowed top management to identify even the lowest level decision maker and hold that person accountable for costs. In the past, only middle managers were held accountable for costs.

Premise controls established more precise guidelines within which decisions are made. The rules that specified the span of control and lines of authority in more detail also made each manager accountable to a more senior manager. Together with budgetary controls, these bureaucratic controls made it possible to push decision-making responsibility down the organizational hierarchy, while holding operating managers accountable for the cost effectiveness of their decisions.

THE EXTENSION OF TECHNICAL CONTROLS

Once the bureaucratic and budget controls were specified in more detail, top management established a decision-making center to implement two inter-related technical controls. These controls facilitated *continuous processing*: the reconceptualization and reorganization of production by moving the product steadily through the manufacturing process (i.e., raw materials to finished steel).[20] Continuous processing increases efficiency by lowering capital investment in unfinished inventories[21] and the energy cost associated with reheating steel at each discrete stage of production. Like bureaucratic and budget controls, the extension of technical control entails the computerization of information flows.

The first technical control is the cybernetically controlled plant planning and scheduling system, which coordinates and integrates the manufacturing process from beginning to end. Once this centralized decision center received an incoming order, it is entered into the computerized plant scheduling model, which determines production lineups.

The second technical control incorporates statistical analysis with computer controls. *Statistical process control* analyzes statistical variances to determine the tolerance capabilities of particular technologies. These tolerance levels are programmed into the production control computer, which measures the product as it is being manufactured, assesses product quality, and automatically adjusts the manufacturing process when levels of error move beyond predetermined standards. That is, if the production process goes out of statistical control, these cybernetic controls readjust the production technology while the product is being manufactured. Technical controls increase standardization by incorporating many operating decisions into the manufacturing process. Like budget and bureaucratic controls, technical controls centralize control over the production process.

The plant planning and scheduling system and statistical process control are components of a three-layer integrated computer system designed to increase *automated management*: the application of cybernetic information processing systems to aid in decision making and controlling the production process. At the first level, statistical process controls standards are programmed into the production control computer, which operates individual pieces of equipment responsible for a single phase of the production process. A second level of the system coordinates the lower-level control computers and integrates the various steps of the process into a smooth and continuous flow. A third level of the system schedules production lineups that generate the fewest semifinished inventories and requires the least number of adjustments in the manufacturing process. The ultimate goal of this multilevel computer system is to provide a fully integrated set of computer controls to reduce inputs into a decision-making process that were previously not specified by the formal control system.

By 1987, the corporation located computer monitors at each work site, which made it possible to transmit the manufacturing specifications established by technical experts in the centralized decision-making center to the shop floor. Centralization was increased by standardizing the information conveyed to all levels of management from operations to sales to general management. The system was an attempt to overcome the contradiction created by budgetary controls and ensure that decisions at all levels were consistent with the profitability goals of the corporation.

Since supervision over manufacturing is built directly into the system itself, technical control reduces the need for human decision makers. As a result, once the multilevel computer system was implemented, the corporation reduced the lower and middle levels of the managerial hierarchy from seven to three layers, and eliminated 20 percent of its managerial workforce. In short, the applications of neo-Fordism reduced both the need for decision-making skills at the point of production and the number of managers necessary in this high-tech manufacturing facility. Neo-Fordist controls also made it possible to eliminate several thousand blue-collar jobs in this corporation.

In addition to setting up controls over information flows in its existing manufacturing facilities—in a joint venture with a Japanese steel company—the corporation constructed a new high-tech steelmaking plant using the most advanced steel-finishing technology in the world. The fully automated facility includes a material handling unit where there are no managers or workers. Robotic trucks are programmed to pick up the spools of steel and computer-controlled cranes place the finished steel in their storage locations.

THE EXTENSION OF TOP MANAGERIAL CONTROL

The intensification of formally rational control to govern information flows ensured that decisions conformed to top managerial agenda. The formally rational controls ensured standardization of manufacturing decisions by programming a wide range of product specifications directly into the production control computer, which automatically adjusted the manufacturing facility to predetermined specifications. In addition, technical experts established decision premises that were transmitted through the computer system to the point of production to establish the parameters within which production decisions were made.

In the past, top managerial decisions were dependent on experience in service and information obtained from the large staff of middle managers.[22] However, with the intensification of formal control, top management and its small administrative staff have the capability to control information flows, thereby governing a wider range of organizational activities. These controls make it possible to reorganize the entire managerial system into one hierarchical system. The corporation has the administrative capacity to centralize decision-making information, and either implement that information directly into the production process or establish the premise of decisions. This system of control centralized authority and reduced the autonomy of both semi-skilled and skilled blue-collar workers, and lower and middle management.

GLOBALIZATION, THE STATE, AND
THE TRANSFORMATION OF THE CORPORATE FORM

After the corporation set up neo-Fordist controls over its managerial and labor processes, it restructured as a *multilayered subsidiary form* (MLSF): a corporation with a hierarchy of two or more levels of subsidiary corporations with a parent company at the top of the hierarchy that uses computerized information flows to manage its subsidiary corporations. This change in the corporate form occurred at a rapid rate after big business pressured the state to change business-tax policy that was passed during the New Deal to restrict the use of subsidiaries. These political-legal changes were included in the Tax Reform Act of 1986 and the Revenue Act of 1987, and extended to more types of corporate organization by the Tax Acts of 1993 and 1996. The new institutional arrangements allow corporations to restructure their corporate entities as subsidiaries tax free, and to transfer capital from its subsidiary corporations to the parent company or from the parent company to its subsidiary corporations tax free.[23] Although corporations have used subsidiaries since the nineteenth century to organize their foreign operations, the MLSF is becoming more widely used as markets become more global and computerized information flows become more widely used to monitor geographically dispersed corporate units.

In contrast to the multidivisional form (MDF) used by most corporations since the 1950s, where the central office (i.e., top management and its staff) and the operating units are part of the same company, subsidiaries are legally separate corporations that are owned and controlled by a parent company. Although there are many implications of this change in the corporate form, a crucial difference is that subsidiary corporations are legally separate entities. This legal separation reduces the parent company's liability for breakdowns such as bankruptcy and faulty products (e.g., prescription drugs, silicone breast implants) in its subsidiary corporations. The independent legal status of subsidiaries allows parent companies to raise capital by selling stock in its subsidiary corporations. The MLSF enables parent companies to operate in foreign countries where variations in institutional arrangements exist (e.g., laws governing corporate behavior) and to compare the performance of its spatially dispersed subsidiary corporations.

In the 1980s, the largest corporations in the United States used the MLSF to transform their domestic corporate units into subsidiaries. Restructuring as an MLSF allowed parent companies to, for example, increase their strategic and financial flexibility. While the MLSF provides a new means to raise capital internally—for example, initial public offerings (IPOs) of subsidiary's stock—it also facilitated setting up an acquisition strategy. Using the MLSF, the parent company can acquire another company through a stock transaction, incorporate it as a subsidiary, and allow the subsidiary corporation to operate as it did before the transaction occurred.[24] In contrast, integrating acquisitions into the same company requires an alignment of the previously independent corporations' managerial and accounting systems, which can be time-consuming and costly. The problems associated with integrating a merger into a company organized as an MDF became more complex as the size of mergers and acquisitions escalated in the 1980s and 1990s (e.g., General Motors acquisition of Electronic Data Systems (EDS), Lockheed Corporation's $9 billion acquisition of Loral Corporation).

By the early 1990s, the parent companies began to use the MLSF to integrate themselves into the global *commodity chain*: the stages of the manufacturing process that contribute to the final product (e.g., raw materials to steel to automobiles and airplanes). At the steel company examined here, this strategy was set up to provide better access to inexpensive input materials and to market its steel products. The parent company created a second-level subsidiary holding company that set up marketing joint ventures in China, India, and South Africa. Then, the parent company created another subsidiary to buy and sell industrial products on the global market. Also, after the North American Free Trade Agreement (NAFTA) was passed in 1993, the parent company set up a joint venture with Mexico's largest steel producer, and established a steel distribution subsidiary in Mexico. A primary task of these subsidiaries was to link the parent company's domestic subsidiaries to the international market. In addition to providing a structure to market its products abroad, the MLSF allows corporations to relocate parts of their manufacturing process in peripheral countries where manufacturing costs are lower due to low wages and the absence of environmental and workplace health and safety controls.

Computerized information flows in the MLSF, further centralized decision-making authority by making it possible for the same person to be the top manager of the parent company and each of its major subsidiary corporations. The CEO of the parent holding company is also the CEO of the steel producing subsidiary holding company, the steel distribution subsidiary holding company, and the subsidiary company where the parent company organizes its international businesses. Top managers and their technical staff in the parent company have the administrative capability to control information flows to its subsidiary corporations, thereby controlling the basis of decisions made in them. Computerized information flows also allow top management to monitor the various subsidiary corporations that are spatially distributed throughout the global economy.

CONCLUSION

Transformation to the MLSF and neo-Fordist computerized information flows have increased the capacity of top management and its administrative staff to establish controls that ensure consensus and standardize decisions. The MDF and Taylorist and Fordist controls were replaced, because their technical limits generated contradictions that restricted capital accumulation in the increasingly competitive economic environment.

A key dimension of this computerized control system is its capacity to transfer information from one part of the corporation to another. There are three interrelated ways in which information is used to control the labor and managerial processes. First, technical control made it possible to incorporate production guidelines directly into the manufacturing computers at the point of production. Second, whereas more precise rules were established to identify the manager or production worker responsible for a specific cost, premise controls stipulated guidelines governing the decisions made by these organizational members. Third, budgetary controls compare the actual cost of specific manufacturing cost to predetermined costs. If managers fail to follow the rules governing manufacturing, the new budgetary/cost controls simultaneously identify the location of the subsequent cost variation and the manager responsible for that cost.

The establishment of decision-making centers placed lower and middle managers at a greater distance from decision making, while providing the organizational capacity to increase surveillance over them. Neo-Fordism increased top managerial control over more spheres of organizational activity, redefined the traditional responsibilities of lower and middle level managers, and reduced operating management's decision-making autonomy.

The emergence of neo-Fordist has far-reaching implications for the distribution of authority. In addition to extending more precise control over production workers, neo-Fordism demands that lower and middle level managers base their decisions on criteria established in a parent company that may be located in a different country on a different continent.

Authority is being centralized, while responsibility is being decentralized. In addition to increasing control over traditional blue-collar work, neo-Fordism extends top managerial control over the technical and social organization of production throughout the global economy. Whereas Taylorist and Fordist modes of control required extensive managerial hierarchies, which limited centralized control over the labor process, the computerized information flows reduce managerial hierarchies and simultaneously establish formal controls to ensure that managers and workers adhere to predetermined decision-making criteria. Efforts to eliminate costs to increase the rate of capital accumulation project the corporation toward a higher level of mechanization, standardization, and centralization of authority.

In this chapter, I have attempted to identify more precisely the lines along which decision making is simultaneously becoming diffused throughout the organization and located in decision-making centers. Although the new mode of control increases participation on the shop floor, the properties of that participation are determined in the decision-making centers. Cooperation, therefore, must be understood as the process of establishing a means of coordination and control under the centralized authority of top management, who, when faced with competition, progressively tightens the authority structures and control mechanisms within the workplace. Although the layers of management within neo-Fordist declined, the authority structures became more formalized and centralized. The presentation of corporate strategies as based on work teams, cooperative decision making, and participation on the shop floor mask the basic relation of domination and subordination that necessarily prevails when centralized controls are implemented.

Premised on production technologies and decision-making criteria, neo-Fordism is more subtle and integrated than the more direct exercise of authority within previous modes of control. Similar to Taylorism and Fordism, neo-Fordist controls may generate new unanticipated forms of workplace conflict. The neo-Fordist mode of control that regulates information flows to increase surveillance not only sharpens the traditional opposition between workers and management by intensifying control over traditional blue-collar occupations, but it may create a new dynamic that generates opposition between operating management and top management. Subjecting previously "unrationalized" areas of the corporation to centralized control may direct attention to the issue of autonomy and give rise to new forms of strain and conflict that may produce future social change.

NOTES

1. Frederick Taylor, *The Principles of Scientific Management* (New York: W. W. Norton & Company, 1967).

2. Capital accumulation is the mobilization, transformation, and exploitation of inputs—labor, materials, and so forth—in such a way that the total capital of the corporation increases. See Paul M. Sweezy, *The Theory of Capitalist Development* (New York: Monthly Review Press, 1942); and Samuel Bowles and Richard Edwards, *Understanding Capitalism* (New York: Harper & Row, 1985). *Capital accumulation* is used here, rather than *profits,* because it reflects the overall financial position of the corporation. In addition to profits, accumulation includes maintaining a strong liquidity position for capital investment and reducing debt. These variables determine the financial strength of the corporation, the value of its stock, and its financial worth. Most important, accumulation includes reinvestment of capital, which is necessary in the long term to realize profits.

3. I use the term *neo-Fordism* because these changes represent continuity with previous scientific management forms of control. This is in contrast to the views of several researchers who characterize the response to global competition as post-Fordism, which suggests that these changes represent a break from previous forms of control. See Michel Aglietta, *A Theory of Capitalist Regulation* (New York: New Left Books, 1979); and Annemieke Roobeek, "The Crisis of Fordism and the Rise of a New Technological Paradigm," *Futures* 19 (April 1987).

4. There are numerous other dimensions of the social change associated with this historical transition in the late twentieth century, including changing consumption patterns, the dwindling power of trade unions, and the deregulation of industry, that cannot be adequately addressed in this essay. See Harland Prechel, *Corporate and Class Restructuring* (Boulder, Colo.: Westview Press, forthcoming).

5. See, for example, Alfred Chandler, *Strategy and Structure: Chapters in the History of the American Industrial Enterprise* (Cambridge, Mass.: The MIT Press, 1962); and Chandler, *The Visible Hand: The Managerial Revolution in American Business* (Cambridge: Belknap-Harvard University Press, 1977); Oliver Williamson, *Markets and Hierarchies* (New York: The Free Press, 1975).

6. George Huber and Reuben McDaniel, "The Decision-Making Paradigm of Organizational Design," *Management Science* 32 (1986), 572–89.

7. Aglietta, *A Theory of Capitalist Regulation*; Martin Kenney and Richard Florida, "Beyond Mass Production: Production and the Labor Process in Japan," *Politics and Society* 16 (1988), 121–58; Charles Sable, *Work and Politics: The Division of Labor in Industry* (Cambridge: Cambridge University Press, 1982).

8. Harland Prechel, "Economic Crisis and the Centralization of Control over the Managerial Process: Corporate Restructuring and Neo-Fordist Decision Making," *American Sociological Review* 59 (1999), 723–45.

9. American Iron and Steel Institute, *Annual Statistical Report* (Washington, D.C.: AISI, 1989).

10. For further discussion on this point, see Harland Prechel, "Irrationality and Contradiction in Organizational Change: Transformations in the Corporate Form of a U.S. Steel Corporation, 1930–1987," *The Sociological Quarterly* 32, no. 3 (1991).

11. Karl Marx, *Capital*, vol. 1 (New York: International Publishers, 1967); Sweezy, *The Theory of Capitalist Development*; Ernest Mandel, *Late Capitalism* (London: Verso, 1975).

12. See Harry Braverman, *Labor and Monopoly Capital: The Degradation of Work in the Twentieth Century* (New York: Monthly Review Press, 1974); Dan Clawson, *Bureaucracy and the Labor Process: The Transformation of U.S. Industry, 1860–1920* (New York: Monthly Review Press, 1980); Richard Edwards, *Contested Terrain: The Transformation of the Workplace in the Twentieth Century* (New York: Basic Books, 1979); Stephen Marglin, "What Do Bosses Do? The Origins and Functions of Hierarchy in Capitalist Production," *Review of Radical Political Economy*, no. 6 (Summer 1974).

13. See Michael Burawoy, *Manufacturing Consent: Changes in the Labor Process under Monopoly Capitalism* (Chicago: University of Chicago Press, 1979); Burawoy, "Between the Labor Process and the State: The Changing Face of Factory Regimes under Advanced Capitalism," *American Sociological Review* 48 (1983).

14. The organizational literature refers to the expansion of organizational complexity beyond the cognitive capacity of managers as bounded rationality. See Herbert Simon, *Administrative Behavior*, 2nd ed. (New York: Macmillan, 1957), 79; James March and Herbert Simon, *Organizations* (New York: John Wiley & Sons, 1958), 168–71.

15. H. Thomas Johnson and Robert S. Kaplan, *Relevance Lost: The Rise and Fall of Management Accounting* (Boston: Harvard Business School, 1991).

16. The definition of *dumping* has varied historically, but generally refers to selling steel below prices the U.S. government negotiated with foreign steelmakers. Harland Prechel, "Steel and the State: Industry Politics and Business Policy Formation, 1940–1989," *American Sociological Review* 55, no. 5 (1990).

17. David Vogel, *Fluctuating Fortunes: The Political Power of Business in America* (New York: Basic Books, 1989); Harland Prechel, *Big Business and the State: Historical Transitions and Corporate Transformation, 1880s–1990s* (Albany, N.Y.: State University of New York Press, 2000).

18. Robert McIntyre and Dean Tipps. *Inequality and Decline* (Washington, D.C.: Center on Budget and Policy Priorities, 1983).

19. William Scheuerman, *The Steel Crisis: The Economics of Politics of a Declining Industry* (New York: Praeger, 1986).

20. Traditionally, steel production was organized in segments.

21. For manufacturing corporations, semifinished inventory cost is a major source of capital investment. For example, in the early 1980s, this corporation had between $750 and $900 million invested into semifinished inventories.

22. See Chandler, *The Visible Hand: The Managerial Revolution in American Business.*

23. Harland Prechel, "Corporate Form and the State," *Sociological Inquiry* 67, no. 2 (1997).

24. Prechel, "Irrationality and Contradiction in Organizational Change." See also Harland Prechel, "Corporate Transformation to the Multilayered Subsidiary Form: Changing Economic Conditions and State Business Policy," *Sociological Forum* 12 (1997), 405–39.

4

Working Women and the Dynamics of Power at Work

Marina A. Adler

Women have entered the labor market in increasing numbers, and they currently make up about 46 percent of the U.S. labor force. In August 1999, 60 percent of women older than 16, compared with 75 percent of men, were employed in the civilian labor force. Women continue to be employed predominantly in white-collar occupations labeled as "traditionally female," such as sales, clerical, and nursing. These occupations are also associated with low income, limited career advancement opportunities, and low levels of authority.[1] Extensive literature documents variations in the work experience and occupational segregation of men and women in the labor force.[2] These studies show that gender affects the differential allocation of individuals into occupations, and that labor market realities and on-the-job experiences vary by gender. Research also documents that women are less likely to be policymakers or supervisors, and have less job autonomy than men.[3] Since women are overrepresented in the working class, they also are more likely to be separated from the labor process than men. In fact, women and men occupy different locations in various hierarchies of power at work. Part of the reason for this pattern is grounded in the traditional gender division of labor, which transcends the patriarchal household and impinges on the organization of work in modern capitalism.

This chapter explores the position of working women in power relations in the workplace. After reviewing various approaches relevant to the analysis of women's power as wage earners, empirical data are presented to support the claim that women continue to occupy a disadvantaged position at work vis-à-vis men.

GENDER AND CLASS

In all societies, an individual's position in the social structure is derived from his/her relationship to economic and kinship systems in general, and control over scarce resources in the market and family in particular. In advanced capitalist societies, there has traditionally been a separation of human activity into a "male-centered" public sphere (labor market) and a "female-centered" private sphere (family).[4] Consequently, conventional stratification analysts have assumed that men gain their class position through their employment in the labor market, whereas women's position is defined by their family ties to men, and hence only indirectly by economic relations. However, by 2000, most women in the United States had become active participants in the labor force, and feminist researchers pose the question of how to incorporate the gender dimension of stratification into a class-based analysis.

Joan Acker has pointed out that "sex stratification always involves economic and power inequalities: These inequalities are produced and maintained within the system of relationships that also constitute the class structure."[5] Consequently, one of the major premises underlying this essay is that power structures and social stratification are not gender-neutral. This argument is grounded in the assumption that there is a division of labor by gender at home and at work, and that access to societal power positions is not equal for women and men.

Although the general social organization of work is defined by class relations, these class structures are internally stratified.[6] Because most women are gainfully employed, the analysis of women's position in the workplace has become a major aspect of gender stratification research. As part of the workforce, women are overrepresented in low-paying, gender-typed occupations with low career advancement opportunities. Therefore, in addition to the inequalities arising from the labor process (social class), sources external to the market (gender, race) serve to divide groups of workers into different jobs and activities, regardless of individual qualifications.

Patriarchy as a form of power based on gender is related to economic domination at work and in the family. Thus, one may argue that ascribed characteristics, such as gender, may facilitate the access to and use of economic control, which then increases the inequality between the genders. These patterns of male privilege are particularly evident in the history of the dynamics between kinship and economic systems. The patriarchal family form in Western society with its emphasis on the male breadwinner role has influenced the social relations of production related to women's employment patterns; consequently, women do traditionally different work than men, are paid on average lower wages, and are less likely to be protected by unions.[7]

Several researchers have recognized the need for increased attention to intraclass variation in worker power and rewards, particularly with respect to gender.[8] It is clear that stratification research grounded in class analytical frameworks needs to confront the linkage between gender and access to work power. In this context, Arne Kalleberg and Larry Griffin search for "additional sources of within-class positional inequality," and Robert Thomas argues that "it is necessary to connect status inequalities external to the labor process more directly with the way in which activities and positions are structured internal to economic organization."[9] In other words, the link between ascribed characteristics, such as gender or race, and work stratification must be made more explicit.

The neo-Marxist position on ascription is essentially one of "class first." In other words, because in modern capitalist societies class is considered the most fundamental social category, the origin of inequality is considered to be located within the labor process, not external to it.[10] This poses the challenge of how to regard gender as a fundamental basis of inequality and stratification, without simultaneously having to reject Marx's analysis of the labor process in its entirety. Thus, Thomas' question is restated: "Can non-class categories impact on the organizational labor process?"[11] To answer this question, one has to accept the view that gender as a nonmarket status distinguishes among workers, regardless of their skill levels. Therefore, the consequences of gender for work stratification include occupational gender typing as well as the division of workers into different jobs and work activities. In addition to separating workers by gender, this selection process ranks "gendered" tasks by importance, resources, and remuneration. "Women's work" is an example of this phenomenon. According to Rosabeth Kanter, occupations containing high proportions of women often come to reflect the gender of the incumbents rather than the actual skill requirements for the job.[12] However, gender not only affects the occupational structure and work content, but it also causes differences in workers' power at work.

ALIENATION AND POWER AT WORK

Work is a fundamental human activity, and most women and men in the United States spend a large amount of time in paid employment. According to Marx, alienation is the separation of the worker from the work process, from the products of work, from fellow workers, and from his or her "species being" (lack of creativity). The literature on alienation contains approaches focusing both on the subjective perceptions of workers and the objective employment conditions that produce these perceptions. Robert Blauner conceptualizes alienation in terms of four dimensions: powerlessness, meaninglessness, isolation, and self-estrangement.[13] Powerlessness refers to the worker's lack of control over the work process, working conditions, and policy decision-making. Meaninglessness of the labor performed is based on routinization and the subdivision of work into minute tasks under capitalism. The worker's isolation is also referred to as social alienation, and self-estrangement relates to lack of creativity and fulfillment in work. Others have developed the concept of "occupational self-direction," which is defined as the "use of initiative, thought, and independent judgment" at work.[14] This concept has three empirical dimensions: substantive complexity, routinization, and lack of supervision.

Most of these empirical analyses stress the subjective expression or social psychological interpretation of alienation. However, one of the Marxist premises related to alienation deals with the underlying objective conditions of the capitalist mode of production: lack of ownership or control of the means of production (hence, control over work) results in worker alienation.[15] Thus, both the process and product of labor become "alien" to workers, and they do not have control over their work activities.[16] The problem arises from the contradiction between the profit requirements of capitalist production and work as being autonomous, nonalienating, and creative.[17] Alienation clearly goes beyond subjective feelings of job satisfaction or control over the immediate work environment because they are rooted in objective employment conditions. However, for the analysis of gender and power at work, the exercise of control over work activities is crucial. Relations of production become exploitive when one group has more power in the workplace in relation to another group. This uneven distribution of power facilitates the extraction of surplus value from those with less power and, hence, less control over the production process. If it can be shown that women are more likely than men to be in a disadvantaged position with respect to work power, they also may be more likely to be alienated.

The Marxist framework views alienation and workers' lack of control over the work process under capitalism as an outcome of the socioeconomic structure of capitalist society (i.e., social relations of production or property-based class relations).[18] The bulk of this literature is concerned with the empowerment of the working class vis-à-vis the capitalist system and its exploitative nature; another focus is on proletarianization and unionization processes as they relate to the collective power (or lack thereof) of workers as a group.[19]

As an extension of traditional class analysis, another approach acknowledges the existence of hierarchies not only between classes, but *within* them; it focuses on the various forms and degrees of worker control over work resources, positions, and personnel. It is argued that "economic inequality is generated by differences in the *power* of economic actors and that inequalities in job rewards are determined both by work structures that reflect the relative power of employers in product markets and by those that represent the relative power of workers in labor markets."[20] Thus, class relations are gendered because gender inequality is a part of the social relations of production. According to Monica Boyd, we have to recognize that "gender is not a separate dimension of inequality but is . . . embedded in . . . the class structure."[21]

In relation to women's disadvantaged position in the labor market, this means that in addition to individual characteristics, such as educational and skill levels, structural factors determine unequal rewards by gender. Members of the working class are differentiated by gender, race, and the characteristics of the firms and markets they work in. It is also acknowledged that individuals may have different amounts of power within these broader categories.

Alienation has also been associated with deskilling processes, proletarianization, and increasing routinization of the modern workplace.[22] Harry Braverman argues that in modern capitalist societies, the separation of mental and manual labor under capitalist relations of production has led to the destruction of "crafts."[23] Conceptual control has become separated from the execution of production, and work tasks increasingly minute; not only blue-collar work but also white-collar work is shown to have become increasingly routinized, menial, and controlled. This has been attributed to a shift from earlier, small-scale manufacturing to large-scale corporate and bureaucratic organizations as the main employers. Bureaucracy has become a part of the capitalist production process, and thus, white-collar skills have been downgraded and their craft dimension destroyed. However, low-level, white-collar work continues to be associated with higher training and educational levels than blue-collar work. Professional white-collar workers, scientific workers, or semiautonomous workers are less alienated than lower level white-collar and blue-collar workers because of education and autonomy.[24]

Since World War II, the service sector of the economy and white-collar work in general have expanded. In fact, most jobs created since the 1980s have been service jobs. According to Val Burris, there has also been a dramatic shift from self-employment to the salaried middle class since 1900.[25] This can be attributed to the large growth in white-collar occupations, which resulted from the transformations in the nature of modern capitalism related to declines in profit rates and consumption. These processes have also led to mechanisms to increase rationalization and control of the labor process. The combination of high demand in the labor market and the opportunity to pay less to women than men has created the feminization of the service sector and the gender segregation of the modern office in terms of male managers and female administrative support staff.[26]

THE DEFINITION OF WORK POWER

In defining *work power,* some authors conceptualize authority as "legitimated control over the work process of others," whereas others specify job power as "control over organizational resources."[27] When specifically addressing women's power in the workplace, emphasis is placed on women's "capacity to shape their work environment."[28] In a similar vein, "empowerment" is seen as crucial for women, because it generates "more autonomy, more participation in decisions, and more access to resources."[29]

The concept of job autonomy or discretion is usually treated as separate from power. However, it can be argued that in the work context, autonomy becomes a form of power because it entails independence and control for the worker. Erik Olin Wright defines *job autonomy* as the "extent to which an individual controls the conceptual aspects of work."[30] Job autonomy or self-direction may be regarded as both a dichotomous or a gradational concept: Whereas the employer/supervisor may categorically have the ability to determine the amounts of responsibility delegated to individual employees, these employees then vary in terms of their degree of job autonomy. Therefore, "autonomy . . . designates a social relationship between supervisor and subordinates which structures the range of activities over which the subordinate has discretion. It is possible to measure this range as a continuous variable while still regarding it as an indicator of the underlying social relation."[31] Thus, whereas employees as members of the working class may not have much power as part of their relationship with the employer, they may have some degree of autonomy in terms of the actual work activities performed. Women are overrepresented in the working class in general, but they may also be disadvantaged in regard to the amount of control they have over their own work, when compared with working-class men.

Autonomy as a structural aspect of work power can be derived from arguments about proletarianization and deskilling. By breaking down comprehensive production into minute tasks requiring minimal skill levels, the contemporary production process has stifled most of the workers' conceptual input. The separation of mental and manual labor under capitalism is a key element in power relations at work.[32] According to Stewart Clegg and David Dunkerly, "de-skilling represents a loss of control by the worker over a given task because of a re-design of the job by which the task is accomplished."[33] In other words, the nature of work in industrial society has changed in as much as it partitions skills originally embodied in one craft and thereby reduces the worker's power, autonomy, and creativity. Nevertheless, industrialization has also created new positions and occupations (professional occupations in particular) that have relatively high levels of autonomy.

Technological innovation is based on efforts to increase the organization's efficiency and, thus, as in the case of authority, is likely to curtail some of the workers' control over their work environment. In other words, the workers' abilities to make decisions regarding their own work processes, pacing, timing, and conceptual structures will be reduced. Increased routinization and regulation, as well as supervision, reduce the independence and responsibilities of the worker. Since the literature suggests that women have historically been closely supervised at work and that women are in jobs characterized by high levels of routinization,[34] one may expect that they have less autonomy at work than men.

Overall, although individuals may be subject to rules, supervision, and control by superiors, they may be able to exert some input on how and when their work is done. Being the "recipient" of authority (supervision) is not necessarily the same as lacking job autonomy. In other words, although authority is "other-directed," autonomy entails workers' immediate decisions about their own work situation or the degree of independence in the performance of the job, and therefore it is self-directed.

OCCUPATIONAL SEGREGATION AND POWER

The literature on gender differences in work power is limited. Nevertheless, studies show that men generally have more power and autonomy at work than women.[35] Although Wright's theory focuses on class relations, his exploitation-centered analysis is relevant to the study of gender inequality. Throughout recent history, women as a group have been systematically subordinated by exclusion from paid labor. Originally excluded from paid labor, women were relegated to the class status of their male family members (fathers or husbands). Upon entering the labor force, women were initially excluded from various occupations, particularly those involving crafts and the professions, and later they were concentrated in certain industries and economic sectors, such as textiles and services, all the while being subjected to lower pay scales than men. Furthermore, as a result of patriarchal capitalist relations, women were not only excluded from the protection provided by unions, but were denied access to power positions, such as supervisors, within factories and organizations. After the barriers of exclusion to paid labor were lifted, women's participation in the labor market was, like child labor, characterized by exploitation and subordination. Women's labor was relegated to cheap, unprotected, and "secondary" labor. Even when doing the same work as men, women were paid lower wages, thereby increasing the employers' profits as well as consolidating the patriarchal family form.[36]

The entire idea of "women's work" bears on this history of exclusion, exploitation, and oppression. Occupations that have traditionally led to high-level power positions or high rewards, such as professional or managerial jobs, have until only recently been out of reach for women. The types of work women have traditionally engaged in are invariably jobs that are not in direct contradiction to the normative "female role." Occupations involving care for children and homes, such as teacher, governess, or maid, exemplify this kind of work. Another occupational category that was opened relatively early for women is factory work. This work is characterized by a lack of unionization, low wages, and limited advancement opportunities to power positions. This combination of disadvantaged conditions is likely to affect the collective position of women, as well as the individual power distributions among men and women at work.

Research demonstrates that "the lower the level of authority considered, the more egalitarian is the process of acquiring that level of authority, at least with respect to education."[37] Wendy Wolf and Neil Fligstein have found that when controlling human capital and family characteristics, women's access to higher levels of authority, as measured by the ability to hire and fire, is restricted. Nevertheless, they argue that generally most of the gender differences in authority returns are due to differences in job characteristics, such as gender typing. Overall, even though different indicators of authority are used, this and other such studies conclude that despite occupational status similarity, men have more authority than women.[38]

In general, women are overrepresented in lower paying, lower authority occupations that lack job ladders. White-collar occupations, such as secretary, for example, have very limited routes for career development. This is consequential for gender differences in power at work, because collectively and individually, women encounter lower ceilings with respect to advancement opportunities than men within occupation and careers. It has been suggested that women forgo career opportunities, authority, and higher wages to "buy" flexible work schedules to accommodate their family responsibilities. In other words, women trade higher paying jobs and increased power for the ability to control, leave, and resume their work. This would explain why women tend to be more satisfied with their jobs despite less desirable working conditions–they expect less from their jobs than do men.

Research also indicates that segregation tends to be higher in those industries that are characterized by higher profitability.[39] These are located in the core sector of the economy, which is the sector with high incomes, unionization, and job stability. Thus, it is argued that these increased assets may offset the costs of inefficient labor practices, such as gender segregation. Another study demonstrates that, in general, firms are highly gender segregated and that the nature of work performed by employees varies by gender: Even when women are in the same occupations as men, they tend to perform different tasks and receive less pay.[40] Those tasks labeled as "women's work" are consistently assigned a lower value than activities considered to be "men's work."

Research on the relationship between occupational gender segregation and wages indicates that when controlling the type of tasks performed, women are paid less than men.[41] Consequently, in an attempt to counteract the negative effect of gender typing on income, the concept of "comparable worth" (i.e., equal pay for equal work) was developed.[42] Work tasks that entail similar skill and educational levels, disregarding the proportion of women in the job, are assigned the same income. This strategy aims at elevating the "systematically undervalued" women's work to equalize male and female incomes.

Consistent findings indicate that part of the income gap between the genders and races is due to differences in access to high positions in authority hierarchies and restrictions of job ladders. Specifically, Charles W. Mueller and Toby Parcel argue that "differential access to authority resources explains racial earnings differences, whereas differential resource efficacy is more important in explaining sex inequality."[43] Thus, power in the workplace contributes to the explanation of the gender income gap by showing that women with similar power as men are not rewarded equally. In other words, black men may generally be barred from power positions, but if they reach them, they are paid the same as white men in those positions. Women, however, even if they do attain high levels of power, cannot convert that power into income to the same extent as men.

Overall, in terms of "span of responsibility" (task and sanctioning authority) and "span of control" (number of subordinates), white males benefit more from authority than women, because they are selectively promoted and rewarded.[44] Thus, gender discrimination exists in both access to and benefits from power. This finding also gives credence to Kanter's analysis of informal power networks and their exclusionary effect on women in organizations.[45] In addition, research on the relationship between work power and income indicates that although both "control over monetary resources" and "control over personnel" are the key work variables determining women's income, men benefit mainly from monetary control alone.[46] This finding somewhat contradicts Mueller and Parcel's, who found control over personnel to be less important for the income of female managers than male managers. One possible explanation may be that female managers are more likely to supervise female employees and thus are rewarded less.

CURRENT EMPIRICAL PATTERNS IN OCCUPATIONAL SEGREGATION AND POWER AT WORK

To assess whether women are less likely than men to have control over the work process, some recent data are presented. It is evident from the data presented in table 4.1 that male and female workers are not equal in terms of rewards for their work and in their occupational distribution. The table shows that although about 64 percent of all women (and 77 percent of all men) in the United States are employed in the labor force, they only earn about 74 percent of men's median annual earnings. Even when taking marital and parental status into account, the majority of women are employed

Table 4.1   **Employment and Family Status by Gender, 1998**

Employment and Family Status	Women	Men
Median annual earnings, full-time workers	$24,973	$33,674
Total % employed	63.6	76.9
>35 hours/week	70.7	86.4
<35 hours/week	29.3	13.6
Percent employed		
Without children	53.9	67.0
Total parents (children <18)	71.8	94.6
Married (children <18)	70.0	95.1
Not married (children <18)	76.7	89.5
Total parents (children 6–17)	77.6	93.5
Total parents (children <6)	64.9	96.1
Percent employed		
Mothers with children <3	57.7	n.a.
Married	58.3	n.a.
Not married	55.6	n.a.
Mothers with children <1	53.6	n.a.
Married	55.2	n.a.
Not married	48.4	n.a.

Source: U.S. Department of Labor, Bureau of Labor Statistics, *Labor Force Statistics from the Current Population Survey, 1999;* U.S. Bureau of the Census, *Current Population Reports,* Series P-60, 1998.

outside the home. In fact, disregarding marital status, more than 70 percent of women with children are in the labor force. This percentage is only about 5 percent lower when the children are younger than school age. For mothers with children younger than three, the labor force participation is between 56 percent and 58 percent, and more than 50 percent of mothers of infants are in the labor force. What becomes obvious from these data is that the traditional "male breadwinner with female mother/homemaker" family form is a thing of the past. Despite the fact that the notion of the "family wage" is clearly outdated, women's annual earnings are only 74 percent of men's.

When comparing the median earnings of men and women in each occupational category (see table 4.2), it becomes clear that women consistently earn less than men, disregarding particular occupations. Table 4.2 shows that in 1998, female full-time wage and salary workers earned about 76 percent of men's weekly earnings. The pay gap is largest in sales (59.8 percent), executive management (68.4 percent), and traditional male blue-collar occupations (69.5 percent). Women do best vis-à-vis men in jobs where wages are relatively low, including the nonprivate household service jobs (90.8 percent of men's wages), some skilled jobs (86.6 percent for mechanics), unskilled labor (85.9 percent for handlers), and agricultural jobs (88.6 percent).

Table 4.2 Occupational Segregation and the Gender Pay Gap, 1998

Occupational Category	% Women in Occupation	Women's Median Weekly Earnings in $	Men's Median Weekly Earnings in $	Women's Earnings as % of Men's
All Occupations	46.2	456	598	76.3
Managerial and professional	49.0	655	905	72.4
Exec., admin., manag.	46.4	626	915	68.4
Professional specialty	51.6	682	895	76.2
Technical, sales, admin. support	61.9	419	606	69.1
Technical & related support	49.4	511	701	72.9
Sales	45.0	372	622	59.8
Admin. support, clerical	76.3	418	518	80.7
Service	50.0	296	389	76.1
Private household	95.0	220	n.a.	—
Protective	22.5	418	613	78.5
Other	57.2	295	325	90.8
Precision, craft, repair	8.1	408	587	69.5
Mechanics	3.8	519	599	86.6
Construction	1.6	408	545	74.9
Other	21.2	392	611	64.2
Operators, fabricators, labor	23.3	327	456	71.7
Machinist, assembly, inspection	35.9	328	472	69.5
Transport, material movers	8.0	373	519	71.9
Handlers, equipment cleaners, helpers, labor	17.7	311	362	85.9
Farming, forestry, fishing	14.0	272	307	88.6

Source: U.S. Department of Labor, Bureau of Labor Statistics, *Labor Force Statistics from the Current Population Survey, 1999.*

Among the sales jobs, those with the highest pay are financial services sales ($758), which are also male-dominated with only about 29 percent women. The lowest paid sales jobs, such as apparel sales ($296), also employ 80 percent women. In the managerial occupations, the highest paid are marketing, advertising, and public relations managers (38.5 percent women). Here men receive an average of $1,128 per week, compared with women's $759, indicating that the highest paid women managers earn only about 67 percent of their male counterparts. In the professions the pay gap is 82 percent for engineers (11 percent women), 77 percent for physicians (26.6 percent women), and 70 percent for lawyers (28.5 percent women). Thus, breaking into the higher paying occupations does not pay off equally for women and men. In traditionally female occupations, such as registered

nursing, teaching, or secretarial work, women receive 95 percent and 90 percent of men's wages respectively, yet these white-collar jobs generally also
do not pay well. Overall, the female/male income ratio is lowest for traditional white-collar jobs categorized as technical, sales, and administrative
support occupations, and it is highest for traditional blue-collar jobs in the
precision, craft, repair and operators, fabricators, and labor categories. Thus,
female workers may do better vis-à-vis male workers in traditional working-
class labor, partly because these jobs are not as "feminized" as the white-
collar support jobs.

Analysis of the occupational distribution of women and men (see table
4.3) reveals evidence of occupational gender segregation. Table 4.3 reflects
the distribution of all workers across white- and blue-collar jobs. While about
59 percent of the U.S. labor force is employed in white-collar work, only
about 47 percent of men are. Women are clearly overrepresented in white-
collar occupations (76 percent) and underrepresented among blue-collar
workers (11 percent). Within these jobs, women are predominantly in "pink
collar" work, such as the semiprofessions (teaching, nursing, and social
work) and clerical support (secretaries and clerks). Again, these can be regarded as extensions of the traditional female "helping, caring, and assisting"
role, and thus, are not associated with high monetary rewards. Some gender
gaps in occupation-specific income seem to reflect society's value system in
a startling manner. For example, a female child-care worker earns on average less ($208) than a male service station attendant ($297); a female kinder-
garten teacher earns less ($398) than a male general maintenance worker

Table 4.3   Labor Market Structure by Gender Distribution of Workers, 1998

Labor Market Category	Percent of All Workers in Category	Percent of All Female Workers in Category	Percent of All Male Workers in Category	Female Distribution All Workers
Total white-collar	59.2	75.8	46.7	16.6
Management	15.1	16.2	14.3	1.1
Professional	15.5	18.6	13.2	–3.1
Technical, sales, admin. support	28.6	41.0	19.2	12.4
Service	11.1	12.8	9.7	1.7
Total blue-collar	28.0	10.8	41.1	–17.2
Precision, crafts, repair	12.2	2.3	19.8	–9.9
Operators, fabricators, labor	15.8	8.5	21.3	–7.3
Farming, forestry, fishing	1.6	0.5	2.5	–1.1
Total percent	100.0	100.0	100.0	

Source: U.S. Department of Labor, Bureau of Labor Statistics, *Labor Force Statistics from the Current Population Survey, 1999.*

($457). On the other hand, the rewards for a female registered nurse ($734) are about equal to those for a male police officer ($738), indicating that both types of work are of equal value.

After providing evidence for gender differences in the occupational distribution, the extent to which control at work varies by gender is assessed. To assess the effect of occupational segregation (traditional female occupations, such as teacher, white-collar service, nurse, secretary) on control at work, tables 4.4 and 4.5 present data on the percentage of men and women having any managing and supervisory capacity by occupation. In 1998, only about 22 percent of all U.S. employees held jobs indicating that they were managers (15.1 percent) or supervisors (6.9 percent). Nearly half of the managers were women and they earned about 68 percent of their male counterparts, indicating a larger wage gap than that among supervisors (79 percent), where women's share is only 34 percent. The gap is largest for educational management (66 percent) and smallest for real estate managers (81 percent). While in the "other service occupations" the pay gap is quite small (women receive about 91 percent of men's wages), becoming a supervisor does not pay off for women in this sector: female food preparation supervisors earn only about 71 percent, and cleaning supervisors about 76 percent, of their

Table 4.4   Managerial Power by Gender and Earnings, 1998

Level of Power	% Women in Occupation	Women's Median Weekly Earnings in $	Men's Median Weekly Earnings in $	Women's Earnings as % of Men's
Management (15.1% of all employees)	46.4	626	915	68.4
Administrators, officials, public administration	48.6	663	957	69.3
Financial managers	51.4	703	1,017	69.1
Personnel and labor relations	63.8	747	947	78.9
Purchasing managers	41.2	724	965	75.0
Market, advertising, public relations	38.2	759	1,128	67.3
Administrative and educational	59.3	730	1,111	65.7
Medicine and health	78.6	679	869	78.1
Food services and lodging	44.1	434	591	73.4
Property and real estate	55.8	518	638	81.2
Management-related	58.6	602	790	76.2

Source: U.S. Department of Labor, Bureau of Labor Statistics, *Labor Force Statistics from the Current Population Survey, 1999.*

Table 4.5 Supervisory Power by Gender and Earnings, 1998

Level of Power	% Women in Occupation	Women's Median Weekly Earnings in $	Men's Median Weekly Earnings in $	Women's Earnings as % of Men's
Supervisors (6.9% of all employees)	33.8	483[a]	612	78.9[a]
Sales and proprietors	42.0	449	649	69.2
Administrative support	59.9	556	679	81.9
Protective services	8.4	674[b]	786	85.8[b]
Food preparation	56.2	304	427	71.2
Cleaning	39.5	348	457	76.1
Mechanics	6.1	652[c]	748	87.2[c]
Construction	0.8	548[d]	709	77.3[d]
Precision production	17.0	478	686	69.7
Motor vehicle operation	22.8	440[e]	625	70.4[e]
Farm managers	14.3	446[f]	486	91.7[f]
Agricultural supervisor	6.3	418[g]	479	87.3[g]

Notes:
[a] estimates
[b] estimates based on the pay gap for public service police officers
[c] estimates based on the pay gap for mechanics and repairers
[d] estimates based on the pay gap for all construction trades
[e] estimates based on the pay gap for all motor vehicle operators
[f] estimates based on the pay gap in all farm occupations
[g] estimates based on the pay gap in agricultural occupations

Source: U.S. Department of Labor, Bureau of Labor Statistics, *Labor Force Statistics from the Current Population Survey, 1999.*

male counterparts. It may be argued that cooking and cleaning are extensions of the traditional female role, and thus women do not have to "train" for it, thereby not warranting the same income that men receive, who work outside their traditional role. Nevertheless, although the numbers of female supervisors in most traditionally male blue-collar occupations are very small, the wage gap is also generally smaller (79 percent). Female farm managers and mechanics supervisors are doing best vis-à-vis men, with wage gaps of 92 percent and 87 percent, respectively. Overall, it appears that women do gain a moderate wage advantage vis-à-vis men by entering male-dominated blue-collar occupations and by becoming supervisors. Although women have moved into white-collar managerial work, they were not able to convert this power into equal rewards. Therefore, to improve the status of women in the labor market, it is insufficient to combat occupational segregation per se. Although it may be advantageous for women to enter less traditional occupations in terms of increased economic rewards, they continue to lack equal control over their work. Consequently, because women have less control at work, they are more likely to be alienated than men. Moving into less gender-typed occupations will not change that fact. One may argue that although the majority of U.S. workers lack significant control over their work environment, gender is an additional dimension that serves to stratify the modern workplace. The dynamic relationship between capitalism and patriarchy has created a gendered division of labor that is evident in occupational gender segregation.

CONCLUSION

The theoretical and empirical literature has produced various approaches to the question of gender as it affects work-related phenomena. The Marxist analysis locates the source of economic inequality in the nature of capitalist relations of production rather than in gender relations. Structural labor-market theorists argue that the capitalist economy has segmented the labor market, industries, and occupations, which in turn compounds women's disadvantages. The Marxist–feminist tradition emphasizes the dynamic cooperation of capitalism and patriarchy in establishing the structures that now place women in an inferior position vis-à-vis men in the labor process. This chapter has attempted to provide some empirical evidence for the effect of one such structure, that is, occupational gender segregation, on discrepancies in power over the labor process.

A fundamental issue revolves around the "place" of women in the class and occupational structure. This chapter has documented that women remain segmented within contradictory class positions as well as segregated in particular occupations. This does not suggest that women voluntarily choose female-typed occupations. Furthermore, women earn less than men even in male-dominated occupations. Overall, it has been shown that women are consistently outranked by men in the labor market.

Another question is: If women workers are in a different structural position vis-à-vis male workers, how does that affect their control over the labor process? The empirical patterns found in numerous studies demonstrate that women are generally less likely than men to have power at work. In other words, not only do women earn less than men and are working in different kinds of occupations than men, women in similar work situations have less power over the process and product of their labor than men. One consequence of this separation from the labor process is increased alienation.

It has been argued in the literature that women are willing to trade high income, power, and career opportunities for flexible work schedules and convenience so that they can more easily combine work and family responsibilities. Another line of thought urges women to pursue nontraditional occupations to combat low incomes, occupational segregation, and lack of power at work. Neither of these arguments seem supported by the empirical evidence presented here. Both the gender wage gap and occupational segregation persist in the face of rising numbers of female professionals. Increased demand for lower level white-collar workers, such as clerical and service workers, continues to reinforce existing occupational structures.

Expansion of the modern workplace continually erodes the control of the workers in general. The empowerment of women at work does not seem to coincide with empowerment efforts of male workers. In addition to creating a work environment devoid of alienating conditions, the gender-based structures related to the traditional division of labor and gender-typing of occupations need to be eradicated. Beyond the requirements of capitalist production, the traditional division of household labor consolidates the existing patters of female disadvantage. As long as women are assigned a disproportionate share of household maintenance and child-rearing responsibilities, their choices in finding creative and nonalienating work outside the home are severely restricted.

NOTES

1. Shelley Coverman, "Occupational Segmentation and Sex Differentials in Earnings," in *Research in Social Stratification and Mobility,* ed. R. V. Robinson (Greenwich, Conn.: JAI Press, 1986); Marina Adler, "Gender Differences in Job Autonomy: The Consequences of Occupational Segregation and Authority Position," *The Sociological Quarterly* 34 (1993).

2. See Francine D. Blau, "Women in the Labor Force: An Overview," in *Women: A Feminist Perspective,* ed. Joe Freeman (Palo Alto, Calif.: Mayfield, 1984); Sharlene Hesse-Biber and Gregg Lee Carter, *Working Women in America: Split Dreams* (New York: Oxford University Press, 2000); Jerry Jacobs and Sue T. Lin, "Trends in Occupational and Industrial Sex Segregation in 56 Countries, 1960–1980," in *Gender Inequality at Work,* ed. J. A. Jacobs, (Thousand Oaks, Calif.: Sage, 1995); Barbara Reskin, "Sex Segregation in the Workplace," *Annual Review of Sociology* 19 (1993).

3. Charles W. Mueller and Toby Parcel, "Ascription, Dimensions of Authority, and Earnings," *Research in Social Stratification and Mobility* 5 (1986); Erik Olin Wright, C. Costello, D. Hachen, and J. Spraegue, "The American Class Structure," *American Sociological Review* 47 (1982); Gart M. McGuire and Barbara Reskin, "Authority Hierarchy at Work: The Impact of Race and Sex," *Gender and Society* 7 (1993).

4. Elise Boulding, "Familial Constraints on Women's Work Roles," *Signs* 1 (1976); Heidi Hartman, "Capitalism, Patriarchy and Job Segregation by Sex," *Signs* 1 (1976).

5. Joan Acker, "Women and Stratification: A Review of Recent Literature," *Contemporary Sociology* 9 (1980), 26.

6. Joe L. Spaeth, "Structural Contexts and the Stratification of Work," *Research in Social Stratification and Mobility* 3 (1984).

7. Coverman, "Occupational Segmentation and Sex Differentials in Earnings"; Tamara K. Hareven, *Family Time & Industrial Time: The Relationship between the Family and Work in a New England Industrial Community* (New York: Cambridge University Press, 1982); Hartman, "Capitalism, Patriarchy and Job Segregation by Sex."

8. Toby Parcel and C. W. Mueller, *Ascription and Labor Markets: Race and Sex Differences in Earnings* (New York: Academic Press, 1983); Robert J. Thomas, "Citizenship and Gender in Work Organization: Some Considerations for Theories of the Labor Process," *American Journal of Sociology* (Suppl.) 88 (1982). See also Arne L. Kalleberg and Larry J. Griffin, "Class, Occupation and Inequality in Job Rewards," *American Journal of Sociology* 85 (1980); Robert V. Robinson and Jonathan Kelley, "Class as Conceived by Marx and Dahrendorf: Effects on Income Inequality and Politics in the United States and Britain," *American Sociological Review* 44 (1979).

9. Kalleberg and Griffin, "Class, Occupation and Inequality in Job Rewards," 765; Thomas, "Citizenship and Gender in Work Organization," S109.

10. Thomas, "Citizenship and Gender in Work Organization." See also Erik Olin Wright, "Race, Class and Income Inequality," *American Journal of Sociology* 83 (1978).

11. Thomas, "Citizenship and Gender in Work Organization," S86.

12. Rosabeth Moss Kanter, *Men and Women of the Corporation* (New York: Basic Books, 1977).

13. Robert Blauner, *Alienation and Freedom* (Chicago: University of Chicago Press, 1964).

14. Melvin L. Kohn and Carmi Schooler, *Work and Personality: An Inquiry into the Impact of Social Stratification* (Norwood, N.J.: Ablex, 1982), 22.

15. Stephen Hill, *Competition and Control at Work: The New Industrial Sociology* (Cambridge, Mass.: MIT Press, 1981).

16. Douglas M. Eichar and John L. P. Thompson, "Alienation, Occupational Self-Direction, and Worker Consciousness: An Exploration," *Work and Occupations* 13 (1986).

17. Beverly H. Burris, *No Room at the Top: Underemployment and Alienation in the Corporation* (New York: Praeger, 1983).

18. Albert Szymanski, *Class Structure* (New York: Praeger, 1983).

19. See Jerry Lembcke, *Capitalist Development and Class Capacities: Marxist Theory and Union Organization* (Westport, Conn.: Greenwood Press, 1988); Rick Fantasia, *Cultures of Solidarity: Consciousness, Action and Contemporary American Workers* (Berkeley: University of California Press, 1988).

20. Arne L. Kalleberg and Ivar Berg, *Work and Industry: Structures, Markets and Processes* (New York: Plenum Press 1987), 29.

21. Monica Boyd, "Feminizing Paid Work," *Current Sociology* 45 (1997), 52.

22. Harry Braverman, *Labor and Monopoly Capital: The Degradation of Work in the Twentieth Century* (New York: Monthly Review Press, 1974); Margery Davies, "Women's Place is at the Typewriter: The Feminization of the Clerical Labor Force," *Radical America* 8 (1974); Evelyn Nakano Glenn and Roslyn L. Feldberg, "Degraded and Deskilled: The Proletarianization of Clerical Work," *Social Problems* 25 (1977).

23. Braverman, *Labor and Monopoly Capital.*

24. See Val Burris, "Capital Accumulation and the Rise of the New Middle Class, *Review of Radical Political Economics* 12 (1980); Erik Olin Wright, *Classes* (London: Verso, 1985).

25. Burris, "Capital Accumulation and the Rise of the New Middle Class."

26. Kanter, *Men and Women of the Corporation.*

27. Wendy C. Wolf and Neil D. Fligstein, "Sex and Authority in the Work Place: The Causes of Sexual Inequality," *American Sociological Review* 44 (1979), 236; Joe L. Spaeth, "Job Power and Earnings," *American Sociological Review* 50 (1985), 603.

28. Dorothy Remy and Larry Sawers, "Women's Power in the Workplace," in *Social Power and Influence of Women,* ed. Liesa Stamm and Carol D. Ryff (Boulder, Colo.: Westview Press, 1984).

29. Kanter, *Men and Women of the Corporation,* 166.

30. Erik Olin Wright, *Class Structure and Class Consciousness Study U.S. Survey, 1980: A User's Guide to the Machine-Readable Data File* (Ann Arbor, Mich.: University of Wisconsin at Madison, Institute for Political and Social Research, 1985), 324.

31. Wright et al., "The American Class Structure," 712, footnote 6.

32. Braverman, *Labor and Monopoly Capital.*

33. Stewart Clegg and David Dunkerly, *Organization, Class and Control* (London: Routledge and Kegan Paul, 1980), 465.

34. Hareven, *Family Time & Industrial Time*; Hartman, "Capitalism, Patriarchy and Job Segregation by Sex"; R. Stolzenberg, "Occupations, Labor Markets, and the Process of Wage Attainment," *American Sociological Review* 40 (1975).

35. Parcel and Mueller, *Ascription and Labor Markets: Race and Sex Differences in Earnings*; Adler, "Gender Differences in Job Autonomy"; Spaeth, "Job Power and Earnings."

36. Hareven, *Family Time & Industrial Time*; Hartman, "Capitalism, Patriarchy and Job Segregation by Sex."

37. Wolf and Fligstein, "Sex and Authority in the Work Place," 244.

38. Wolf and Fligstein, "Sex and Authority in the Work Place," 244. Also see Patricia Roos, "Sexual Stratification in the Workplace: Male-Female Differences in Economic Returns to Occupation," *Social Science Research* 10 (1981).

39. William P. Bridges, "The Sexual Segregation of Occupations: Theories of Labor Stratification in Industry," *American Journal of Sociology* 88 (1982).

40. James N. Baron and William T. Bielby, "The Organization of Work in a Segmented Economy," *American Sociological Review* 49 (1984).

41. Paula England and Steven D. McLaughlin, "Sex Segregation of Jobs and Income Differentials," in *Discrimination in Organizations,* ed. Rudolfo Alvarez et al. (San Francisco: Jossey-Bass, 1979).

42. Ronnie Steinberg, "From Laissez-Faire to a Fair Wage for Women's Work: A Technical Fix to the Labor Contract," *Contemporary Sociology* 13 (1984).

43. Mueller and Parcel, "Ascription, Dimensions of Authority, and Earnings," 212. See also Adler, "Gender Differences in Job Autonomy."

44. Mueller and Parcel, "Ascription, Dimensions of Authority, and Earnings."

45. Kanter, *Men and Women of the Corporation.*

46. Spaeth, "Job Power and Earnings."

5

Race, Nationality, and the Division of Labor in U.S. Agriculture

John C. Leggett

Farmworkers by the hundreds of thousands migrate annually from both north-central Mexico and the U.S. Southwest to the California southlands—the Imperial and Coachella valleys. Then up the West Coast they motor through either Pacific central coastal California or the San Joaquin Valley to the American Northwest. There they labor in the vegetable rows and on the orchard ladders of Oregon and Washington. Subsequently, they return, either to northwestern Mexico or southern California.

Toward south-central United States, and residing largely in Texas during the winter, can be found hundreds of thousands of Mexicans—some are "legals," and others "illegals." They move north each year to work the fields in southern Michigan, Wisconsin, Minnesota, and the Dakotas. Once through working the crops, most return to Texas. Still, many of these working-class Mexican-Americans have left this Texas-based farm labor behind to settle in northern Midwestern communities, such as Chicago, Minneapolis, and Omaha, to work in steel mills or meat-packing houses. In some cases, they have settled to labor as permanent small-town residents inside service employment, plus the occasional seasonal bout within fruit or vegetable harvesting, as in northwestern Ohio and southern Michigan.

On the East Coast, the major migratory farmworker groups are African Americans, Jamaicans, Puerto Ricans, Mexicans, Laotians, Cambodians, and Vietnamese, although a residual group of whites can be found winter-based in Florida, Georgia, and the Carolinas. Also, like their Texan-Okie-Arky cousins in California, these whites have descended from an essentially Scot-Irish background. They have worked the ripened green vegetable produce and fruits, from southern Florida up through the Carolinas, the Chesapeake Bay, on into Delaware and New Jersey, and from there to upstate New York, into Connecticut, and even onward for the few to join local high school children in the potato harvest of northern Maine.[1]

Here it should be noted that the type of work done generally depends on nationality grouping. For example, on the East Coast, African Americans and Haitians work the vegetables; Belle Glade Florida Jamaicans serve as contract laborers for six months every year to harvest the sugar cane; Mexicans work fruit and vegetables; and Philadelphia-based Indo-Chinese labor primarily in vegetable fields in southern New Jersey.

Out West, the same patterning occurs in the San Joaquin and Imperial valleys, where corporate farms, such as those owned by DiGiorgio Corporation, have channeled each nationality grouping into a limited range of crop-producing occupational choices. Thus, there has been cross-nationality competition for the better, high-paying manual jobs, and a largely contained but nonetheless real animosity has developed among the various nationality groupings, thereby limiting possibilities for labor solidarity within agriculture—a situation that benefits the white growers.[2]

RACE, NATIONALITY, AND THE ORIGINS
OF COMMERCIAL FARMING IN CALIFORNIA

During the eighteenth century, the Spanish colonialists came to California as conquerors, took the land, entrusted the reworking of the agricultural division of labor to the Franciscan missions, and enslaved Indians within this division of labor. The Franciscan missionaries gave way during the Mexican governmental period (1821–1846) to Spanish nonclerical ownership of estates whose secularized division of labor continued to focus on production of many agricultural products rendered by Indians. The Anglo-Americans began to arrive during the 1840s, adopted the Mexican large estate structure, and eventually imposed a violent and rapacious servitude-based division of labor on the California Indians. The subordination of the Indians by Anglo-Americans within a division of labor where Indians had no choice but to accept their ranch field supervision without pay became a causal precedent for white ranch owners' violent treatment of nonwhite laborers in general.

In the early 1860s, the Anglo-American land owners began to substitute Chinese tenantry for the diminished Indian quasi slave labor force. By 1870 much of white dependence on Indian labor had all but disappeared—a situation that coincided with a 95 percent decline of the Native American population in northern California between 1840 and 1900.

The Chinese succeeded the American Indians on both Anglo-American and residual Spanish haciendas. These essentially non-Han Chinese from China's Kwangtung and Fukien provinces cut a path quite different from this country's indigenous native population.[3] In the main, the arriving Chinese worked initially for pecuniary rewards as California land tenants.

The Anglo-Americans leased subsections of land to Chinese tenants who, in turn, employed free, noncoolie Chinese field gang labor procured for the tenants by labor contractors also of Chinese descent. The labor contractor system rested on wages and occupied a crucial link within the all-Chinese vertical chain of command, except at the very top where the owners were generally white.

Barred from almost all California labor unions, the Chinese laborers employed by the Chinese tenant farmers were able to shield themselves somewhat by way of their cross-class Chinese protective associations, the "tongs."[4] From the 1860s until World War I, Chinese laborers and their fellow Chinese allies did fashion for themselves a modest amount of protection through these self-help associations made up exclusively of Chinese. These tongs were used as the bases for bargaining with white owners to obtain better wages for Chinese workers.

Violence against the Chinese plus anti-Chinese immigration legislation (most notably the 1882 law passed by the U.S. Congress to forbid further Chinese immigration) paved the way for extensive 1890s Japanese emigration into California agriculture.[5] Initial, turn-of-the-century Japanese migration into California agriculture essentially overlapped with widespread Chinese participation in agricultural production, although between 1910 and 1920, the Japanese surpassed the Chinese in terms of numbers and importance within California's agricultural division of labor, often settling side by side within spatially proximate communities, such as those established in the Sacramento and San Joaquin Delta region.[6]

Carey McWilliams has noted how, in the Sacramento, Santa Clara, San Joaquin, and Imperial valleys, it was the Japanese who for the most part proved responsible for the reclamation of waste lands. The hardships they experienced in the course of this pioneer activity took a stunning toll; in many cases, the Japanese laborers worked under exceedingly unhealthful conditions—in swamps, river deltas, and marshes. In Fresno County alone, during one period when water and sanitary conditions were bad, an estimated 3,000 Japanese lost their lives.[7]

Still, the Japanese farm laborers were able to build up small, informal, work-group solidarity teams that, through strikes, made insistent wage demands on the growers. Frequently, the Japanese laborers made their wage demands known at the time of the harvest; they would declare a strike and walk out at that crucial moment of crop-gathering.

The gang labor, tenantry, and land ownership success of the Japanese moved California populists during World War I to use the state government to sponsor the settlement of whites only on lands to be purchased by U.S. military veterans. The intent was to use these new properties to erect cooperatively based agriculture as an answer to large white holdings and their practice of leasing/selling properties to Asians, especially the Japanese. By the late 1920s, this racialist experiment in white agrarian co-ops had failed, mainly because white large-scale agribusiness came to rely successfully on Filipinos, Sikhs, Hindus, blacks, and most important, Mexicans.

During the 1930s, agribusiness turned increasingly toward the recruitment of hundreds of thousands of "dust-bowl refugees" from the U.S. Southern Great Plains (e.g., "Okies," "Arkies," and "Texans"); however, they did not become the labor base for California agriculture.[8] By the early 1940s, white agribusiness moved simultaneously toward the realization of two objectives: (1) the absorption of Japanese-owned and leased landholdings, as the Japanese were escorted by the federal government to the detention camps, and (2) the importation of unlimited numbers of *bracero* labor from Mexico.[9]

Hurriedly sent to barbed-wire enclosed prison camps by the federal authorities, the relocated land-owning Japanese had no choice but to sell their properties at a fraction of their value, while other lands rented by Japanese from whites were left behind. In effect, Japanese landholdings were garnered by whites as all 110,000 Japanese, noncitizens and citizens alike, were forcibly moved to ten so-called internment camps. Tens of thousands of Japanese were thereby pressed from the overall agricultural division of labor.

In 1942, the federal government initiated the widespread importation of *bracero* labor from Mexico to take the place of Japanese farm labor. This, coupled with the growth of large agricultural firms acquiring sizable plots of land during this period, gradually transformed the twentieth-century ranch into a modern day white-owned hacienda based largely on Mexican labor.[10]

With the proliferation of late-twentieth-century corporate farming, involving thousands of acres of absentee-owned ranches, most of the arable land in the United States has become the property of the great banks and oil companies. These production facilities have evolved into veritable factories in the field dependent overwhelmingly on nonwhite labor drawn from a variety of nationalities, but fundamentally most dependent on Mexican Indian/ Mestizo farmworkers.[11]

Racism against Native Americans, Chinese, and Japanese left an indelible mark on the California agricultural division of labor. That past historical condition, socially patterned and legitimated over the decades by dominant white institutions, functions as an ongoing causal force for the cruel treatment of and minimal pay for today's Mexican farmworkers. As a consequence, these nonwhite farmworkers obtain but a fraction of what they have produced for large farms owned by white growers, and when these farmworkers protest against such conditions through union struggles, their actions are met with violence.[12]

Hence, history appears to have come full circle. For today this patterning of battered exploitation has been reinforced by the fact that an ever-growing number of California field laborers derive their identity from a native heritage rooted in the northwestern Mexican countryside.[13] Over the centuries—from the exploitation of the first Native American farm laborers to their present-day Mexican counterparts—race, racism, nationality, exploitation, and profits have all become inseparable.

CORPORATE FARMING AND THE DIVISION OF LABOR IN CALIFORNIA AGRICULTURE

In California during this century, certainly since World War II, the coordination of the agrarian subgroups has moved forward under circumstances of increased concentration and centralization of capital and control.[14] As the number of farm owners has shrunk from many millions to but a fraction of that number over the past century, the concentration of land ownership has become more pronounced and, consequently, decisions about the use of land and investment in water sources, seeds, fertilizers, pesticides, herbicides, general land improvements, soil conservation, and overall crop production are made by an ever-smaller minority of corporate owners whose bottom line is to secure the highest rate of profit possible, whatever the human cost. These changes in the structure of ownership parallel the enlargement of farm size, reduction in overall farm count, and decrease in farm laborer employment. Thus, although by 1989 there were 2.95 million people who owned 833 million acres of private farmland, only 124,000 owners (or 4 percent of the total) held 47 percent of the land. Meanwhile, owners whose holdings were less than 50 acres, accounted for 30 percent of the total number of owners but held only 2 percent of the total acreage.[15]

Modern corporate agriculture involves a complex web of social relations that are based on the division of farm labor and the multilayered structure of work relations at the point of crop production in the fields. We find here and nearby the workers, crew leaders, farm labor contractors, growers, and boards of directors, as well as the judges, legislators, and the police. The essential elements of this collection of multiple interests come together in a contradictory way to generate foods to be marketed for private profit. The division of labor in corporate agriculture, as in other sectors of the capitalist economy, thus has as its end product the continued accumulation of capital—a process that facilitates further control and exploitation of labor in the fields, as on the shop floor.

Robert J. Thomas, in his study of lettuce cultivation in the Salinas Valley, California, in the late 1970s, provides some observation on the situation of farmworkers, the role of the farm labor contractors, and the nature of the industry itself.[16] He observes how the large lettuce-producing firms have organized production around a large number of low-paid workers who labor much the same way as those in construction and mining operations, in an industry dominated by highly capitalized, bureaucratically administered, multinational corporations. Thomas notes how lettuce harvesters work under physically destructive conditions, suffer the social and economic costs of seasonal migrations, and lack legal protections within the large community.[17]

A most informative book by William Friedland, Amy Barton, and Robert Thomas, titled *Manufacturing Green Gold: Capital, Labor, and Technology in the Lettuce Industry*, published in 1981, offers additional insight into the division of labor in California agriculture and documents the labor process at the point of production by providing a detailed description of lettuce cultivation in California's Salinas Valley.[18] In their depiction of supervised thinning and weeding operations in the lettuce harvest, the authors note that these tasks are performed by workers external to the lettuce firms, "sometimes by the grower-shippers who hire workers on a daily basis or often by specialists in the recruitment and management of temporary workers, for example, labor contractors."[19] This externalized labor force, they point out, is drawn from three major sources: (1) unskilled workers seeking to develop regular employment; (2) people who are not regularly or continuously in the labor force; and (3) casual workers who work only as forced to economically.

Unlike the thinning and weeding laborers, the higher status harvesters occupy a position as "the semi-internalized labor force."[20] This group consists of harvest workers. Harvesting activities have included two major kinds of arrangements, and therefore involve different kinds of workers and work organizations. The most significant category of harvest workers, although now in decline because of mechanization, has been those involved in the ground pack of lettuce—the cutting and packing of lettuce into cartons. Here the workers have been organized into crews usually consisting of thirty-six workers.

Cutters lead off the crew and move, stooped, through the rows cutting and trimming heads of lettuce, while the packers follow behind and squeeze the heads into empty cardboard cartons. The packer leaves the filled carton in the rows. He is followed by a sprayer who sprays the lettuce with water. The cartons are then glued, stapled, and loaded on trucks for transport out of the field. The truck (and any other equipment used) remains in the furrows so that heads left behind will remain undamaged and thereby permit future picking. With the exception of simple mechanical aids, all work is done by hand.

Crews are paid per carton. Among crew members, the emphasis is on speed and coordination of their actions. Although the length of the workday may vary according to weather, field, or market conditions, the physical exertion required in the work is tremendous. The arduousness of the work can be compared to walking stooped for eight to ten hours a day or doing more than 2,500 toe-touches over the same period. The speed and endurance required in harvesting take their toll on workers. Careers in the industry are short, because the length of a worker's career ranges from ten to eighteen years.[21] Most common among the physical complaints and reasons for quitting the harvest are back injuries, arthritis, hernias, and slipped disks.

During the early 1980s the average adult farmworker made $186 a week for twenty-three weeks, or $4,300 per year. The same average worker obtained another two weeks of nonfarm work for an additional $320 per year, for a total income of $4,620. A typical family of four worked on the average for a total of forty-nine weeks per year and earned less than $9,000, whereas the poverty level in 1983, as defined by the federal government for a family of four, was $10,178. According to Philip Martin, by 1996 there had been few if any improvements in the earnings of California farmworkers, especially when compared with manufacturing wages—$6 to $8 versus $12 to $14 per hour. As Martin points out, the average hourly earnings reported by USDA in its Farm Labor publication include the earnings of supervisors, which pulls up average hourly earnings. In January 1999, for example, average hourly earnings for all hired workers in California were $7.88. However, average hourly earnings for field workers were $7.08. Farmworkers average about 1,000 hours of work per year, about half as many as manufacturing workers. As a result, farmworkers in California have annual earnings that are one-fourth the $24,000 to $28,000 annual average earnings of factory workers. Of this farmworker income, an amount is also taken by the labor contractor, leaving even fewer dollars in the hands of the farmworkers.[22]

According to a survey by Mines and Martin, more than 70 percent of the 168 four-member households in the sample were in poverty. They commented that although the hourly rate ($5.10) and weekly wage ($186) for farmwork may seem "high," yearly cash income levels have been low because of long periods of farmworker unemployment. Although workers do take advantage of governmental "transfer payments," including unemployment compensation and welfare, the tendency to do both has been much less the case among Mexican men who have migrated up from Mexico. These "undocumented" Mexican males almost never use welfare, perhaps because of a fear of county and state administrators, as well as the police. Thus, despite Cesar Chavez's past drives to organize farm labor through the United Farm Workers (UFW) union to improve their condition, the situation of the farmworkers has steadily deteriorated, especially during the 1980s and 1990s. By the late 1990s, the condition of farmworkers had become worse than some twenty-five years earlier at the height of their initial unionization struggles.

THE GROWERS AND THE FARM LABOR CONTRACTOR

Whatever the changes in farm ownership and control, one role has proven to be central to the division of labor in California agriculture. Here we must stipulate as centrally powerful the coordinating activity of the farm labor contractor. Over the centuries, the division of labor in California agriculture has moved through several broad stages until one has emerged triumphant, and each stage has made a contribution to an overall, current definition of the contractor's role in the larger agrarian division of labor.

To impose proper controls on farm labor, both away from work and in the fields, the owners of the great estates, railroad construction sites, and placer mining ventures saw fit to accept the Mexican farm labor contractor. Being a member of the exploited nonwhite group in question, the labor contractor had the cultural understanding and leadership skills to impose order and to guide his labor gangs—and to do so within limits he could judge to be properly flexible, thereby avoiding rebellion among his charges.

He knew his subordinates well, for he had initially selected them into his work team not only annually, but often recurrently, over decades. His intimate knowledge of field work allowed him over the years to examine and select the ones he preferred: for crew leaders, he often selected from his relatives; for work crews, he chose from an array of fellow nationality subjects. In the process, he could drop those he considered to be goldbrickers, reprobates, or troublemakers. He thus became an informal personnel manager for white ranchers as he made these complicated evaluations and choices.

Spirited by a personal survival animus into the fields to guide the task performances of others, the often intelligent labor contractor soon learned of his indispensability in the eyes of the Anglo growers. That being the case, he has over the decades found himself in a position where he can be ethically derelict, if only modestly by ranch norms, as long as these gain-seeking proclivities did not go so far as to seriously antagonize his crew members. Crude transgressions could provoke labor stoppages and, consequently, harm the profit margins of the growers. So the contractor's gains from his flock proved to be measured, small in each instance, spaced to minimize the buildup of underlying anger, yet self-enhancing in amount in the long haul. As we shall see, the labor contractor's inspirations came to include the gleaning of small but over time significant amounts of spending money held by his twenty-five to thirty-five subordinates. These were the very ones he had brought together to labor on behalf of a whole string of growers. Composed by the contractor in late winter for the forthcoming year's long field-to-field march, these labor gangs moved from south to north, and returned in the fall, in effect both up and down as well as back and forth, zigzagging as it were, within a collective traverse, all sweated within the continent's particular crop-picking circuit.

At first glance, given the rationality of his coordination, the labor contractor's nationality may seem to be incidental. There is good reason, however, for there to exist an interrelationship among the nationality of the labor contractor, crew leader, and work team members, and this tie has been advantageous to growers. When the labor contractor belongs to the same nationality as the bulk of his crew, he can use his intimate knowledge of its cultural norms, values, and beliefs to manipulate the crew toward exact sought outcomes, such as high labor productivity.

Richard Mines and Phillip Martin have noted how, given the preponderance of short-term jobs, the rapid turnover of Mexican immigrants through the farm labor market, and the language barrier between white employers and Mexican crews, the contractors and crew leaders do the labor recruiting and managing for the growers.[23] Both the contractors and the crew leaders keep track of the demand for workers in the area, and both scout and secure an adequate supply of laborers at a wage to meet the growers' demands.

The contractor (or crew leader, where a contractor is absent) has become an irreplaceable link in the rural employment chain. Also, employers, instead of hiring individuals no doubt culturally incomprehensible to them, hire labor contractors who are bilingual, personally ambitious, and culturally sensitive managers who oversee the productive process in the fields and are directly responsible to the owners.

The labor contractor decides who will work and who will not, as he recruits and transports crews to the work site. At the point of production, he is the one who lines up his subordinates to be paced through specialized tasks. These he maps in his head before he walks into and about the fields. Later, he directs that expending of labor power among the vines, trees, and furrows, on occasion deciding that some of his charges should be fired and new ones hired. Although the contractor role takes multiple and complex forms, he ordinarily obtains a simple lump sum from the grower to hire workers and then deploys his blue-collar subordinates into field labor. With the all but total disappearance today of the UFW from California agriculture, the labor contractor has returned to positions of commanding heights at the point of production within almost every agricultural setting, but especially in the Imperial and San Joaquin valleys.[24]

In the overall labor process, the labor contractor arranges housing for crew members, sells work tools, sets up sources of food, and mediates conflicts among crew members. Also, he encourages agricultural workers to use the company (or nearby) store to purchase food and clothing essentials. He loans money to the farmworkers, charges interest, and sells the workers food as they work in the fields. He pays them about three-fourths of the money given to him by the growers for crew member pay. He keeps the remaining one-fourth of the cash for the real and imagined services he provides to the growers and the crew members. In addition, he collects lump-sum money from the growers for the skilled labor provided—in effect charging the owners an added labor price for obtaining and directing crew members and crew leaders.[25] Altogether, he sets aside a goodly portion of the overall compensation for himself at the end of a work period—be it a day, week, or season—and often his crew's net wages are not much once he has subtracted deductions.

Then there is debt peonage. When the migratory farmworkers go into debt, the contractor proves eager to provide loans. In California, crew leaders also engage in money lending to crew members. Especially common on the East Coast is the propensity for workers to obtain loans just as they initiate their trip up from Florida, Georgia, or the Carolinas. The cash advances come in handy, because the field laborers' meager savings from the previous year have been spent to survive during the winter layovers. Given the usurious profits involved, the labor contractor will grant loans at the kick-off point of the north migration, plus many stops during the course of the trip, including the ride home. As a consequence, not a few farmworkers end their winter-approaching harvests without any savings.[26]

These nonwhite field workers sometimes become permanently bound to the labor contractor through debt. Like bonded peasants of the eighteenth and nineteenth centuries, many of today's indebted laborers remain firmly linked to the contractor until they have paid off their debts. That payback becomes difficult, given the excessive interest rates. Unable to pay down the principal and subordinated to the contractor until that sum is paid, the indebted become locked indefinitely to their bosses.

The labor contractors also make difficult the enforcement of federal and state laws designed to protect farmworkers from toxic chemicals. Often the contractors force workers to enter fields too soon after the application of carcinogenic herbicides and pesticides. Further, the contractors make clear to their crew members that should they question any work site practices that do in fact violate the law, such as entering sprayed fields too soon or borderline illegal acts (e.g., recruitment of strike breakers to take farm laborers' jobs in an upcoming labor dispute), they can be dismissed or deported by the U.S. immigration service if they are foreign-born.[27] In fact, Mexican farmworkers of U.S. citizenship status have been "deported" to Mexico during the course of agricultural strikes. Such episodes have happened repeatedly, as James Crockcroft has documented.[28] Time and again, it has been the labor contractor who has singled out those eligible for deportation.

Most important, the labor contractor will go out of his way to destroy any bonafide union-organizing activity among his crew members and to purge those judged by him to be ringleaders,[29] because unionization by legitimate unions means the elimination of the contractor role and the substitution of the union hiring hall. The contractor role was eliminated wherever the UFW won union contracts during the 1960s and 1970s.

The growers have been absolutely opposed to nonsweetheart unionization of farmworkers, especially those laboring in the fields where work stoppages risk the harvest and indicate the questioning of white grower power. Thus, the growers have traditionally counted on the contractor to function as a detective and to be able to scent the faint beginnings of unionization. The growers also fear that unionization can only lead to the purge of the labor contractor—the person on whom the grower has staked his point-of-production division of labor. Thus, the grower uses the contractor, as both field leader and labor spy, to stand alert against bonafide unions.

The net result of these injustices for the farmworkers is clear. They are both humiliated and made to earn less by the presence of the labor contractor.

THE WORK CREW: FARM LABOR AND
THE ORGANIZATION OF WORK IN THE FIELDS

The general portrait of farm labor should be broken down into specialties within the agricultural division of labor. In doing so, we should keep in mind both crop and task to give the reader a better idea of how work is allocated by time of immigration, plus gender and age, as well as nationality.

California agriculture crew members are, with few exceptions, of Mexican extraction. Most are probably still Mexican citizens, many being legal immigrants to the United States, whereas others are undocumented workers. Although many crew members make their permanent home in Mexico, directly across the border from the Imperial Valley, especially in cities such as Mexicali, an increasing number of farmworkers are beginning to settle down in the United States (e.g., in the Salinas Valley).

Among farmworkers, there are definite patterns of blue-collar job assignments. For example, the most recent immigrant workers do the most toilsome labor, whereas the other immigrants and the long-term U.S. residents obtain less laborious tasks. The longer farmworkers remain in California, the more likely it is that they will find and become involved with mature immigrant social networks. These mature, locally and job-site integrated members have more experience and hence are better able to find both themselves and newly arrived friends in higher paying jobs. The aid is meted out generally to like workers of middle age.

Meanwhile, the young men tend to avoid such traditional social networks, and seek to dominate most of the heavy harvesting tasks in ground citrus, tree fruits, melons, and piece-rate vegetable harvesting. This physically demanding labor requires youth and strength, and hence, surplus of energy needed to stoop, climb, wrench, carry, and heave. It is not difficult to imagine how, after ten to fifteen years, this cartilage-pulling labor would take its toll on workers' backs. Hence, aging workers must move along to jobs more in keeping with depleted tendons and vertebrae. Also, as they grow older, they seek and find supportive social networks to confirm their laboring in work slots where they can survive.[30]

Older workers specialize in the harvesting of strawberries, carrots, and certain vegetables, such as cauliflower; these crops are cut, placed on a conveyor belt, and packed in the field. In addition, the older men dominate in the semiskilled tasks of operating machines, supervising, irrigating, and tree pruning.

Farmworker children and women do a large share of the hoeing, thinning, and sorting. Older men may also be involved in these relatively lighter tasks. However, many of the older males drop out of farm work altogether by age forty-five. Very few of them remain after they reach age fifty-four.[31]

Crew members were recruited, in the past, through existing members of crews, their crew leaders, and their farm labor contractors. When a new person was required, an individual crew member could bring a candidate into the crew. The crew member became, in effect, the new person's sponsor and was considered responsible for the work of the candidate. If the new person's work was insufficient, (e.g., an inability to maintain the pace), the sponsor was responsible for making up the deficiencies. This system of recruitment placed serious obligations on crew members who did not take such responsibilities lightly. Crews work at high speed, and careless sponsors might find themselves subsidizing a share of the income of unworthy candidates. Sponsorship appears to have been based on kinship and friendship patterns.

Work crews develop norms for themselves with respect to earnings. In any given crew, there is what can be called a "target earnings level" of so many dollars per hour for each crew member. Some crews work much harder than others and therefore earn more. Thus, there is a hierarchy of work crews in terms of earnings that establishes the basis for individual movement among crews. Mobility, through this system, consists of individuals initially joining slower crews and then moving into crews with higher earning potential. Young individuals can work their way through a hierarchy of crews by gaining experience and maintaining their strength. However, as they grow older and are less capable of maintaining the pace, they begin to descend the hierarchy. The need for the reversal of such conditions has become an important factor in farmworker organizing efforts to unionize the fields.

Unionism and its concomitants, especially seniority rights, have been instrumental in breaking down the self-recruitment and self-regulation of the crews, and have initiated the integration of workers into various agricultural firms. Several processes give rise to these changes. First, unionization tends to encourage restriction on "runaway" piece rates. Unions encourage situations in which earning levels are homogeneous and regular. Second, the establishment of seniority under union contracts creates the basis for an entirely different crew organization in which workers are assigned to work based on length of individual service rather than membership in a crew or the length of the crew's service. This process also affects the situation in which crews used to determine their target earnings levels and therefore intercrew mobility. Once intercrew movement declines, the tendency toward homogenization of crew earnings also accelerates. Prior to the destruction of the UFW during the 1980s, the unionization of the fields had in this sense played an important role in bringing about the uniformity of farm labor in California agriculture.

FARMWORKER UNION STRUGGLES

The history of major farmworker organizing efforts and unionization struggles during this century goes back to the 1930s. As agricultural laboring conditions deteriorated appreciably between 1929 and 1931, and as the United States plunged into the Great Depression of the 1930s, the developing labor struggles of this period spread to the farms and fields of California and other states around the country.

By 1933, the California Communists had begun to use greater (however scant) resources to recruit significant numbers of agricultural workers to militant union locals. Relying partly on Carey McWilliams's full account of farm labor struggles in California during the 1930s, Walter J. Stein observed in his book *California and the Dust Bowl Migration* that California's Filipino and Mexican field workers had dropped their accustomed docility to generate a temporary alliance with multinational union organizers of left-wing commitment and considerable organizational skill. Stein noted that the massive 1933–1934 agricultural strikes mounted and directed by the Communist Party within the Imperial and San Joaquin valleys provided the "immediate background" against which the California growers gratefully received the essentially nonunion Great Plains migrants as replacements for the Mexicans and Filipinos. The growers were glad to see these Okies and Arkies, at least until the desperation strikes of 1938, when the dust bowlers proved to be the key participants within a "united front" labor drive.[32]

The Trade Union Unity League (TUUL), the affiliated Cannery and Agricultural Workers Industrial Union (CAWIU) of 1933–1935, and the United Cannery, Agricultural, Packing and Allied Workers of America (UCAPAWA) of 1938–1939 went all out but failed to win against their opponents, despite the at-times massive participation of workers, especially in the 1933–1935 fights waged throughout California's Central Valley. In these extraordinary disputes, even though many farmworkers no doubt believed they had little chance of winning, fight-or-starve laborers nonetheless organized and struck. As Stein noted when commenting on the conflagration of 1933, when the Mexican farmworkers' demands for higher cotton-picking wages were refused, the field workers shut down the San Joaquin Valley's cotton industry. Stein has commented: "Unheralded, indeed ignored, by historians of industrial labor, the San Joaquin cotton strike was a major labor conflict." According to Stein, from 15,000 to 18,000 workers went out on a 120-mile front for twenty-four days. The strike was ended through outside mediation, and the strikers returned to the fields.[33]

Stein has observed how the Communists, buoyed by their victory, moved south into the Imperial Valley. The following year they supplied leadership in a strike of 3,600 Mexican vegetable workers and organized a host of lesser strikes throughout the state during the 1933–1934 period. In fact, by 1934, at the height of the great strike wave, the Communist-led drive had drawn 70,000 farmworkers into a union as yet unmatched in U.S. farm labor history for its commitment to labor militancy.[34]

Three decades later, in the 1960s, another resurgence of farmworkers militancy and unionization struggles took hold in the California fields. In the mid- and late 1960s, California Central Valley farmworkers rebelled and tried to organize. In September 1965, thousands of Delano farmworkers joined either the Agricultural Workers Organizing Committee (mainly Filipino) or the National Farm Workers Association (overwhelmingly Chicano), and participated in the great marches and demonstrations that mobilized hundreds of thousands of supporters in favor of the farmworkers' cause.

By 1970, the UFW launched and won a series of offensive and successful strikes against the growers of the San Joaquin and Salinas valleys. These victories brought tens of thousands of farmworkers under UFW contracts. However, when UFW contracts came up for renewal in 1973, the growers adamantly opposed their renewal. To aid the growers and to destroy the UFW, the Teamsters hired professional strike breakers, many of them Chicanos, to beat up UFW workers. The Teamsters were joined by police in coming down hard on pro-UFW workers, whatever their nationality.[35]

In the 1980s, Latino farmworkers scored a number of successes. Among them is the spring 1986 triumph of the Mexican-American Farm Labor Organizing Committee (FLOC) against Campbell Soup and Vlasic Pickles, not to mention their supplier growers situated in both northwestern Ohio and southern Michigan.[36] More recently, unionized farmworkers in New Jersey won a historic pact. A southern New Jersey, Cumberland County farm has been the first to grant a contract to farmworkers.[37]

Still, very real problems face farmworker unions today. For example, the California-centered UFW has lost 70 percent of its membership in seventeen years, in large measure because of Teamster raids against the UFW, because of the courts, and in part because of the hostility expressed by successive state administrations at the local and national levels.[38]

Corporate agribusiness conflict with farmworkers and their unions became most intense between the mid-1960s and 1973, at which time an alliance of growers, California government agencies, and the Teamsters Union soundly defeated but did not eliminate entirely the fledgling Mexican/ Filipino-based UFW union. Between 1974 and 1981, in particular, the UFW both conducted union drives and fought strikes intermittently, but the phantom alliance of the governor's office, the state legislature, the courts, the federal government, the growers, the banks, the mass media, the county and local governments, and the Teamsters Union simply overwhelmed the UFW. The decline in union activity and strikes by the UFW accompanied the union's propensity to give up on the impossible—namely, a fight for lasting union contracts for farmworkers. Rather, the UFW turned to educating the public about the dangers of chemicals, especially those sprayed on grapes. Although in the 1980s the UFW relied on contributions from its many supporters to keep the union afloat, today the union is less than one-fourth of what it was thirty years ago, and its overall strategy seems to be one of surviving until times more conducive to labor organizing make their appearance in the California fields.

Historically, in the United States, farm labor battles, like struggles of U.S. labor in general, have coincided with cyclical economic hard times. This cycle of economic downturn and social resurgence seems to recur every thirty years: the early 1900s, the 1930s, the 1960s, and the late 1990s.

The 1990s turned out to be a bad time for farmworker unions, certainly in California. Key leaders continued to leave the farm labor movement. Charismatic leaders like Cesar Chavez died, faded, or quit and moved to Los Angeles. Many activist leaders were simply fired by the chief union boss. Labor contracts all but disappeared. Still, some of the faithful have remained loyal. For good reasons, these true believers have loathed traditional bureaucratic labor unionism, because it eschews the ABCs of militant, direct-action, progressive unionism.[39]

Yet successful union bureaucracy does breathe day-to-day nutrient into union organizations. Think of the Teamsters as a prototype. Union strike victories, collective bargaining recognitions, and successfully negotiated contracts improve workers' material benefits and hence do make workers believe in unions. Successive defeats can erode such faith, but not necessarily forever. Take the situation facing UFW workers at the time of Chavez's death in 1993. The residual membership total of 15,000 was but a fraction of what it had been in 1973. In the early 1990s UFW members seemed dispirited. Since then, however, the UFW membership has actually doubled to become a little more than 30,000.

In the United States, capitalist growers have for decades used their corporate and state powers to hammer the farmworker movement to oblivion. Under contemporary conditions of corporate-sought UFW union disaggregation, union members staff and organizers have also been expected to accept union dictates from above. Those who have stayed with the UFW and its top-down structure have remained the frayed silent marchers for the union cause. Perhaps a majority of them must feel frozen into hopeless structures from which there can be no proud exit.

Yet, there is hope. Given the much publicized and increasing shift of California continental geological plates, what California farmworkers may get is an economic disaster rendered by ecological catastrophe under conditions of serious economic recession. As in China, historically, that cataclysmic shake-up within the substructure might indeed launch the entire exploited population into a general movement for revolutionary change.

APPENDIX: CHEMICALS IN THE FIELDS

The agricultural division of labor proceeds out of doors. With the enormous quantity of dangerous chemicals sprayed on crops, workers' bodies absorb liquid and vaporous toxins through the lungs and skin as they labor in the fields.

The additive and the synergistic toxic effects of herbicides and pesticides fail to redound to the betterment of either underpaid workers or the consuming public. In fact, these chemical compounds are often deadly.

Among the most carcinogenic chemicals are the following:

Methyl bromide is extremely poisonous to all forms of life. This fumigant is reportedly responsible for more occupationally related deaths than any other pesticide; even nonfatal exposure can cause severe, irreversible effects on the nervous system, with permanent brain damage or blindness.

Parathion and *phosdrin* are work-site chemicals that can be fatal, producing illnesses in workers in as few as twenty minutes. These poisons are usually sprayed aerially and endanger the surrounding populations as well as the farmworkers, since as much as 90 percent of aerially sprayed pesticides miss their targets.

Dinoseb induces a poisoning at first resembling heatstroke; subsequently, cumulative doses cause extensive illnesses, including loss of vision. *Capatan* is sprayed on table grapes at the rate of 344,000 pounds each year. The residue of this compound is the most frequently discovered material on grapes in stores. Not only can capatan cause cancer, but it also originates birth defects and changes in body cells; it is structurally similar to thalidomide, which several decades ago caused thousands of babies in the United States and Europe to be born without arms and legs.

The result of the use of such deadly chemicals in the fields has been disastrous to the farmworkers. An estimated 78 percent of Texas farmworkers studied in one survey had chronic skin rashes, 56 percent had kidney and liver abnormalities, and 54 percent suffered from chest-cavity problems. Nationwide, more than 300,000 farmworkers are made ill every year through pesticide exposure, with pesticide poisoning incidents doubling in the last ten years. The miscarriage rate is seven times the national average. Disability days associated with pesticide illnesses have increased by 53 percent and hospital days by 61 percent since 1979.[40] That trend remains the case as we enter a new century.

NOTES

1. See Gladys K. Bowles, "The Current Situation of the Hired Farm Labor Force," in *Farm Labor in the United States,* ed. E. E. Bishop (New York: Columbia University Press, 1967); Carey McWilliams, *Factories in the Field* (Santa Barbara and Salt Lake City: Peregrine Publishers, 1971); Dorothy Nelkin, *On the Season: Aspects of the Migrant Labor System* (Ithaca, N.Y.: New York School of Industrial and Labor Relations, 1970).

2. John G. Dunne, *Delano, the Story of the California Grape Strike* (New York: Farrar, Straus & Giroux, 1967); Alec Wilkinson, *Big Sugar: Seasons in the Cane Fields of Florida* (New York: Vintage Books, 1989).

3. See Sucheng Chan, *This Bittersweet Soil: The Chinese in California Agriculture, 1860–1910* (Berkeley: University of California Press, 1989); Stanford Lyman, *Chinese Americans* (New York: Random House, 1974).

4. Chan, *This Bittersweet Soil;* also see Richard E. Lingenfelter, *The Hardrock Miners: A History of the Mining Labor Movement in the American West, 1863–1893* (Berkeley: University of California Press, 1974).

5. Harry Kitano and Roger Daniels, *Asian Americans: Emerging Minorities* (Upper Saddle River, N.J.: Prentice Hall, 1988).

6. Chan, *This Bittersweet Soil.*

7. McWilliams, *Factories in the Field.*

8. See James Gregory, *American Exodus: The Dust Bowl Migrations and Okie Culture in California* (New York: Oxford University Press, 1989).

9. Ernesto Garlarza, *Merchants of Labor: The Mexican Bracero Story, an Account of the Managed Migration of Mexican Farm Workers in California* (Santa Barbara, Calif.: McNally and Lofton, 1964).

10. Kevin F. McCarthy and Burgiaga Valdez, *Current and Future Effects of Immigration in California* (Santa Barbara, Calif.: Rand Corporation, 1985).

11. Garlarza, *Merchants of Labor: The Mexican Bracero Story;* James D. Cockcroft, *Outlaws in the Promised Land: Mexican Immigrant Workers and America's Future* (New York: Grove Press, 1986).

12. McWilliams, *Factories in the Field;* John C. Leggett, *Mining the Fields: Farm Workers Fight Back* (Dix Hills, N.Y.: General Hall, 1998).

13. Richard Mines and Philip L. Martin, *A Profile of California Farm Workers* (Berkeley, Calif.: The Giannini Foundation of Agricultural Economics, University of California, Berkeley, 1986); Cockcroft, *Outlaws in the Promised Land.*

14. Harland Padfield and William E. Martin, *Farmers, Workers and Machines* (Tucson: University of Arizona Press, 1965); Gigi M. Bernardi and Charles M. Geisler, *The Social Consequences and Challenges of New Agricultural Technologies* (Boulder, Colo.: Westview Press, 1984).

15. Cited in Chan, *This Bittersweet Soil.*

16. Robert J. Thomas, "The Social Organization of Industrial Agriculture," *The Insurgent Sociologist* (Winter 1981), 5–20.

17. Thomas, "The Social Organization of Industrial Agriculture."

18. William Friedland, Amy Barton, and Robert Thomas, *Manufacturing Green Gold: Capital, Labor, and Technology in the Lettuce Industry* (Cambridge: Cambridge University Press, 1981), 58.

19. Friedland et al., *Manufacturing Green Gold,* 58.

20. Friedland et al., *Manufacturing Green Gold.*

21. See Mines and Martin, *A Profile of California Farm Workers.*

22. Mines and Martin, *A Profile of California Farm Workers,* 38–41. For 1996 data, see Philip Martin, *Promises to Keep: Collective Bargaining in California Agriculture* (Ames: Iowa State University Press). Professor Martin provided the 1999 data to John Leggett through a detailed December 1999 personal communication.

23. Mines and Martin, *A Profile of California Farm Workers.*

24. Truman Moore, *The Slaves We Rent* (New York: Random House, 1965); William Friedland and Dorothy Nelkin, *Migrant Workers in America's Northeast* (New York: Holt, Rinehart and Winston, 1971); Nelkin, *On the Season: Aspects of the Migrant Labor System*; Leggett, *Mining the Fields: Farm Workers Fight Back.*

25. Dunne, *Delano, the Story of the California Grape Strike;* Mines and Martin, *A Profile of California Farm Workers.* On the East Coast, the migratory crew chief takes on the contractor role and charges accordingly. See Dale Wright, *They Harvest Despair: The Migrant Farm Workers* (Boston: Beacon Press, 1965); Friedland and Nelkin, *Migrant Workers in America's Northeast.*

26. Moore, *The Slaves We Rent*; Nelkin, *On the Season: Aspects of the Migrant Labor System*; Herman L. Emmet, *Fruit Tramps* (Albuquerque, N.M.: University of New Mexico Press, 1989).

27. See Murray Campbell, "Withering on the Vine: As Conquests Fade, a New Nightmare Haunts Grape Pickers," *The Globe and Mail* (Toronto) (27 November 1991), A1, A10.

28. See Cockcroft, *Outlaws in the Promised Land.*

29. Cockcroft, *Outlaws in the Promised Land*; Campbell, "Withering on the Vine," A1, A10.

30. Campbell, "Withering on the Vine," A1, A10.

31. Only 5 percent of the females and 10 percent of the males studied by Mines and Martin were 55 or older. See Mines and Martin, *A Profile of California Farm Workers.*

32. Walter J. Stein, *California and the Dust Bowl Migration* (Westport, Conn.: Greenwood Press, 1973).

33. Stein, *California and the Dust Bowl Migration,* 224.

34. Stein, *California and the Dust Bowl Migration,* 224–26; McWilliams, *Factories in the Field,* 211–29.

35. Cockcroft, *Outlaws in the Promised Land,* 183; Linda C. Majka and Theo J. Majka, *Farm Workers, Agribusiness, and the State* (Philadelphia: Temple University Press, 1982).

36. Donald Warshaw, "Campbell and Workers Reach Pact," Newark *Star Ledger* (21 February 1986), 56; Kenneth Barger, *Hasta LaVictoria, a Farm Labor Movement in the Midwestern U.S.* (Austin: The University of Texas Press, 1992).

37. Donald Warshaw, "Unionized Migrant Workers Win Historic Pact," *Newark Star Ledger* (7 May 1986), 33.

38. Cockcroft, *Outlaws in the Promised Land*, 184. The estimated figures used by Cockcroft cite a drop from 100,000 to 30,000.

39. Why the farmworker unions in California failed during the second half of the twentieth century has been addressed with acumen by a number of authors. See Ernesto Galarza, *Farm Workers and the Agribusiness in California, 1947–1960* (Notre Dame: University of Notre Dame Press, 1977); J. Craig Jenkins, *The Politics of Insurgency* (New York: Columbia University Press, 1985); Patrick H. Mooney and Theo J. Majka, *Farmers' and Farm Workers' Movements: Social Protest in American Agriculture* (New York: Twayne Publishers, 1995), especially 184–215. Diana Hembree, ed., *The Fight in the Fields: Cesar Chavez and the Farmworkers Movement* (New York: Harcourt Brace, 1997); Robert Gordon, "Poisons in the Fields: The United Farm Workers, Pesticides, and Environmental Politics," *Pacific Historical Review* 68, no. 1 (1999), 51–78.

40. See Gordon, "Poisons in the Fields"; Daniel M. Berman, *Death on the Job: Occupational Health and Safety Struggles in the United States* (New York: Monthly Review Press, 1978); Harry Weinstein, "The Health Threat in the Fields," *The Nation* 240 (11 May 1985), 558–60; V. Wilk and D. M. Hancock, "Farmworker Occupational Health and Study in the 1990s," *New Solutions* 1 (Spring 1991), 6–10.

6

The Global Economy and Changes in the Nature of Contingent Work

Robert E. Parker

This chapter explores the continuing expansion of the "contingent" workforce in the United States in recent years. With the increasing globalization of production, the 1990s has witnessed several important developments in the use of contingent workers that characterize the global economy, the most notable of which is the sheer growth in their number.

The global expansion of capital and the transfer of production to the peripheral regions of the world economy has brought about a deindustrialization process in the United States that has shifted the employment structure from the goods-producing sector to the service sector and brought with it growth and expansion of the low-paid, part-time, contingent workforce.

While the growth in number of contingent workers has been an important development in the U.S. labor force, another important trend has been the increasing occupational diversity of these workers. When the decade began, contingent workers were typically peripheral members of the U.S. working class, disproportionately employed in clerical and industrial positions. But by the end of the 1990s, contingent workers were plainly visible in occupying a variety of temporary positions in U.S. workplaces.

Also examined in this chapter is the growing number of legal cases and government regulations involving the use of contingent workers. These legal and regulatory impediments faced by corporations using contingent workers, along with the active resistance of some workers to their underemployed status, appear to be slowing the growth of contingent work.

In recent years, temporary workers have organized to improve their conditions and several court cases involving contingent workers have arrived at decisions favorable to the fledgling resistance movement. Before any of these trends can be more fully understood, however, a brief conceptual and

historical groundwork is warranted given the differing contemporary views
of what constitutes contingent work.

A CRITICAL CONCEPTUALIZATION OF CONTINGENT WORK

Although the use of a narrow official conception of the contingent workforce
makes it appear that U.S. capitalism is providing an abundance of opportunities for work, it deviates sharply from the daily reality experienced by millions of underemployed workers in the United States. It is this underemployed status that truly segregates the contingent workforce from the
permanent, full-time, year-round labor force. When considering the size of
the contingent labor force, it is fundamental to understand that there are millions of contingent workers in the country who share more in common than
simply meeting a set of convenient governmental criteria. Most important,
contingent workers share a "secondary labor market" status, characterized
by low wages, low skills, and few if any fringe benefits—conditions exacer-
bated by the accelerated globalization of capital.

Since Audrey Freedman of the Conference Board (a business research
group) first coined the term in the mid-1980s, *contingent work* has evolved to
mean different things to different people. The result has been a proliferation
of wide-ranging estimates of the size of the U.S. contingent workforce. Most
significant in terms of its social and economic implications is the definition
used by the Department of Labor's Bureau of Labor Statistics (BLS). Its definition and conceptual framework is the one most frequently cited by academic
and popular authors. Over time, the way the BLS has framed contingent work
has gained growing uncritical acceptance. Scholars publishing in peer-
reviewed journals have used BLS definitions without hesitation or scrutiny.

The Department of Labor has developed three estimates of the number of
contingent workers in the U.S. labor force. In February 1995, the BLS first
enumerated a survey of this population in a supplement to its monthly Current Population Survey (CPS). The three estimates begin with a minimalist inclusion of types of contingent workers that excludes many temporary workers. The broadest of the three estimates includes additional *workers who do
not expect their jobs to last indefinitely.* Yet this broader conceptualization
does not differ significantly from the most narrow of their definitions. The
BLS's main criterion is whether a worker expects a job to last indefinitely. Although they acknowledge a host of emerging workplace arrangements including growing numbers of independent contractors, on-call workers, employees provided by contract firms, and workers supplied by temporary help
agencies, they could just find 5.6 million contingent workers in their follow-
up study in 1997.[1] Not only does the total number seem understated but the
1997 CPS supplement further asserted that despite corporate America's

growing use of temps, part-timers, and independent contractors, the number of "official" contingent workers declined, from 4.9 percent of the labor force to 4.4 percent.[2]

In short, since the mid-1990s, a very narrow view of contingent work has become the operational definition used in both popular discourse and academic research. The result is an overly sanguine assessment of the conditions faced by a growing army of workers saddled with a contingent status in the U.S. labor force. For example, in a recent summary of contingent work studies, Richard M. Devens, writing in *Monthly Labor Review* draws the conclusion that with the decline in contingent work, workers are feeling increasingly secure in their current positions.[3] Devens draws this conclusion in spite of substantial public opinion polls showing that U.S. workers have never felt so insecure about their jobs as they do at the end of the twentieth century.[4]

At the outset of the 1990s, following the conventions adopted by critical scholars of the U.S. labor force, I estimated that the contingent workforce in the United States had surpassed one-quarter of the workforce and could well be as high as one-third.[5] In late 2001, identifying one-third of all U.S. workers as contingent would appear to be a conservative estimate, rather than an alarmist exaggeration.

The government and conservative econometric estimates are not without competitors in conceptualizing contingent work. In an article in *Social Policy*, Edie Rasell and Eileen Appelbaum, following Arne Kalleberg et. al., emphasize the concept of "nonstandard" employment over contingent work and include in their estimate independent contractors, contract workers (e.g., janitors employed at a building custodial services firm who spend their working hours at other work sites), part-time workers, and on-call/day laborers.[6] Using this framework, the authors suggest that in 1995, 29.4 percent of all U.S. workers held contingent jobs, a figure considerably greater than the government's official estimate of less than 6 percent. Without comprehensive data to precisely document trends in the contingent labor force, this definition more nearly approximates the true condition of workers in the United States as the new century begins.

Yet, even this more expansive conceptualization leads to an understatement of the number of contingent workers. In the U.S. labor force, there are subpopulations of employees that are all but neglected by labor statistics; workers whose jobs are certainly not going to last indefinitely, such as migrant farmworkers and temporary agricultural workers allowed into the United States under the H-2 visa program. Contrary to public perception, the numbers of these workers has not declined in recent years. Indeed, the number of workers with temporary work visas grew officially from 60,000 to nearly 120,000 in the late 1990s.[7] To reiterate, to avoid the impression that absolute precision can be determined, this chapter casts an even broader net in conceptualizing contingent work (or those in nonstandard working arrangements). It links contingent workers by highlighting that the vast majority face uncertain working tenures, lower pay, and lesser levels of fringe benefits than full-time workers performing the same tasks, and whose physical location at the workplace typically isolates them from permanent or full-time workers. Additionally, this chapter stresses that the contingent workforce is a demographically distinctive one—disproportionately composed of nonwhites, women, youth, and the elderly.

TYPES OF CONTINGENT WORKERS

The expression *contingent work* does not refer to a single monolithic type of employee–employer arrangement and is not restricted to any specific economic sector. Instead, contingent workers are found throughout the economy, and include employees of the temporary help industry, part-time workers, day laborers, and others outside of the permanent workforce.[8] Although some workers choose a contingent working status (often for family or other personal reasons), a large and growing percentage of these workers are finding contingent positions their only option as U.S. corporations continue to restructure their operations on a global basis.

Employers have increasingly turned to contingent workers to cut labor costs, gain greater control over the labor process, and increase their profits. This strategy can also thwart unionization efforts, because contingent workers are inherently more difficult to organize. Together, these factors have led to the creation of a more transient and contingent workforce.[9]

As noted, virtually all the workers considered share several important characteristics: Most are paid less for working at part-time jobs than full-time employees earn on standard schedules. The majority are excluded from receiving any type of fringe benefits, except those mandated by federal law. Except for a section of the working class that can afford intermittent employment, contingent workers face a future of limited upward occupational mobility and very few have opportunities to exercise discretion over how their work is performed, or to upgrade their existing skill levels.

The corporate search for a cheap, docile, and flexible workforce in the global economy is closely related to the process of control and exploitation of labor, and the movement toward a contingent workforce is the result of changes in the capitalist labor process now taking place on a global scale—changes that have an enormous impact on the working class as a whole.

The transition to an increasingly contingent workforce provides U.S. businesses with greater flexibility and higher rates of profit, but it means lower wages, reduced health care protection, and the loss of pension and retirement benefits for workers.[10]

Temporary Workers

Like others among the contingent labor force, temporary workers are largely made up of full-time job seekers. And like independent contractors and involuntary part-time workers, temporary workers are an underemployed segment of the labor force, enduring uncertain hours, inadequate income, and a profound mismatch between their existing skill levels and the working opportunities offered by the temporary help industry. According to BLS data, the number of workers in the help supply services industry (the vast majority of whom are "temps") grew by an annual rate of 17 percent between 1992 and 1995, and has since slowed to a yearly growth rate of 9 percent.[11] The BLS also reveals that of the more than 18 million nonfarm jobs created between 1992 and 1998, 1.4 million were in the help supply services sector of the labor force.[12] In the final quarter of 1998, the average number of individuals employed daily in temporary help jobs "officially" peaked at an estimated 2.9 million workers.[13] Because temporary jobs are supposed to last indefinitely, logic would suggest that all those working on such a schedule would be a part of the BLS's "contingent workforce." But, as noted above, a significant number of temps are not counted as contingent workers.

In terms of industrial distribution, the six major sectors within the staffing services industry include office/clerical, industrial, technical, professional, health care, and marketing. The office/clerical sector of the industry continues to dominate as it has for decades. In 1998, wages paid to such workers reached $17.6 billion, or slightly more than 40 percent of all staffing services' payroll. It is, however, a declining sector of this increasingly diversified industry. In 1991, clerical workers made up nearly 48 percent of industry payroll. The technical sector of the industry held its own during the 1990s, with wages paid to workers in the industrial sector reaching $15 billion in 1998. Another area to show increased growth in the past decade has been the independent professional. Experts in areas such as law, sales, marketing, and management have steadily grown in prominence among the ranks of temporary workers. Between 1991 and 1998, the number of such professional workers in the industry grew eight-fold, with payroll reaching nearly $3 billion.[14] Technical workers, including computer programmers, designers, and engineers are another rapidly growing sector, doubling in payroll during the 1990s.

One area that has declined in significance has been in health care, where payroll has dropped from 8.4 percent of the total in 1991 to 2.2 percent in 1998. According to the National Association of Temporary and Staffing Services (NATSS), the decline is attributable to the rise of managed health care. Finally, marketing workers have emerged as a distinct niche in the temporary labor force as the demand for telemarketers and product demonstrators has increased.

As a group, temps are similar to other segments of the U.S. working class. Indeed, many have had experience working full-time in the U.S. economy. But despite the BLS's reassurances that job displacement is on the decline in the United States, the fact remains that nearly 700,000 permanent jobs were cut by U.S. corporations in 1998, the most of any year in the decade. Corporate America, in spite of the steady drumbeat about U.S. prosperity and the stock market's dizzying performance, continues to downsize and outsource its personnel as a quick and ostensibly painless way to cut costs, increase profits, and heighten productivity. In short, as corporations continue to pursue a lean-and-mean profile, it should come as little surprise that an industry founded on the notion of worker interchangeability, and jobs that by definition have short tenures is growing as rapidly as the temporary help sector of the economy. It is an industry that neatly complements American business practices as the new century unfolds.

Taken together, the temporary help services industry is a financially formidable and steadily advancing one, with 1998 being the seventh consecutive year of double-digit growth (as measured by receipts collected). In 1990, the industry collected roughly $20 billion for its services, with the total reaching nearly $60 billion in 1998. Manpower Inc. and Kelly Services are the industry's giants in terms of payroll, employees, and number of offices. It is truly a sign of the times that Manpower is not just the industry's leader, but also the United States's single largest private employer.

Part-Time Workers

Part-time work has constituted a major portion of the contingent workforce for decades. Like other underemployed workers, part-timers generally endure low wages, poor, if any fringe benefits, and uncertain working futures. And as with other segments of the contingent labor force, the high proportion of part-timers in the economy largely reflects corporate America's desire to minimize workers' wages and benefits. For conceptual purposes, the part-time workforce in the United States can be broken down into two categories—those who work part-time because they prefer that type of schedule and those who are known as "involuntary part-time workers." The latter are made up of workers who ordinarily work full-time but who are temporarily on a reduced schedule as well as those who accept part-time employment because it is the only work they can find.

Since the late 1960s, the number of part-time workers and their percentage of the U.S. labor force as a whole has increased substantially. During the Reagan administration in the 1980s, part-time work grew particularly rapidly. Between 1980 and 1988, the number of part-time workers increased by 21 percent (from 16.3 million to 19.8 million) at a time when the total U.S. labor force grew by only 14 percent. As Susan McHenry and Linda Lee Small have observed, more than 25 percent of the "much heralded 10 million jobs created during the Reagan era were part-time."[15] By the end of the 1980s, the part-time workforce had expanded to roughly one-fifth of the entire U.S. labor force. Involuntary part-time workers figured prominently in the uptick during this period. For example, between 1972 and 1982, when voluntary part-time employment was advancing by 33 percent, the growth in involuntary part-time work increased by 166 percent, from 2.19 million to 5.8 million.[16] During the 1980s, growth in the involuntary part-time workforce slowed significantly, but there were still some 5 million officially recorded involuntary part-time workers in 1990. During the early part of the 1990s, the number of part-time and involuntary part-time workers continued to rise. In 1994, however, the BLS redesigned its traditional survey of the labor force, adding a question that resulted in a higher percentage of part-timers being categorized as voluntary and a smaller percentage as involuntary. Since that time, both types of part-time workers have shown a downward trend as a percentage of the labor force.

It is noteworthy that the conceptual change attenuated the number of part-time workers for the BLS, but it could have just as easily implemented changes that would have officially increased the number and percentage of part-time positions. For example, if the BLS enumerated part-time jobs, rather than the number of part-time workers, they would have arrived at a larger number. Many part-time workers are, in fact, multiple job holders, officially counted as full-time workers because they work more than 35 hours per week, but who are really patching together two or more part-time jobs to produce a living wage for their households. In short, the Department of Labor has made a number of conceptual changes in the 1990s that have consistently resulted in an understatement of the number of workers who are officially identified as contingent. In this instance, the number of part-time workers who endure low wages, substandard fringe benefits, and uncertain working futures are increasingly being counted as voluntary members of the part-time workforce. In contrast to the BLS's figures, consider the findings of a CBS–New York Times poll in 1995 that asked part-time workers if they prefer part-time or full-time schedules. Whereas the BLS survey concluded that only 20 percent of part-timers would prefer to be on a full-time schedule, this poll found that 47 percent of all part-timers would prefer full-time schedules.

In 1998, despite a growing number of conceptual criteria that effectively limits the number of part-time workers identified as involuntary, 3.6 million workers still reported being employed on a part-time basis because of "economic reasons," including "slack work," and part-time work being the only type of employment available. In addition to these, the bureau identified 23 million workers who were employed on a part-time shift voluntarily. In both cases, the numbers, even given the BLS's caveats, seem sizable given the steady economic expansion that has characterized the 1990s. One could reasonably ask: How many years into a recovery does it take to provide full employment for all of those who want it? After years of economic expansion, tens of millions of U.S. workers, disproportionately female and nonwhite, still cannot find full-time, year-round, permanent jobs. Even those who say their schedule is voluntary are not necessarily saying their lower wages and lessened benefits are accepted on a voluntary basis.

Clearly, the BLS has adopted a very narrow view of what constitutes contingent employment. Instead of focusing on a fragment of the working class that shares low wages for performing the same work as permanent employees, who have little in the way of health insurance and other fringe benefits, and who share an uncertain working future, the BLS had constructed a view of contingent work that fits neatly into their existing methodological procedures. Arriving at a seemingly precise official count of the contingent workforce has taken priority over understanding the fundamentally underemployed character of contingent employment.

Day Laborers

In virtually every medium to large U.S. city, there are specific sites (typically streets where homeless shelters are located) where workers gather daily to try to secure work as landscapers, construction workers, or manual laborers. Many citizens in these areas have witnessed men trying their luck at flagging down construction or landscaping contractors to find day work.[17] Generally, day laborers are lesser skilled, less educated, and are therefore more vulnerable to the vagaries of the local labor market and to arbitrary and capricious treatment by employers. Compared with other members of the growing army of contingent workers, day laborers are also more susceptible to the possibility of on-the-job injuries by more frequently exposing themselves to truly hazardous working conditions. Construction contractors pursuing cheap labor for manual jobs routinely use day laborers to fill their needs. According to Arne Kalleberg, et. al., there were nearly two million day laborers employed in the U.S. labor force in 1995.[18]

In Atlanta, which has seen its day-labor population balloon in the past two decades from roughly a thousand to tens of thousands, race has become a salient issue for local residents and authorities. As is true in most other U.S. cities, the day-labor population is disproportionately nonwhite, and increasingly Latino in its demographic composition. And frequently most day laborers are undocumented workers. To control the day-labor population, Marietta, Georgia, following other communities in and around Atlanta, adopted an ordinance in 1999 that prohibits day laborers from congregating on public land.[19] It also bans day laborers from waiting on private property without permission. Unlike other communities, however, Marietta's day-labor corners, heavily populated with workers from El Salvador, Guatemala, and Mexico, have been the locus of an intensive crackdown on illegal immigrants. Despite the adverse conditions faced by workers getting day labor from the corner, for some, especially newly arrived South American and Mexican immigrants, it remains the only work they can find.

In other communities, the increasing reliance on day labor to build U.S. cities has attracted attention because of the dangerous nature of the work and of the blatant abuses day workers routinely endure. In perhaps the clearest example of the difficult, dangerous activity day laborers perform, and a pattern of incidents which U.S. Attorney General Janet Reno labeled "shameful human exploitation," untrained homeless day laborers are being recruited to remove asbestos from demolition projects around the country. Asbestos, long-used (and still manufactured in the United States) for insulation, is hazardous even when handled by highly skilled professionals. Asbestos fibers can easily become imbedded in the lungs, causing respiratory illnesses, including asbestosis. Careful removal requires special precautions, including protective masks and respirators. Removal procedures include wetting down the material and putting it into special containers. None of these precautions has been evident in the day-laborer cases. Clearly, this aspect of day labor is a nationwide problem and while several building contractors have been caught and punished, it is unclear how many similar incidents involving hazardous work and day labor go undetected.

Less dramatic evidence, but still demonstrative of the dirty, dangerous, and often unrelenting pace of day labor can be found in accounts from Texas, North Carolina, and California. For instance, in Houston, according to one contractor, it is the industry's little secret that illegal immigrants do the hard, concrete-busting, ditch-digging jobs at many construction sites. Hispanic immigrants are popular there because they have the reputation of being good workers willing to perform backbreaking tasks without complaint.[20] In Raleigh, N.C., inexperienced, untrained day laborers were employed to stuff sticks of dynamite down a metal tube and ignite them to clear land for a golf course.[21] And in Los Angeles, where the most comprehensive survey of day laborers has been undertaken by UCLA's Center for the Study of Urban Poverty, more than half of the day laborers interviewed at eighty-seven Los Angeles sites reported being abused by their employers.[22]

In short, not only are day laborers a sizable and important part of the U.S. contingent workforce, they are one of the most vulnerable and least protected groups. An irony surrounding the day-labor issue is that demand for such employment has been strongest in the same communities where resistance to their presence has been greatest (especially in southern California, where day laborers are intensively used for landscaping and other residential-type work).

Labor pools that routinely employ day laborers, much like labor corners, are particularly prominent in rapidly growing southern and southwestern states such as Louisiana, Texas, Georgia, Nevada, and California. This very bottom sector of the temporary employment industry, together with the rapidly expanding practice of communities constructing facilities for day laborers and their employers, is leading to the institutionalization of day labor. Labor pools thrive on the work provided by low-skilled manual laborers, often entrapping them in an endless cycle of temporary day jobs that prevents them from escaping poverty.[23] Working for a labor pool usually involves hazardous, uncertain, arbitrary, and undesirable working conditions, features often shared with other segments of the contingent labor force. Labor pools attract workers from among large numbers of the urban poor, a population that is disproportionately nonwhite.

Other Types of Contingent Work

Many observers of the labor process in the United States have spent the bulk of their research efforts on the more prominent and publicized categories of the burgeoning contingent workforce. But many neglect more specialized subgroups in the working population who share all of the same fundamental features as temporary workers and involuntary part-time workers. These include groups such as independent contractors, on-call workers, and subcontracted employees.

In recent years, subcontracted employees have become increasingly common in U.S. workplaces as corporate officials pursue maximum flexibility in managing their workforces. Often, subcontracted employees work at jobs that were previously held by workers employed by the very same employers. For example, a growing number of subcontracting firms are providing "business services" such as janitorial and food service workers. Although the industrial sector known as "business services" includes companies with expertise in everything from advertising to engineering, the typical subcontracting scenario involves a corporation paying a (subcontracting) firm to landscape its physical plant or to provide custodial services.

It is difficult to precisely estimate how many subcontracted workers may be employed in the U.S. labor force on any given day, but the numbers are clearly on the rise. The BLS, in a special survey of subcontracting patterns among manufacturing companies, discovered that a majority were using some type of subcontracting arrangement. The canvass showed consistent increases among manufacturing companies in the use of subcontracting for a range of services, including accounting, machine maintenance, secretarial work, engineering and drafting, janitorial work, and trucking.[24] Subcontracted workers share many characteristics with other members of the expanding contingent workforce. They tend to be paid less than permanent, directly employed workers, have minimal access to fringe benefits, have short and unstable tenures with their employers, and are seldom a part of any collective-bargaining agreement. Kalleberg et al., in their study of "insecure" or nonstandard work, estimated there were a total of 1.4 million part-time and full-time workers employed by contract companies in 1995.[25]

On-call workers represent another sizable group of employees that tend to go neglected by analysts of the contingent work phenomenon. Generally, on-call workers refer to a pool of employees that employers may draw on as the need arises, often for relatively extended periods. In the U.S. labor force, employees such as construction workers, often supplied by a union hiring hall, and substitute teachers, employed and supplied by local school districts, are quintessential examples of on-call workers. Again, despite the lack of certainty surrounding the length of these types of work, neither the BLS nor private researchers generally include them in their count of the contingent workforce.

Independent contractors have become a particularly controversial part of the contingent workforce. Generically, independent workers are freelancers who offer a product or service to individuals, a company, or the government. Many of these workers are actually self-employed; offering their services as freelancers or consultants, some are doing very well. In their study of nonstandard work arrangements, Kalleberg et al. estimated there were more than 1 million wage and salaried contractors and 6.5 million self-employed independent contractors in 1995.[26] It should be emphasized that though the number of self-employed individuals is high, their economic fortunes are generally less favorable than full-time wage or salaried workers. Self-employment allows workers to exercise discretion over their own labor, but that often means overwork and relatively little income. Many are able to remain self-employed only for short periods, eventually seeking out permanent full-time work.

In recent years, the "independent contractor" type of arrangement has been grossly abused by employers. Many—the most infamous of which has been the Microsoft corporation—have engaged in the practice of terminating permanent, full-time employees en masse and then rehiring the same workers as independent contractors. For employers, this kind of subtle change in job status reaps significant financial rewards. In one simple stroke of the pen, and without losing any of their trained workers, employers have been able to cut their labor costs by one-third.

Few among the millions of workers discussed here enjoy the kind of health insurance coverage, vacation, or retirement plans that full-time permanent workers still expect to receive. This survey, which parallels the work of Rasell and Appelbaum, as well as Kalleberg et al., nonetheless omits additional groups that share an indefinite employment future and whose daily lives in every other way share much in common with the above cited segments of the workforce. But these workers seldom receive the same attention when the topic of contingent work surfaces.

SLOWING THE SHIFT TO CONTINGENT WORK

There are a host of reasons that may attenuate the growth of contingent work. Employers who rely on temporary and other contingent workers are likely to suffer from a variety of organizational "human resource" problems.[27] Many managers have begun to discover that contingent work is neither efficient nor cost-effective. Clearly, workers who have a more tangential association with their employers care less about tardiness, absenteeism, and even sabotage on the job than permanent full-time workers. Although a host of additional reasons surely play a role, a 1998 survey by CCH of 401 human-resource officials revealed that worker absenteeism was up 25 percent over the same period a year earlier (with dollars lost to companies as a result increasing 32 percent).[28]

Other managerial concerns have been published with regularity in the business press during the 1990s. In 1995, in surveying the swelling numbers of contingent workers, *HR Focus* (a publication of the American Management Association) asked its business readers "Are Contingent Workers Really Cheaper?"[29] In *Computerworld,* Barb Cole-Gomolski documents problems from relying on contingent workers, especially for extended periods.[30] She quotes a worker who had been at Microsoft for more than six years (employed as a "permatemp") who spoke of temps creating a stratified workplace dividing permanent and temporary staff, making teamwork problematic, along with others who spoke of issues surrounding morale and frustration. Moreover, even temps or part-timers who are filling important, relatively well-paid positions tend to terminate their contingent status when full-time employment becomes available. For managers, this is a potential time bomb as growing numbers of temps work as highly-skilled technicians. According to the BLS, the number of computer systems analysts and engineers working as temps or contract workers increased from 76,000 in 1995 to 107,000 in 1997 (an increase of nearly 41 percent). Besides Microsoft, other household names in the information systems industry such as Compaq, maintain about one-fifth of their workforce on a contingent basis. Cole-Gomolski warns that information systems designed and implemented by "permatemps" will be more difficult to upgrade or repair in the future because the same contingent workers are unlikely to remain employed at the same firm. As one temp database administrator expressed it, "[I] really don't want people pestering me months down the road" once they have accepted other employment.

Still another reason the movement toward contingent work may slow substantially is the growing number of regulations and local laws that involve and often uphold the rights of workers. As Susan Massmann notes, some employers have found that the short-term benefits of hiring temporary workers and other contingent workers is being transcended by lengthy and costly litigation.[31] Key to much litigation has been the (nonmandatory) Equal Employment Opportunity Commission's (EEOC) issuance of guidelines for employers who use contingent workers. Though the guidelines are not legally binding, courts in many jurisdictions uphold its standards. Meanwhile, other corporations are being penalized for misclassifying their employees as independent contractors and temporary workers in an attempt to reduce labor costs.

L. Braff, for instance, outlines the kinds of legal pitfalls involved in classifying and misclassifying workers.[32] The author notes that while there are significant advantages to employers who use contingent workers, such as being exempt from making contributions to Social Security and minimizing the likelihood of union activity, they may encounter problems with the Internal Revenue Service, the Department of Labor, the National Labor Relations Board, and may find themselves in violation of governmental regulations such as the Consolidated Omnibus Budget Reconciliation Act, the Worker Adjustment and Retraining Act, and the Family and Medical Leave Act, should they carelessly misclassify workers to secure short-term gains.

In recent years, Microsoft has exemplified the potential problems that corporations are encountering in their attempt to use contingent workers to cut costs. As noted, U.S. corporations like Microsoft, with the stroke of a pen, have been relabeling their workforces as independent contractors, thus permitting them to avoid fringe benefit costs and regulatory liabilities. For much of the 1980s and 1990s, Microsoft has increased its independent contractor and temporary workforce, and reaped a windfall in increased profits as a result. But in October 1996, the Ninth U.S. Circuit Court of Appeals in San Francisco, following an investigation by the Internal Revenue Service, ruled in favor of contingent workers in a class-action lawsuit. The suit accused Microsoft of wrongly classifying many of their workers as independent contractors, therefore unfairly denying benefits to those who were actually full-time employees.

In the Microsoft case, most of the plaintiffs were software testers and writers of technical manuals. They had worked for years at the same company, worked under the same supervisors as regular workers, performed the same kind of work in the same offices as other employees, and even had similar company badges. But Microsoft hired them as temps, and had them sign agreements in which the workers accepted responsibility for paying their own withholding taxes and all fringe benefits. After it was initially fined and penalized in 1990 by the IRS over the practice, Microsoft began intensively using private-sector temporary staffing companies. These workers were given the option of continuing to be Microsoft employees if they agreed to be hired by the temporary agency. The workers refused and the class-action suit was filed. In reaching its 1996 decision, the court explicitly scorned the "large corporations" that hire temporary employees "as a way of avoiding payment of employee benefits, and thereby increasing their profits."

The Microsoft case illustrates that the corporate obsession of using independent contractors to save money may actually cost firms more in penalties, fines, and back payments (not to mention employee morale and loyalty) than if they were classified correctly at the outset. More recently, Microsoft suffered another legal blow in its continuing efforts to deny benefits to temporary workers.[33] In early 1999, a three-judge panel of the Ninth Circuit Court of Appeals in San Francisco ruled that thousands of previously excluded workers were eligible to buy discounted stock in the company. The decision potentially adds millions to the company's past and current compensation costs. Despite Microsoft's best efforts, this ruling expanded their liability from hundreds to thousands of workers, many of whom may eventually buy company stock and be paid for the appreciation of shares they were unable to buy.

Again, the business and legal literature makes it plain that Microsoft is not the only company involved in such illicit practices, nor are theirs the only tactics being used against contingent workers. In October 1998, the Labor Department filed suit against media giant Time Warner Inc. for denying benefits to its temporary employees, and in June 1999, contingent hospital workers in California's Santa Clara County sued the county government for denying them benefits. In their case, roughly one-third of the 3,500 employees at Valley Medical Center have been classified as temporary, even though many have been employed by the hospital for years.[34] And according to the General Accounting Office (GAO), between 1994 and 1998, the IRS conducted more than 11,000 Employment Tax Examination Program audits that resulted in the assessment of $751 million in taxes and the reclassification of nearly 500,000 workers.

In short, the 1990s has presented numerous obstacles to U.S. corporations in their quest to create a flexible, disposable, contingent workforce. Although victories are being scored on both sides, the issue of contingent work has been raised to an unprecedented point of contention between workers and their employers. The U.S. legal and regulatory apparatus, then, provides one important reason to believe contingent work may slow in the near future.

But at the same time, it is important to emphasize that workers have not simply been passive in the transition to a contingent labor force. As individuals, in organizations, and in labor unions, workers have resisted the trend to nonstandard work arrangements.[35] Workers have been proactive and are showing that they are willing to invest heavily to protect the more marginalized members of the U.S. workforce.

Perhaps the industrial dispute involving contingent work that gained the greatest national profile recently was the successful August 1997 strike of workers employed by the United Parcel Service (UPS), a labor action that was heavily influenced by the contingent work issue. Earlier in the 1990s, UPS had been hiring disproportionate numbers of contingent workers. Indeed, of 46,000 unionized workers the company added from 1993 to 1997, fully 38,000 were hired as part-timers. By that point, the UPS part-time workforce had reached 110,000 workers.

In negotiations with UPS, the union rejected the company's rationale for its growing reliance on contingent workers. With revenues that exceeded $22 billion in 1996 and the market dominance it enjoyed, UPS officials' argument that it needed more part-time workers to remain competitive appeared dubious. During the process, the Teamsters emphasized the savings the company was accumulating from the lower earnings of part-time workers who were paid $9 to $10 hourly compared with $20 by full-timers. In early August 1997, with little sign of progress in the negotiations, 185,000 UPS drivers and package sorters went on strike. It was the largest strike in the United States in three decades and, according to a Gallup/CNN poll, 55 percent of Americans surveyed supported the Teamsters while just 27 percent backed UPS.

The Teamsters won major concessions as a result of the contentious fifteen-day strike, including higher wages for both part-time and full-time workers, more full-time jobs, and worker control over their pension plan. With respect to the use of contingent workers, UPS agreed to convert 10,000 part-time positions into full-time jobs (compared with the 1,000 figure initially offered by the company). Additionally, the company gave ground on the use of subcontractors—agreeing to phase out their use over six months (except during holidays). Taken together, then, important legal victories involving contingent workers, the regulatory environment of the United States, and the resistance of organized labor represent significant constraints in U.S. corporations' continuing efforts to implement contingent work arrangements.

CONCLUSION

In this examination of current issues surrounding contingent work in the U.S. labor force, we are left with some important conclusions and many unanswered questions. Clearly, one point that deserves reiteration is that the efforts of government bureaucrats and unreflective academics to define and measure the magnitude of the contingent workforce has led to a significant understatement of the true nature of the problem. In the quest to precisely operationalize and enumerate this marginalized segment of the workforce, government statisticians and independent researchers omit large and significant groups in the U.S. labor force. In this chapter, attention was drawn to groups of contingent workers who have come to serve a function for employers in facilitating management control within the workplace. In addition, it was shown that the creation of a contingent workforce has served to divide workers. It has erected an obstacle to communication and mobilization among workers, and pitted one group against another. The use of temporary workers, part-time employees, subcontractors, and others who are paid less, receive significantly fewer benefits, and have a loose affiliation with their employers undermines the pay and working conditions of all workers. In this way, the use of contingent workers has been a highly effective management tool for employers—a strategy that, in the short run at least, has facilitated management's control over the labor process and assured the maximization of the potential output of every hour of paid labor.

However, despite the tremendous economic and political power of U.S. corporations, a combination of their own narrow self-interest and the ongoing contest with organized labor may actually hinder and slow the advance toward contingent work in the twenty-first century.

NOTES

I would like to gratefully acknowledge the assistance of Joan Rozzi, supervisor of medical resources, James Dickinson Library, University of Nevada, Las Vegas.

1. Steven Hipple, "Contingent Work: Results from the Second Survey," *Monthly Labor Review*, November 1998, 22–35.

2. Bureau of Labor Statistics, "Press Release: Contingent and Alternative Employment Arrangements, February 1997" (Washington, D.C.: U.S. Department of Labor, 1997).

3. Richard M. Devens, "Gains in Job Security," *Monthly Labor Review*, March 1998, 74–75.

4. Cited in "Livelihood," PBS Documentary Series. See especially "Shift Change."

5. Robert E. Parker, "The Labor Force in Transition: The Growth of the Contingent Work Force in the United States," in *The Labor Process and Control of Labor: The Changing Nature of Work Relations in the Late Twentieth Century,* ed. Berch Berberoglu (Westport, Conn.: Praeger Publishers, 1992), 116.

6. Edie Rasell and Eileen Appelbaum, "Nonstandard Work Arrangements: A Challenge for Workers and Labor Unions," *Social Policy* 28, no. 2 (1997): 31–36.

7. Walter Colon, "Iowa Needs Immigrants," *Des Moines Sunday Register,* 26 September 1999, 2A.

8. Robert E. Parker, *Flesh Peddlers and Warm Bodies: The Temporary Help Industry and Its Workers* (New Brunswick, N.J.: Rutgers University Press, 1994); Kevin D. Henson, *Just a Temp* (Philadelphia, Pa.: Temple University Press, 1996); Chris Tilly, *Half a Job* (Philadelphia, Pa.: Temple University Press, 1996).

9. William Serrin, "Up to a Fifth of U.S. Workers Now Rely on Part-Time Jobs," *The New York Times* (14 August 1983), 1.

10. Polly Callaghan and Heidi Hartmann, *Contingent Work* (Washington, D.C.: Economic Policy Institute, 1991).

11. Bureau of Labor Statistics, 1999.

12. Bureau of Labor Statistics, 1999.

13. Timothy Brogan, *Staffing Services Annual Update* (Alexandria, Va.: National Association of Temporary and Staffing Services, 1999), 1.

14. Brogan, *Staffing Services Annual Update,* 4.

15. Susan McHenry and Linda Lee Small, "Does Part-Time Pay Off?" *MS,* March 1989, 88.

16. William Serrin, "Up to a Fifth of U.S. Workers Now Rely on Part-Time Jobs," *The New York Times,* 14 August 1983, 1.

17. Brad Schrade, "Hispanics Oppose Roswell Crowd-Control Effort after Arrests," *Atlanta Journal and the Atlanta Constitution,* 7 April 1999, B3; Howard Henry Chen, "The Working Corner," *The News and Observer* (Raleigh, N.C.), 16 March 1997, E1; Denise Cardinal, "Council Bans Pickup of Day Laborers," *Las Vegas Sun,* 24 June 1997, 1; and "Day Laborers Ignore Law," *Las Vegas Sun,* 7 March 1998, 1; Kate Berry, "Laborers Work Hard for Their Pay," *The Orange County Register,* June 22, 1999, C1; Parker, *Flesh Peddlers and Warm Bodies.*

18. Arne L. Kalleberg et. al., *Nonstandard Work, Substandard Jobs* (Washington, D.C.: Economic Policy Institute, 1997), 77.

19. Will Anderson, "INS Arrests Day Laborers in Marietta," *Atlanta Journal and the Atlanta Constitution,* 23 June 1999, F1.

20. Jenalia Moreno and L. M. Sixel, "A Day's Work: Immigrant Laborers Are Lining Up to Take Hard, Risk-Filled Jobs," *Houston Chronicle,* 17 May 1998, 1.

21. Chen, "The Working Corner."

22. Nancy Cleeland, "Many Day Laborers Prefer Their Work to Regular Jobs," *Los Angeles Times,* 19 June 1999, A1.

23. Parker, *Flesh Peddlers and Warm Bodies,* 73–78.

24. Bureau of Labor Statistics, 1987.

25. Kalleberg et al., *Nonstandard Work, Substandard Jobs,* 77.

26. Kalleberg et al., *Nonstandard Work, Substandard Jobs,* 77.

27. Parker, *Flesh Peddlers and Warm Bodies.*

28. Stephanie Armour, "Workplace Absenteeism Soars 25 percent, Costs Millions," *USA Today,* 6 November 1998, 1A.

29. "Are Contingent Workers Really Cheaper?" *HR Focus,* September 1995, 1.

30. Barb Cole-Gomolski, "Reliance on Temps Creates New Problems," *Computerworld,* 31 August 1998, 1.

31. Susan Massmann, "Temporary Workers Can Leave Employers with Some Long-Term Liability Headaches," *National Underwriter,* 9 August 1999, 6, 31.

32. L. Braff, "Legal Pitfalls of Classifying Workers," *HR Focus* 74, no. 12 (1997): S9.

33. Ralph T. King, Jr., "Microsoft Loses Ruling over Temporary Workers," *Wall Street Journal,* 14 May 1999, A3.

34. Merrill Goozner, "Longtime Temps Want Some Perks, Now Some Are Suing for Benefits," *Chicago Tribune,* 22 June 1999, 1.

35. Michael A. Verespej, "What's behind the Strife?" *Industry Week,* 1 February 1999, 58–62.

7

The Political Economy
of Global Accumulation and Its
Emerging Mode of Regulation

Behzad Yaghmaian

The international capitalist economy is undergoing a process of fundamental transformations, in both its structure and its institutional/regulatory counterparts. This chapter is an inquiry into the underlying causes of some of the institutional changes, and their interrelations with structural transformations. I contend that recent institutional and regulatory developments are rooted in the global restructuring of capitalism and transformations in the organization of production. The global dominance of neoliberalism (pioneered by Thatcher and Reagan), the Structural Adjustment Policy of the World Bank and the IMF, and the new GATT Accord constitute the important building blocks of the new institutional and regulatory requirements of transnational capitalism.

The methodology used in this chapter conceptualizes these transformations by synthesizing the theory of the Internationalization of Capital,[1] and the Theory of Regulation developed by the French Regulation School.[2] The Regulation School provides a useful framework for introducing the role of institutions and social structures into the theory of capital accumulation. Once placed within the logic of global capital accumulation, the regulation framework can be used to theorize the tensions between national and international regulation and accumulation.

My analysis is informed by the (uneven) process of internationalization of the total social capital and its fragments—individual autonomous capitals. Its view of the transformation of regulation and the role of nation-states draws on the competition of capitals (intraclass conflict) and their competing and often conflicting demands on state policy; the class struggle between labor and capital; and the competition among national sites (to maintain and increase shares of global surplus value and capital).

In the first section of this chapter, I present a critical assessment of Regulatory Theory. The second section puts forth a theory of transnational capitalism and state regulation. These sections lay the foundation for a political-economic analysis of recent international policy and institutional changes. The third section includes an assessment of neoliberalism, the GATT, and the Structural Adjustment Policy of the World Bank/IMF within the framework developed earlier.

THE THEORY OF REGULATION: A CRITICAL READING

Though not a homogeneous body of work, Regulation Theory provides a systematic attempt to introduce the role of institutions and social structures into the theory of capital accumulation.[3] Capital accumulation is regarded as a complex process of intertwining social, economic, and cultural forces; it presupposes harmony and balance among forces that are often contradictory and conflicting in nature. Regulation Theory makes possible investigation of the interconnections between the labor process, labor control—the disciplining of labor power for the purpose of capital accumulation—and social and cultural institutions, as integral parts of a regime of accumulation and mode of regulation. The regime of accumulation is defined as "the stabilization over a long period of the allocation of the net product between consumption and accumulation; it implies some correspondence between the transformation of both conditions of production and the conditions of reproduction of wage earners."[4]

The accumulation of total social capital is a contradictory process. It requires conformity and correspondence among its fragments, the individual capitals. The accumulation of individual fragments of the total social capital must strike a balance that secures a smooth expansion of the system. The tension between the interests of the fragment (individual capital) and the collective (total social capital) needs to be sorted out and resolved by market and extramarket forces and institutions. "There must exist a materialization of the regime of accumulation taking the form of norms, habits, laws, regulating networks, and so on that ensure the unity of the process, i.e., the appropriate consistency of individual behaviors with the schema of reproduction. This body of rules and social processes is called the '*mode of regulation*.'"[5]

The mode of regulation concept is a useful framework for analyzing the complexity of the state regulation of accumulation. This complexity arises, on one hand, from the competition of capitals, and the conflicting interests and demands of individual capitals upon the state. But it also reflects the inherent nature of capital as a social relation of production and the class struggle between capital and labor (the level of total capital). State regulation is framed by different levels of competition and class conflict, and their consequent contradictions.

The regulation of the capitalist system is a social creation. Its structural crises are manifestations of the nonconformity between economic and social institutions, the incoherence of the schema of reproduction, and the balance between accumulation and consumption. Production (including capitalist commodity production) is always the production of social relations, in addition to material objects. Crises are therefore ruptures in the continuous reproduction of social relations, and lead to the restructuring of the system and the gradual emergence of a new regime of accumulation.[6] Recovery from crisis requires restoration (over a long period of time) of a coherent relationship between the economic and social institutions and the formation of a new mode of regulation that corresponds to the underlying (transformed) regime of accumulation.

The primary concern of Regulation Theory has been explanation of the patterns of accumulation in the post–World War II period. Postwar accumulation benefited from a combination of market and extramarket arrangements and institutions that can be captured by what David Harvey has aptly called the "Fordist–Keynesian" regime.[7] According to most regulation theorists, the Fordist regime reached its internal limits in the 1960s, while the oil crisis of 1973 sounded its death knell and marked the beginning of the transition to a new regime of accumulation.

The increasing dominance of neoliberalism on a world scale in the past two decades has produced a debate about the ability of neoliberal policies to resolve the crisis of the national unit (individual nation-states). Can neoliberalism generate sustained national growth and resolve the Fordist crisis? Has there emerged a "post-Fordist" regime of accumulation and mode of regulation? This has been an emerging line of debate within the regulation school.[8] While Bob Jessop regards neoliberalism as one possible way out of the crisis of national Fordism,[9] Jamie Peck and Adam Tickell view it as the politics of crisis, promoting "systemic instability, both temporarily and geographically."[10] Peck and Tickell along with Lipietz argue for the development of alternative nonliberal productivist solutions to the crisis (of the national economy).

Crises and the consequent economic restructuring and corresponding regulatory changes are national phenomena in Regulation Theory.[11] In most regulationist writings the international economy is viewed as the sum total of various national units. In more recent years, attempts have been made to introduce "the international factor" into the analysis of the crisis of national accumulation in advanced capitalist countries.[12]

By contrast to earlier Regulation School works, in which accumulation and its crisis rested solely on "domestic" forces, in the internationalized version of the theory, the smooth reproduction of the wage system in the central capitalist countries also requires the existence of a hegemonic state in relation to other nation-states in the world economy. Here, the hegemonic state is the "external" factor that secures smooth national accumulation in the context of a national regime of accumulation/mode of regulation pair. Hegemony is seen as the "main form of cohesion within a system of nations."[13] The Fordist crisis, Peck and Tickell argue, is essentially a crisis of international hegemony in a system of globally connected national units.[14] As Aglietta contends, the internationalization of the theory of regulation "rests on the primacy of the national dimension and regards the world economy as a system of interacting national social formations."[15] In more recent Regulation theorizing, Bob Jessop speaks of national modes of growth and their insertion into the international hierarchy constituted through the global division of labor.[16] Here again, the starting point is the national unit within the context of the global division of labor.

This juxtaposition of accumulation and regulation within the "national" site introduces an ideologically constructed constraint that ultimately limits ability to theorize the emerging regulatory arrangements that are responses to the spatial duality of accumulation and regulation. The development of a theory of global accumulation and regulation, I argue, requires the removal of the nation-centeredness of Regulation Theory. The appropriate point of departure in the analysis of accumulation and regulation is total social capital and its fragments (individual capitals). The spatial dimension is important only to the extent that it affects the relations between accumulation and regulation.

In this sense, the debate about the "national" role of neoliberalism is essentially misplaced. The controversy will be resolved once the theory of regulation is freed from its national straitjacket and placed within the framework of global accumulation. That is, deconstruction of the theory of regulation through removal of the national unit as the starting point of analysis leads to entirely different questions about accumulation and regulation. In what follows I will demonstrate that neoliberalism is the regulatory configuration meant to facilitate the smooth accumulation of the most globalized fractions of capital. But the smooth accumulation of capital(s) does not necessarily imply the resolution of the crisis of national sites. In fact, securing the accumulation of (fractions of) capital on the global scale can, in some cases, lead to the deepening of the crisis of the nation-state.

INTERNATIONALIZATION OF CAPITAL AND THE POLITICAL ECONOMY OF TRANSNATIONAL CAPITALISM

The internationalization of capital is an uneven process leading to different forms and degrees of integration of fragments of capital in international accumulation. The diversity of form and scope of internationalization, in turn, results in competing and contradictory demands for nation-state policy (regulation) by different capitals. With the intensification of the internationalization process, nation-states and their regulation of the conditions of accumulation become increasingly framed by the competing interests of unevenly internationalized capitals.

Despite the uneven nature of the internationalization of capital, certain historically specific patterns and phases of internationalization[17] can be observed, leading to identification of the relative dominance of certain forms of international accumulation in different stages of capitalist development. In this sense, theorizing accumulation and regulation requires concretizing of the stages of internationalization of capital, the forms of international accumulation, and identification of the dominant form of international accumulation at each stage. The struggle between labor and capital for state regulation, intraclass conflict among fractions of capital, and the tension between local and international regulation are framed by the evolving forms (regimes) of accumulation. The theory of the state and state regulation of accumulation must address these dimensions of internationalization.

Stages of the Internationalization of Capital

The analysis in this section focuses on the internationalization of total social capital. In the following subsection, I will discuss the uneven internationalization of fragments of total social capital (individual capitals). The theorizing of global accumulation and regulation emerges from the synthesis of these two levels of analysis and a theory of the state.

Capital as a social relation of production has been international in its basic character (its essential reality) from its inception. The partial confinement of capital to national sites—the national form of capital—has been a changing phenomenon, declining in scope with the development of the forces of production.

The early globalization of capital was marked by the spatial expansion of capitalism in precapitalist societies through the mobility of capitalistically produced commodities.[18] At this earlier stage, the internationalization process was closely intertwined with the so-called primitive accumulation of capital. It was the internationalization of capitalist class relations through the internationalization of the circuit of commodity capital $(C - M - C \ldots P \ldots C')$.[19] Even at this early stage of development, accumulation is partially international. Though production and investment occur within the confines of the national economy, realization, at least in part, takes place internationally in the world market.

The internationalization of accumulation advances with the internationalization of other moments of the circuit of industrial capital. The true realization of the international character of capital occurs through that spatial mobility of money capital (M – C . . . P . . . C' – M') and productive capital (P . . . C' – M' – C . . . P). But this further spatial mobility of other forms of capital is achieved only at a certain stage of capitalist development. The creation of credit money and share capital, and a consequent deepening of the centralization of capital, were the historical prerequisites for the spatial mobility of all forms of capital—the internationalization of the circuit of industrial capital.

The internationalization of production and the integrated use of multiple sites for single production processes occurs in progressive phases. Early internationalization of production occurs through the spatial movement of a part of a single production process to a "foreign" site. The circuit of industrial capital is completed when production and the realization of the value of commodity capital take place in the new site. This phase of international production coincides with the strategy of import-substitution industrialization.[20]

This limited form of internationalization of production requires state intervention in formulating national trade, exchange-rate, industrial, and labor policies. The national regulation of accumulation in developing countries helps enhance the international accumulation of capital by securing the conditions of accumulation through seemingly antiglobal (national) policies, i.e., exchange control and exchange rate overvaluation, protectionism, and so on. The protection of infant industries (differentiated rates of protection of finished, semifinished, and capital goods) fulfills the dual task of developing local industries (serving the national interest in the developing country), while paving the way for further internationalization of production and accumulation.[21]

Internationalization accelerated in the 1970s and 1980s and assumed qualitatively new dimensions. The computer revolution, the advance in communications technologies, and the reduction in transport costs[22] led to increasing internationalization of production and finance and a move towards more complete integration of the world market through unprecedented spatial mobility of capital and resources. Transnational capital, in the institutional form of transnational corporations, now disaggregates and disperses production to take advantage of global differentials in labor regimes, labor processes, and industrial organizations, and to maximize its international profitability. The internationalization of production is carried out through direct investment, outsourcing and subcontracting, joint ventures, strategic alliances, and so on.

The sketch of the stages of internationalization presented here is informed by the movement and development of the total social capital. The historical forms outlined above represent a general but uneven pattern of internationalization of the circuit of industrial capital. The periodization does not imply the existence of only one form of internationalization or accumulation in any stage. Different forms coexist and accordingly affect nation-state policy. Individual capitals' uneven integration into international economic activity and their various forms of international accumulation become the context of fierce competition of capitals and their conflicting demands on state policy.

The analysis now requires specification of the forms of competition of capitals and the regulatory responses of the state to individual capitals' demands. Here we move from the level of the total social capital to that of the individual capitals. The starting point is an appropriate differentiation of capitals and the articulation of their positions, interests, powers and demands for regulation.

Forms of Internationalization and the Competition of Capitals

Analysis of the effects on nation-state policy of the increasing internationalization of capital in recent years requires concretizing of different forms of international accumulation, and articulation of the dominant form. Dick Bryan provides a very useful differentiation of capitals based on their involvement in international accumulation.[23] Four forms of international integration based on different spatial combinations of production, reproduction and realization are described: the national circuit; the global circuit; the investment-constrained circuit; and the market-constrained circuit.[24] The four circuits constitute four forms of international accumulation, despite their spatial difference in investment, reproduction, and realization. Bryan's taxonomy can be used as a point of departure for studying the competition of capitals and their conflicting demands for nation-state regulation of international accumulation.

The circuit of national capital is one in which production ($C \ldots P \ldots C'$), realization ($C' - M'$), and reproduction ($M' - C'$) occur within the nation. Capitals in this circuit tend to be small and involved in service and naturally protected industries, and are likely to demand a combination of protectionist trade and exchange-rate policies and low interest rates from the nation-state. The state's securing of domestic effective demand is essential for the moment of realization within this circuit.

The investment-constrained circuit depicts a form of international integration in which only realization occurs internationally. Capitals in this circuit are integrated into international accumulation at the level of exchange, but not production. The investment constrained circuit is the first form of international accumulation in the historical process of the internationalization of capital. Essentially, capitals involved in this circuit demand free trade and an exchange-rate policy that enhances the international competitiveness of domestically produced commodity capital.

The market-constrained circuit involves international investment but national production and realization. The capitals in this circuit produce import-competing commodities. Like the national circuit, the state's protective exchange-rate and trade policies, social wage, and public expenditures in securing the conditions of realization, and so on, are essential to accumulation within this circuit.

This was the dominant TNC strategy during the period of import-substitution industrialization. The Fordist regime of Regulation Theory depicts the period in the internationalization of industrial capital in which the market-constrained circuit is the dominant form. The post-Fordist era, I argue, coincides with a more developed stage in the process of internationalization, in which the market-constrained circuit gradually loses its dominance to the global circuit.

The global circuit depicts the most developed form of internationalization, in which both realization and reproduction are international. Accumulation in this circuit requires unrestricted cross-national mobility of commodity capital and money capital. The state not only must facilitate conditions of unfettered cross-national movement of commodity capital; it must also guarantee unrestricted conditions for international investment. Accumulation requires structural and institutional flexibility, and unrestricted capital mobility. Capitals involved in international production gained a competitive advantage and greatly benefited from the protection provided by the national state policies of capital recipient countries in the earlier phase of internationalization. But such policies fetter international accumulation and capitals' ability to secure their global profitability at the more developed stage of globalization.

The ascendancy of global accumulation is reflected in the growing importance of intrafirm trade, sales by the foreign affiliates of TNCs, outsourcing, and so on. The increasing importance of intrafirm trade and sales by foreign affiliates of TNCs in recent years is a sign of the deepening of international production and global resource allocations of transnational capital. Between 1984 and 1993, intrafirm trade in the world increased by almost 95 percent. Sales by foreign affiliates of TNCs exceeded exports of goods and nonfactor services throughout the period (table 7.1). In 1992, sales of affiliates exceeded the exports of goods and nonfactor services (excluding intrafirm trade) by almost 65 percent. The extent of the globalization of production and the growing dominance of global accumulation is further revealed by aggregating sales of foreign affiliates, sales associated with licensing, and intrafirm trade. Throughout the 1980s, the sum of these transactions exceeded the exports of goods and nonfactor services (excluding intrafirm exports) by more than 100 percent (see column 6 in table 7.1).

Available data also reveal that only one-third of international transactions are not associated with international production.[25] A more complete analysis of the globalization process necessitates the consideration of international subcontracting and TNC trade with nonaffiliate subcontractors. In industries like ground transportation, clothing, and electronics, this form of international transaction has become increasingly important. What is required is disaggregation of international trade data to separate international transactions

Table 7.1   Forms of International Transactions in the World, 1984–1993 (in billions of dollars)

Year	Sales of foreign affiliates (1)	Licensing with unaffiliated firms (2)	Sales associated with exports of goods and nonfactor services (3)	Intrafirm exports of goods and nonfactor services (4)	Services excluding intrafirm exports (5)	Exports of goods and nonfactor Service (1) + (2) + (3) – (5) divided by (5) (6)
1984	2581	30	816	2449	1632	109%
1985	2400	40	734	2202	1468	117%
1986	2675	50	819	2458	1638	116%
1987	3492	60	971	2912	1941	133%
1988	4090	80	1109	3327	2218	138%
1989	4640	80	1202	3606	2404	146%
1990	5089	110	1399	4196	2797	137%
1991	5373	120	1482	4446	2964	135%
1992	5235	120	1646	4939	3293	113%
1993	—	—	1587	4762	3175	—

Source: UNCTAD: *World Investment Report,* 1995, 37.

that emanate from TNC outsourcing to enterprises outside their structural organization.

The degree and form of internationalization of production varies among countries. Today, more than 50 percent of imports and exports of the United States and Japan are international exchange of finished and semifinished commodities within TNCs. Nearly four-fifths of the United Kingdom's manufactured exports are intrafirm trade.[26] The share of intrafirm exports in the total exports of the United States increased from 34 to 44 percent between 1983 and 1993.[27]

The increasing globalization of production and the gradual ascendancy of global accumulation are also reflected in the growing importance of imports of intermediate inputs. In the mid-1980s, the share of intermediate inputs in manufactured imports ranged from about 50 percent for Canada, Germany, the United States, and the United Kingdom to nearly 60 percent for France and 70 percent for Japan. Between the 1970s and the mid-1980s, the same countries substantially increased their foreign sourcing of intermediate inputs.[28]

In 1995, sales by overseas Japanese manufacturers exceeded Japan's total merchandise exports by $17 billion (for the first time in Japan's history). The Japanese TNCs are now developing production networks in Asia whose finished products are to be sold in Asia, Europe, and North America. These networks coordinate and unify the activities of geographically dispersed production units and link them with networks of global distribution. Similar networking by U.S. and European manufacturers is occurring across the world. All of these, in turn, require the removal of investment and trade restrictions among countries and regions.

The emerging international accumulation requires the formation of suitable regulatory mechanisms to guarantee free spatial mobility of all forms of capital and the removal of spatial constraints on the circuits of money, productive, and commodity capital. The internationalization of capital requires the creation of global (supranational) institutions and regulatory arrangements to guarantee the smooth reproduction of internationalized wage relations, and secure the regime of international accumulation. *The regulatory requirements of international accumulation are institutionalized through the ascendancy of global neoliberalism.*

NEOLIBERALISM: THE REGULATORY AND INSTITUTIONAL CONDITIONS OF GLOBAL ACCUMULATION

Using the analysis advanced above, I argue in this section that the victory of neoliberalism in Britain and the United States (and more slowly in most European nations) in the 1980s, and its hegemony in the developing world through the Structural Adjustment Policy of the IMF and the World Bank, and the formation of WTO, constitute the fabric of the emerging regulatory mechanism of global accumulation.[29]

A supranational state (though tenuous and riddled with contradictions) is in the making, with a mandate to (de)regulate the conditions of accumulation on a worldwide basis by removing the national regulation of accumulation. The formation of an effective supranational state, however, is constrained by the competition of capitals, the class struggle between labor and capital, and the competing interests of nation-states. Despite the internationalization of wage relations, class relations are largely reproduced in geographically separated fragments in specific national sites. Nation-states and national state policies remain crucial for the legitimation of capitalist relations of production on national sites. Nation-states will remain viable political entities with contradictory and tenuous and economic objectives and tasks.

The intensification of class struggle and the emergence of various forms of resistance to the mandates of global accumulation (local struggles against international accumulation) lead to tenuous relationships among nation-states, and destabilize the nascent apparatus of the supranational state. In addition, the competition of capitals and their respective demands on state policy formation lead to further contradictions and tensions in the development of a stable global regulation. Thus, global neoliberalism—the (de)regulation of accumulation on a world scale—is an unstable emerging trend reflecting the major contradictions of capitalist production relations.

In what follows I will outline some of these contradictions, for the case of the United States. The United States has played a determining role in the creation of these regulatory and institutional mechanisms. Guided by the interest of the most globalized segments of U.S. capital, the United States has been a leading force in the formation of institutional mechanisms that facilitate global accumulation in general.

The United States and the Move toward Neoliberalism

A widespread restructuring of U.S. industries has been occurring in the past two decades. This restructuring is marked by increasing internationalization and the gradual ascendancy of the global circuit in various leading industries. Capitals originating from the United States have been aggressively extending their investment and production facilities in various sites across the globe. In addition, capitals choosing the United States as the site of investment and production have been increasingly relying on an extended network of geographically dispersed subcontractors for the production of intermediate goods. There has also occurred a substantial rise in the formation of strategic alliances between U.S. firms and firms from other national spaces in the automobile and other industries.[30] Guided by conditions of international profitability, U.S. firms have been using a network of diverse sites for both investment and realization.

Increasingly, leading firms within the country regard the United States as one of many available sites. While the U.S. share of world manufacturing exports declined from 17.1 percent in 1966 to 11.7 percent in 1986, the share of the foreign subsidiaries of U.S. firms increased from 8 percent to 9.8 percent during the same period. The U.S. share of the world output of automobiles declined from 51.4 percent in 1960 to 18.2 percent in 1989, while the top U.S. manufacturers have been increasing their share of the world production of automobiles. Ford and General Motors now produce 58.7 percent and 41.8 percent, respectively, of their total output outside of the United States.[31] This picture is replicated in other industries as well. The entire world output of dynamic random access memory was produced in the United States in 1974. By 1988, the U.S. share of the world market had declined to less that 20 percent. The same patterns are found in consumer electronics, textiles, clothing, banking and finance, and many other industries. The internationalization of production has also affected the fast food industry—the most "national" of all industries. For example, a Hong Kong-owned toy factory produces giveaway toys for McDonald's (including *101 Dalmatians*) in Da Nang, Vietnam (to be distributed in the United States).

This extensive internationalization of accumulation demands regulatory policies from the state that are at odds with the policy demands of other capitals and of labor. Successive U.S. administrations, including the recent Democratic government, have used their power to secure conditions of international profitability for the most internationally mobile and entrenched section of capital. It is these capitals that require freedom of movement on a world scale as a condition of their accumulation.

While the state has systematically attempted to reduce the tax burden on corporations and gradually dismantle the social wage as a way of increasing international competitiveness within the country (competitiveness of national sites), it has, at the same time, through the promotion of NAFTA, the WTO, and other investment and trade policies, *led the international movement* for securing the unfettered mobility of all forms of capital. The neoliberal policies of the 1980s and 1990s, market liberalization, the increasing privatization of government-provided services and activities, attacks on unions, and so on, have been part of a systematic state effort to lower the (social) value of labor power in the United States and provide the flexibility demanded by international accumulation. Labor has been asked to carry the burden of the internationalization of capital and increase U.S. international competitiveness by accepting wages that are compatible with those in nonunion and unprotected production sites in other countries.

The path of securing the conditions for international accumulation has been contested terrain, constrained by various tensions and contradictions. A fundamental tension in policy making of recent U.S. administrations (especially the Clinton Administration) has arisen from the effects of such policies on national macroeconomic realities—the trade deficit, unemployment, etc. Capital mobility and the increase in intrafirm and intraindustry trade have aggravated the balance of trade deficit and swelled the ranks of the structurally unemployed.[32] The so-called natural rate of unemployment increased to 5.6 percent from 4 percent in the 1980s. The loss of industrial jobs in the past two decades and the "deindustrialization" of the U.S. economy[33] are, in part, the consequence of an active coalition of the state and the most internationalized of the U.S.-based capitals in securing the conditions of international profitability and accumulation.

The effects of international accumulation on national economic conditions have been a major source of tension for state policy in the past decade and a half. Hence, we see attempts by the state to present its internationally induced policies as policies in the "national" interest, which will generate jobs and improve the standard of living. These attempts were most visible during the policy debates concerning NAFTA and the WTO. The U.S. government role in creating and shaping the WTO represents the victory (however temporary) of the most internationalized capitals over the working class and other fractions of capital. This being so, the new GATT Accord is the manifestation of the victory of the global circuit in formulating the regulatory conditions of accumulation on a world scale.

It is important to note that the terms *regulation* and *deregulation* are used here in a context that differs from the common use of the word. For our purposes, *regulation* is the creation of institutional and legal arrangements that enhance capital accumulation. Regulation can therefore imply either the imposition or the removal of certain norms and laws, depending on the requirements of accumulation. In this sense, global (de)regulation (neoliberalism) is, in fact, a form of regulation that facilitates the accumulation of the most internationalized capitals. This form of regulation necessitates the creation of new institutions and the enactment of new (international) *laws*. The new laws are enacted and enforced by the WTO and the World Bank/IMF through international trade and investment agreements and the Structural Adjustment Policy.

International Accumulation, WTO, and the Structural Adjustment Policy

The formation of the WTO marks an important development in the life history of the GATT. The evolution of the GATT from the Geneva Round (1947) to the Uruguay Round (1986–1994) is rooted in the evolution of international economic activity, and the increasing internationalization of accumulation. The earlier GATT accords were regulatory regimes conducive to the infancy of international production. The United States and other industrialized countries' primary focus was to reduce the constraints on the mobility of commodity capital. To this end, the earlier GATT agreements were successful in achieving a noticeable reduction in tariffs, slashing the average tariff on goods from 40 percent in 1940 to 5 percent by 1986.[34]

More than being an agreement about international trade, the Uruguay Accord was an agreement about international investment. The accord's central orientation was the creation of an unfettered and unregulated network of interconnected sites for investment and realization. It was an attempt to generalize and enforce the regulatory requirements of the global circuit: flexibility and mobility across the world.

The Uruguay Accord substantially broadened the focus of the GATT by including provisions for the elimination of trade-related investment measures (TRIMs) and nontariff barriers. A 1996 WTO report outlined the objectives of this attack against TRIMs as "not only promoting the expansion and progressive liberalization of world trade but also the *facilitation of investment across international frontiers.*"[35] It is beyond the scope of this chapter to present detailed discussion of the new provisions and their impact on different economies (especially the developing countries). My objective here is to demonstrate that the included provisions are components of a regulatory policy that corresponds to the internationalization of production and the requirements of broadened international accumulation.

The agreements on TRIMs and nontariff barriers are provisions to eliminate the regulation of foreign direct investment, especially in developing

countries where various restrictions remain important pillars of their strategies of development. Such restrictions are obstacles to the free mobility of
capital (commodity, money, and productive capital), and the ability of international capital to make location decisions based on conditions of international profitability. Although nontariff barriers to trade and TRIMs are not entirely identical, they overlap and constitute the same restrictions on the
activities of international capital. Nontariff barriers include import quotas,
import licenses, special packaging and labeling regulations, customs procedures and documentation requirements, health and safety regulations, sub-
sidies to domestic procedures of import competing goods, local content requirements, and exchange-rate manipulation. Strict local content requirements
were used by South Korea, Brazil, Mexico, Argentina, India, and Spain to
deepen the backward linkage effects of import-substitution industrialization.[36] Local contents were set at between 50 percent to 90 percent in these
countries.

It is the accumulation of capital in this circuit that demands unfettered flexibility and mobility. TRIMs limit the ability of capital in the global circuit to
make location decisions with respect to investment and realization based on
the conditions of international profitability.[37] Local content requirements restrict the ability of transnational capital to develop a comprehensive strategy
of global resource allocation and profit maximization. Similarly, import restriction can impede the importation of parts and semifinished products to
the host country from transnational capital's affiliates located on other (foreign) sites. Trade balancing measures impose export activities from a particular national site, an activity that might fall outside the global resource allocation strategy of the transnational capital involved.

In addition to including TRIMs and nontariff barriers, the new GATT
Agreements also incorporated the General Agreement on Trade in Services
(GATS). The inclusion of services in the new GATT is due to the increasing
internationalization of banking, insurance, and finance in general, and the
significant role of international financial transactions for the overall circuit of
industrial capital. The computer and telecommunications revolution has
added new and unforeseen dimensions to the mobility of money capital. International investment is increasingly financed through the international
money and credit markets. The internationalization of money and its link
with international investment and accumulation requires unrestricted flexibility, access, and mobility and a true integration of the world financial markets. The inclusion of services in the GATT Agreement institutionalizes this
mobility worldwide.

The creation of the World Trade Organization was an important step toward the formation of a supranational state and the formulation and enforcement of the regulatory conditions of international accumulation. As
discussed earlier, the wholesale (multilateral) liberalization of production, in-

vestment, finance, and exchange is fundamental to securing the conditions of international profitability in the emerging regime of accumulation. Conditions of international profitability are also being secured through "unilateral" but uniform regulatory policies, enforced in different national sites by supranational institutions. In this context, the World Bank/IMF Structural Adjustment Policy helps shape national wage regulation and the national institutional restructuring conducive to international accumulation. It facilitates the integration of the world market by enforcing unilateral nation-state actions for the restructuring of national sites.

Structural adjustment is an integral part of the internationalization of neoliberalism through enforcement of neoliberal trade and macroeconomic policies in loan-seeking countries. Though taking specific forms at different national sites, Structural Adjustment Policy in general constitutes liberalization of prices, imports, the financial sector, foreign exchange, and labor markets. This liberalization creates the institutional configuration and the regulatory arrangements necessary for international accumulation.

It is beyond the scope of this chapter to discuss the effectiveness of structural adjustment in achieving its stated macroeconomic goals.[38] My intention here is to locate structural adjustment in the regulatory configuration of international accumulation, and demonstrate its role in securing the conditions of international profitability of transnational capital. I argue that market liberalization is informed by the mobility/flexibility requirements of transnational capital and complements the broader global liberalization of investment and production enacted by the WTO. The new GATT agreement generalizes the various "unilateral" market liberalization components of the Structural Adjustment Policy in a multinational and "multilateral" policy package. Trade liberalization, the creation of a friendly environment towards transnational investment (inward direct foreign investment) by deregulating local markets and offering low wages, the privatization of state-owned enterprises, and the reduction of government expenditures—all of these are policies aimed at reproducing the regulatory conditions of accumulation, similar to those pioneered by Thatcher and Reagan in advanced capitalist countries in the 1980s. In the developing world, structural adjustment replaces the regulatory and policy configurations of import-substitution industrialization (the market-constrained circuit) with those more compatible with the global circuit by removing differential exchange rates, liberalizing imports, and pursuing an "outward-oriented" development policy. In this sense, structural adjustment, along with the WTO, enforce the (at least partial) uniformity of (de)regulation across national sites in different parts of the world.

An essential component of the mobility/flexibility phenomenon is the restructuring of the labor market and the creation of flexible labor regimes. Labor market liberalization is the path to increased control by capital over labor through the "flexibility" of task assignments, hiring and firing of workers, and so on. The liberalization of the labor market is, in essence, a "euphemism for the disempowerment of labor."[39] Flexible labor regimes allow the existence of diverse labor processes, and forms and layers of exploitation of labor by capital. It is this flexibility that has helped attract transnational capital to various industries in developing countries (including textiles, clothing, and electronics) under the policy of export-led growth and structural adjustment.

In addition to the institutional restructuring of the labor market, structural adjustment leads to a decline in real wages through both nominal wage reductions (in some cases) and foreign exchange market liberalization and the depreciation of the local currency. Real exchange rate depreciation is used to increase the international competitiveness of the national site by lowering the real cost of labor. Capital-short and loan-seeking states compete to increase the attractiveness of their national economies as a site of investment and production. Real wage reduction and flexible labor regimes are local competitive policies informed by the requirements of international accumulation. Structural adjustment is the institutionalization of these policies across nation-states: an attempt to change capital–labor relations by reducing labor's bargaining power against capital.

Structural adjustment also enforces the free international mobility of commodity and productive capital by mandating trade liberalization and removing state control of foreign direct investment. Loan-seeking states are required to accept the structural and regulatory conditions of capitals in the global circuit by removing national obstacles to international accumulation. As in the case of advanced industrialized countries, these regulatory policies are presented as policies in the "national" interest. And labor, with forced decline in real wages and changes in the labor regime, is the designated bearer of the burden of international accumulation. It is labor that should win the battle (for capital) of international competitiveness through lower real wages and higher productivity, and turn the national space into internationally profitable site for investment.

CONCLUSION

The continuing internationalization of accumulation and the gradual dominance of global production has led to the gradual ascendancy of neoliberalism—the regulatory mechanism for global accumulation. Institutional arrangements and apparatuses conducive to the needs of the emerging hegemonic regime of accumulation and its regulation are being developed, leading to the formation of a nascent supranational state.

The international regulation of accumulation is a tenuous enterprise, embedded in various intraclass and interclass contradictions and conflicts. The contradiction between labor and capital, and the resulting competition of capitals and conflict among nation-states are inherent destabilizing factors that function as countertendencies within the emerging global regulatory trend. In developing countries, the regulatory requirements of international accumulation are enforced through the GATT and Structural Adjustment Policy of the IMF and the World Bank. For the most part, the implementation of these policies has resulted in the deterioration of the living conditions of the working poor and the increase in absolute poverty,[40] and political tension, conflicts, and instability in loan-seeking developing countries. As a result of these tensions, a relatively powerful social and political countertendency is developing alongside the internationalization of accumulation and regulation. In developed and developing countries a new wave of nationalism is emerging among the working classes and segments of the bourgeoisie.

Can capital resolve its contradictions and institutionalize the regulatory requirements of global accumulation? The fate and stability of the new regime of accumulation and mode of regulation depend on the intensity of these contradictions and the way they are played out in the future. Capital accumulation remains a tenuous process riddled with contradictions. International accumulation broadens the scope of these contradictions and internationalizes the space within which they develop.

NOTES

This chapter first appeared as "Globalization and the State: The Political Economy of Global Accumulation and Its Emerging Mode of Regulation" in *Science & Society* 62, no. 2 (1998) and is reprinted here with permission. I would like to thank Phil McLewin, Paresh Chattopadhyay, Fikret Ceyhun, Ann Davis, and the anonymous referees of *Science & Society* for their insightful comments on an earlier draft.

1. Christian Polloix," The Internationalization of Capital and the Circuit of Social Capital," in *International Firms and Modern Imperialism,* ed. Hugo Radice (Harmondsworth: Penguin, 1975); Christian Polloix, "The Self-Expansion of Capital on a World Scale," *Review of Radical Political Economics* 9 (1977); Patrick Clawson, "The Internationalization of Capital and Capital Accumulation in Iran and Iraq," *Insurgent Sociologist* 7, no. 2 (1977); James Cypher, "The Internationalization of Capital and the Transformation of Social Formations: A Critique of the Monthly Review School," *Review of Radical Political Economics* 11, no. 4 (1979).

2. Michel Aglietta, *A Theory of Capitalist Regulation: The U.S. Experience* (London: New Left Books, 1979); Robert Boyer, "Wage Formation in Historical Perspective: The French Experience," *Cambridge Journal of Economics* 3, no. 2 (1979); Alain Lipietz, *Mirage and Miracles: The Crisis of Global Fordism* (London: Verso, 1987).

3. Aglietta, *A Theory of Capitalist Regulation;* Michel Aglietta, *Regulation and the Crisis of Capitalism* (New York: Monthly Review Press, 1982); Boyer, "Wage Formation in Historical Perspective"; Robert Boyer, *Labor Flexibility in Europe* (Oxford: Oxford University Press, 1987); Robert Boyer, "Regulation," in *The New Palgrave: Marxian Economics,* ed. John Eatwell, Murray Milgate, and Peter Newman (London:

Macmillan, 1990); Robert Boyer, *The Regulation School: A Critical Introduction* (New York: Columbia University Press, 1990); Alain Lipietz, "Post-Fordism and Democracy," in *Post-Fordism: A Reader,* ed. Ash Amin (Oxford: Blackwell, 1994); Alain Lipietz, "New Tendencies in International Division of Labor: Regime of Accumulation and Mode of Regulation," in *Production, Work, Territory: The Geographical Anatomy of Industrial Capitalism,* ed. A. Scott and M. Stroper (London: Allen & Unwin, 1986); Alain Lipietz, "Beyond the Crisis: The Exhaustion of the Regime of Accumulation: A 'Regulation School' Perspective on Some French Empirical Works," *Review of Radical Political Economics* 18, nos. 1 and 2 (1986); Lipietz, *Mirage and Miracles;* David Harvey, *The Condition of Postmodernity* (Cambridge: Blackwell, 1991); Jamie Peck and Adam Tickell, "Searching for a New Institutional Fix: The After-Fordist Crisis and the Global-Local Disorder," in *Post-Fordism,* ed. Amin; Bob Jessop, "Post-Fordism and the State," in *Post-Fordism,* Amin.

4. Lipietz, "New Tendencies," 19.

5. Lipietz, "New Tendencies," 19. Each regime of accumulation requires its corresponding mode of regulation, "the way in which the system as a whole functions, the conjunction of economic mechanisms associated with a given set of social relations, of institutional forms and structures." Robert Boyer, "Wage Formation in Historical Perspective."

6. Aglietta, *A Theory of Capitalist Regulation.*

7. Harvey, *The Condition of Postmodernity.*

8. Jessop, "Post-Fordism and the State"; Peck and Tickell, "Searching for a New Institutional Fix"; Lipietz, "Post-Fordism and Democracy."

9. Jessop, "Post-Fordism and the State."

10. Peck and Tickell, "Searching for a New Institutional Fix."

11. The crisis and subsequent transformation are caused by profit squeeze and a decline (or slowdown) in the rate of accumulation. The demise of the Fordist system was the result of the intensification of class struggle (wage-earners' challenge to Fordism at the point of production) and the inability of the Fordist labor process to secure the earlier productivity increases. Aglietta, *A Theory of Capitalist Regulation,* 162. In sum, it was caused by the crisis of Fordist accumulation (mass production and consumption) and Keynesian regulation (the welfare state). Jessop, "Post-Fordism and the State"; Peck and Tickell, "Searching for a New Institutional Fix"; Lipietz, "Post-Fordism and Democracy." David Harvey calls attention to the multifaceted rigidity of the Fordist system as the driving force behind the crisis of Fordism. Harvey, *The Condition of Postmodernity,* 142.

12. Aglietta, *Regulation and the Crisis of Capitalism;* Aglietta, "World Capitalism in the 1980s"; Amin, *Post-Fordism;* Alain Lipietz, "Towards Global Fordism," *New Left Review,* no. 132 (1982); Peck and Tickell, "Searching for a New Institutional Fix."

13. Aglietta, *Regulation and the Crisis of Capitalism,* 6.

14. Peck and Tickell, "Searching for a New Institutional Fix."

15. Aglietta, *Regulation and the Crisis of Capitalism,* 6 [emphasis added].

16. Bob Jessop, "Neo-Conservative Regimes and the Transition to Post-Fordism: The Case of Great Britain and West Germany," in *Modern Capitalism and Spatial Development: Accumulation, Regulation, and Crisis Theory,* ed. M. Gottdiener (New York: St. Martin's Press, 1988); Bob Jessop, "Regulation Theory, Post-Fordism and the State: More than a Reply to Werner Bonefeld," in *Post-Fordism and Social Form: A*

Marxist Debate on the Post-Fordist State, ed. Werner Bonefeld and John Holloway (London: Macmillan, 1991); Jessop, "Post-Fordism and the State."

17. Polloix, "The Internationalization of Capital and the Circuit of Social Capital"; Palloix, "The Self-Expansion of Capital on a World Scale"; Clawson, "The Internationalization of Capital and Capital Accumulation in Iran and Iraq"; Cypher, "The Internationalization of Capital and the Transformation of Social Formations"; John Weeks, "Epochs of Capitalism and the Progressiveness of Capital's Expansion," *Science & Society* 49, no. 4 (1985); Behzad Yaghmaian, "Development Theories and Development Strategies: An Alternative Theoretical Framework," *Review of Radical Political Economics* (1990); Ryth Jenkins, *Transnational Corporations and Uneven Development* (London: Methuen, 1987); Dick Bryan, "The Internationalization of Capital and Marxian Value Theory," *Cambridge Journal of Economics* 19 (1995).

18. By no means should one minimize the importance of nonmarket forces in the process of primitive accumulation and the early globalization of capital. Colonialism, wars, coercion, and brute force played a significant role in this process (see the chapters on primitive accumulation in *Capital,* vol. 1, and Marx's writings on India and China).

19. "Hand in hand with the centralization, or the expropriation of many capitalists by few, develop, on an ever-extending scale, the cooperative form of the labor process, the conscious technical application of science, the methodical cultivation of the soil, the transformation of the instruments of labor into instruments of labor only usable in common, the encompassing of all means of production by their use as the means of production of combined socialized labor, the entanglement of all peoples in the net of the world market, and with this, the international character of the capitalist regime." Karl Marx, *Capital,* vol. 1 (New York: International Publishers, 1975), 763.

20. In this early phase of the internationalization of production, capitalist relations of production rapidly expand in noncapitalist regions and accelerate the dissolution of the remaining precapitalist relations. Immediate producers are separated from their conditions of labor at an unprecedented rate as compared with the earlier era of the internationalization of commodity capital. The commodification of labor power enters its final stages on a global scale.

21. Being trapped in the old theory of comparative cost and the stage of the internationalization of commodity capital, neoclassical theory has failed to understand the reinforcing effect on capital accumulation (on a global scale) of deviating from trade based on "comparative advantage" and pursuing import-substitution industrialization. Neoclassical theory fails to grasp the concrete reality of a world in which social capital is rapidly internationalized.

22. Peter Dicken, *Global Shift: The Internationalization of Economic Activity* (New York: The Guilford Press, 1992).

23. Dick Bryan, *The Chase across the Globe: International Accumulation and the Contradictions for Nation States* (Oxford: Westview Press, 1995).

24. Bryan, *The Chase across the Globe,* 89.

25. World Trade Organization (WTO), "International Trade Trends and Statistics," WTO Web site, www.wto.org.

26. Dicken, *Global Shift,* 49.

27. UNCTAD, *World Investment Report: Investment, Trade and International Policy Agreements* (New York: United Nations, 1996).

28. WTO, "International Trade Trends and Statistics."

29. John Holloway appropriately argues that Thatcherism and Reaganism must be viewed as part of a global shift in the relations between the state and the market. See John Holloway, "Transnational Capital and the National State," *Capital & Class* 52 (1994). In addition to Holloway, David Harvey as well as Philip McMichael and David Myhre make passing references to the necessity of locating the analysis of the policies of the World Bank and the IMF in the regime of global accumulation. None of the authors, however, carry out this important inquiry. See Harvey, *The Condition of Postmodernity* and Philip McMichael and David Myhre, "Global Regulation vs. the Nation State: Agro-Food Systems and the New Politics of Capital," *Review of Radical Political Economics* 22, no. 1 (1990).

30. See Dicken, *Global Shift* for details.

31. See Dicken, *Global Shift* for details.

32. G. K. Helleiner and R. Lavergne, "Intra-Firm Trade and the Industrial Exports of the United States," *Oxford Bulletin of Economics and Statistics,* 41 (1979); DeAnne Julius, *Global Companies and Public Policy: The Growing Challenge of Foreign Direct Investment* (London: Pinter, 1990).

33. Barry Bluestone and Bennett Harrison, *The Deindustrialization of America* (New York: Basic Books, 1982).

34. Dicken, *Global Shift,* 153.

35. WTO, "Trade and Foreign Direct Investment" [emphasis added]. WTO homepage: www.wto.org.

36. Dicken, *Global Shift.*

37. For a detailed account of different forms of the global dispersion of production and exchange in various industries (automobile, electronics, and banking and other services) and for different transnational capitals (firms), see Dicken, *Global Shift.*

38. See Paul Mosley, "Decomposing the Effects of Structural Adjustment: The Case of Sub-Saharan Africa," in *Structural Adjustment and Beyond in Sub-Saharan Africa,* ed. R. van der Hoven and F. Vender Kraaij (London: James Currey, 1994); Paul Mosley and John Weeks, "Has Recovery Begun? Africa's Adjustment in the 1980s Revisited," *World Development* 21, no. 10 (1993); Paul Mosley and John Weeks, "Assessing Adjustment in Africa," *World Development* 23, no. 9 (1995); Manuel Pastor, "The Effects of IMF Programs in the Third World: Debate and Evidence from Latin America." *World Development* 15 (1987), 249–62.

39. Eva Paus, "Economic Growth through Neoliberal Restructuring? Insights from the Chilean Experience," *The Journal of Developing Areas* 28 (1994), 43.

40. Pastor, "The Effects of IMF Programs in the Third World."

8

Women's Work and Resistance in the Global Economy

Julia D. Fox

Historically, capital has always attempted to achieve complete control over labor and the labor process. In fact, the intent to establish control mechanisms provided the impetus for the introduction of the factory system and the decline of the putting-out system in the early stages of industrial capitalism.[1] Similarly, in the advanced phases of monopoly capitalism, worker autonomy and solidarity may be mitigated by shifting the most labor-intensive operations to peripheral countries where the employment of a cheap and a docile female labor force guarantees hegemonic control of labor on a world scale.

Throughout modern history, women have constituted one of the lowest paid segments of the population. Just as young single women were incorporated into the low-wage labor market in the earlier phases of industrial capitalism in Europe and the United States, transnational corporations have in recent decades tapped the international female labor pool.

The incorporation of women into the "new" international division of labor is the focus of this essay. A fundamental question is posed: Why have traditionally marginal workers—women—been selectively recruited and integrated into the transnational labor force? In an attempt to explain the emergence of the international sexual division of labor, an analysis of transformations in the labor process will be undertaken. Although it will be argued that women provide a cheap source of docile labor, the analysis will transcend the profit motives of individual firms or managers. The incorporation of Third World working women into the transnational labor force will be placed in the structural context of capital accumulation on a world scale as it is currently manifested in the use of female labor in Export Processing Zones (EPZs) throughout the Third World—in particular, in Mexico, South Korea, and the Philippines.

The recruitment of low-wage women workers not only increases the international labor pool, but it concomitantly employs the most powerless segment of the population to establish total control over the labor force and thus increase the rate of exploitation. In the early phases of industrial capitalism, women and children served as the "industrial reserve army of labor"; today, young women from Third World countries represent this new labor reserve. The production scheme employed to achieve this transnational objective in global capital accumulation has been export processing. The disproportionate representation of women workers in transnational export processing must therefore be placed in this context of the labor process at the global level—one that segments and fragments the working class and creates a special relationship of superexploitation in which labor is forced to work below the value of labor power.[2]

To explain the gender feature of export processing, two dimensions will be analyzed. First, the genesis of export processing will be examined. If world capitalism requires a reduction in the cost of production especially in times of crisis, how do export-led models provide the structural exigencies of capital accumulation on a world scale? Second, given the demand of crises, what specific features of female labor facilitate capital accumulation?

THE NEW INTERNATIONAL DIVISION OF LABOR

With the development of export-processing industries in the Third World, the production process has become global. This investment strategy involves shifting the labor-intensive portion of the manufacturing process to peripheral countries where labor costs are lower, while the more capital-intensive portion of the process is completed in core countries. Hence, the export-processing strategy is developed for increased exploitation of labor and the maximization of profits within the framework of capitalist control of the labor process on a world scale.[3]

The international sexual division of labor can be located within the context of the new international division of labor, which operates at the level of the world capitalist system and, more concretely, at the level of particular nation states in which the specific institutional arrangements create the conditions for one of the most exploited sectors of the working class—Third World working women. Thus, an analysis of global capitalist expansion can be developed that incorporates both the international division of labor driven by the exigencies of capital accumulation on a world scale and the more concrete processes of work relations at the point of production at the national level in which the social, economic, and political factors interact to create the cheapest and most repressed forms of labor.

Repressive labor policies that outlaw strikes and trade unions and the lack of laws for environmental protection, workers' health and safety, and labor conditions in general are compelling forces that attract foreign capital to the Third World.

Given these mediating conditions in Third World countries, women are selected for export-processing employment because they are among the most exploited and most "vulnerable" sectors of the population that the transnationals think they can most easily control. However, the internal contradictions of profit maximization and exploitation of Third World working women in a given social formation foster labor militancy and resistance to repressive labor control. As export processing has rapidly created a "female proletariat," the contradictions of labor repression and female oppression have combined to produce a militant female working class that is challenging the traditional images of female docility and compliance of Third World female labor.[4]

Export Processing and Female Labor

In recent years, there has been a major shift in transnational investment policies. In the past, transnationals followed a pattern of direct investment via corporate-owned subsidiaries or joint ventures. However, in an attempt to increase the rate of profit, a new investment strategy—export processing—has been adopted. This strategy involves the division of the manufacturing process into two stages. Initially, high-skill, high-wage workers (usually in the United States or another advanced capitalist country) assemble a portion of the product. Then this partially completed product is exported to one of the Third World countries where low-skilled, low-wage workers complete the product, which is re-exported to advanced capitalist markets. This process is tantamount to subcontracting on an international scale.[5]

Export Processing Zones (EPZs) are a growing worldwide phenomenon. The first EPZ was created in 1960, and by 1970, fewer than ten countries had established these zones. By 1986, however, more than fifty countries had created some 175 zones. Today, there are 845 export processing zones worldwide.[6] The North American Free Trade Agreement (NAFTA) has especially had an impact on the growth of export processing zones in Mexico. The number of *maquiladora* jobs more than doubled in the 1990s to 1.1 million and the number of *maquiladoras* soared to 2,600.[7] Latin America is another major site for export-processing investments. In 1998, the Dominican Republic had thirty-five zones; Honduras, fifteen zones; Colombia, eleven zones; Costa Rica, nine zones; and Brazil, eight zones.[8] In addition, the former Soviet bloc countries and China have followed the export-processing development strategy. In 1998, there were eight export-processing zones in Bulgaria and Slovenia and 124 zones in China. In the Asian region, the Philippines, with thirty-five zones, and Indonesia, with twenty-six zones, are the countries with the largest number of export-processing zones after China. Africa, especially Kenya, with fourteen zones, is another site for export processing. Likewise, employment in EPZs has grown immensely compared with earlier periods, from 50,000 in 1970 to 27 million in 1997.

There are three salient features of export processing. First, unlike other investment policies, labor is the primary resource. Second, women are disproportionately represented in export-processing industries, ranging from 90 percent of total EPZ employment in Belize, Barbados, and Jamaica to 66 percent in Mexico and Morocco; Korea and the Philippines represent the middle range of female employment in EPZs with 77 percent and 74 percent, respectively.[9] The most recent report from the ILO concludes that EPZs continue to hire a higher proportion of women than nonzone enterprises.[10] Third, technological innovations have been applied to the forces of production. The introduction of new technology not only made export processing feasible, but it provided the necessary conditions for the fragmentation and internationalization of labor.[11] That is, the new technology allowed the manufacturing operation to be subdivided into simpler components. Export processing is an investment strategy that is designed primarily for the standardization of commodity production and the division of the labor-intensive and capital-intensive operations. This is why three major industries (textiles, garment, and electronics) constitute the highest percent of investment in export-processing strategies.[12] Based on the operations of these three industries, it can be seen that export processing is a labor-intensive strategy that involves not only the increased division of labor via technological innovations, but also the international sexual division of labor.

In South Korea, for example, single young factory women are disproportionately represented in the export-processing industries. Since the emergence of these industries, young women (generally between the ages of 16 and 24) have been targeted for employment in the EPZs. Currently, women constitute 77 percent of export workers, with the highest percentage in garment, textiles, and electronics.[13]

In the Philippines, women currently constitute 74 percent of the total EPZ employment.[14] The male–female wage differentials in the EPZs indicate that female workers receive only 54 percent of male wages.[15] The pattern of hiring young Filipino females and the disproportionate representation of women in the three major industries is consistent with other export-processing strategies.

In Mexico, the *maquiladora* factories represent the export-processing industries. Although the *maquiladora* operations were first established in 1965 as an outgrowth of the Border Industrialization Program, the rapid growth of these factories occurred in the early 1980s. Between 1982 and 1988, the number of *maquiladora* plants increased from 558 to 1,500, with a correspondent increase in the number of workers from 122,500 to 390,000.[16] After the implementation of NAFTA in 1994, the *maquiladora* sector grew precipitously.[17] Today, *maquiladoras* are the fastest growing industrial sector in Mexico. The number of *maquiladoras* increased from 2,129 in 1993 (one year before the signing of NAFTA) to 2,600 in 1998.[18] Employment in the *maquiladora* industry increased from 511,000 in 1993 to 1.1 million in 1998.[19]

Historically, the transnational *maquiladora* industry has selectively targeted young single females (aged 16 to 24), and in the early stages of *maquiladora* development, women workers constituted up to 90 percent of the export-processing labor force.[20] Currently, men constitute 42.6 percent and women 57.4 percent of *maquiladora* employment. Since 1982, the number of women in the *maquiladora* workforce has been declining. There are many interpretations of this trend, but the most frequently cited explanations are that the female labor force is "drying up," and there has been a shift in production from "light assembly" products to "heavy manufacturing" products (e.g., transportation equipment).[21] Despite the disagreements about why the percentage of females in the *maquiladora* industry has been declining, there is consensus that employment for women in the *maquiladora* sector is an economic necessity. Approximately 60 percent of the female workers in the Border Industrialization Program provide the sole source of family income, and in the export-processing industries in general, 30 percent of the women were the head of the household.[22] A recent *Human Rights Report* concluded that "the labor force at the border contains a larger proportion of single women than the Mexican average, and their income is essential to their own and their children's support."[23]

The logic underlying the predominance of female employment in export processing is that transnationals take advantage of indigenous male–female wage differentials in Third World countries. Given the increased application of standardized technology in the world economy, the transnationals extract the highest rates of surplus value by employing the lowest paid sector of the foreign labor market. In the quest for the cheapest source of labor, capitalists selectively recruit Third World working women as a reserve army of labor. In this context, class and gender create a segmentation within the new international division of labor to lower the cost of labor below its value. Hence, producing a special relationship of superexploitation.

Recent studies of South Korean male–female wage differentials have pointed out that there is a "bifurcated wage structure" in which women are employed in the most labor-intensive sectors, such as export processing, which pay the lowest wages.[24] The male–female wage gap is also illustrated by the disproportionate percentage of women earning wages that are less than the minimum cost of living. Overall, the majority of the South Korean working class earns less than the 507,254 Won (U.S. $638) that the government estimates to be the minimum cost of living for a family of four. In 1985, for example, 87 percent of South Korean workers earned less than this minimum.

However, when these statistics are broken down by sex, there is a male–female differential for single workers' minimum cost of living. Based on the most recent data, 13.2 percent of the male workers earn wages below this minimum, while 63.9 percent of the females earn wages below this level.[25] Thus, conclude the authors of a recent study, "if there is any sector of the working class that approaches this condition of extreme poverty, it is single women factory workers."[26]

LABOR RELATIONS IN EXPORT-PROCESSING INDUSTRIES

Although Third World male–female wage differentials allow transnationals to generate greater surplus value by employing women workers, hence maximizing profit, the fundamental economic logic of capital accumulation only partially explains the genesis of export processing and the gender-specific nature of labor relations under this form of global accumulation. The other condition that compelled transnationals to relocate production sites in Third World countries and tap female labor reserves involves the component of control. The labor process, in particular work relations at the point of production, should be analyzed to isolate the control mechanisms that ensure the docility of the workforce. More important, we need to examine how these institutional arrangements predispose women to be more easily controlled than men.

The docility of female labor should not be underestimated in addressing the feminization of Third World export processing. This can be explained by the prevalence of four interrelated components: (1) a social component (low levels of female participation in union organizations); (2) a cultural component (patriarchy); (3) an organizational component (bureaucratic managerial strategies); and (4) a political component (repressive governmental labor policies). The docility of female labor, together with its cheapness, has come to define the unique nature of the new international division of labor—the gender-specific character of Third World export-processing labor.

Control of Labor

The labor process associated with export processing led to a highly controlled workforce. More important, women are selectively recruited because of the potential for greater managerial control and exploitation.[27] The conjuncture of social, cultural, organizational, and political components of control bolsters the coercive labor relations of export processing which affect, first and foremost, Third World working women.

Patriarchy and its ideological component, paternalism, has had an important impact on managerial policies and the selective recruitment of women.

Those espousing the advantages of export processing argue that women are preferred because they have "nimble fingers," "small hands," "higher levels of productivity," and "a greater tolerance for tedious work."[28] Although these justifications are stereotypical notions of female labor, empirical studies of managerial strategies indicate that employers incorporate numerous such features of extant patriarchal structures to ensure female subordination.[29] The demographic profile of female workers indicates that age is an important factor as well. Managers point out that managing these young women is similar to "running a high school." In addition, managerial hegemony has been further reinforced by the establishment of dormitories in the EPZs.[30]

One of the most important features of managerial policies is the selection of novice workers. A recent U.S. Department of Labor report concludes, "EPZ employers express a clear preference for hiring women workers between the ages of 17–25—sometimes explicitly stating this preference in job advertisements."[31] Michael Van Waas in his study of the *maquiladora* program found that 60 percent of the females had never been hired before; managerial rationalizations for hiring "virgin" workers were that "they haven't picked up bad habits" and "we want to train them from the ground up in our way of thinking."[32] The significance of this policy is that novice workers lack organizational experience to counter managerial control.

Another way managerial control is achieved is through the use of Taylorist strategies. The Taylorist approach, employed as the dominant managerial strategy during the early phases of industrial capitalism, has been revitalized in Third World EPZs. Under Taylorism, the application of technological innovations promote fragmentation, deskilling, and control of labor and the labor process.[33] However, the introduction of new technology does not inherently lead to the control of labor; rather, it is through the application of bureaucratic managerial strategies to increase exploitation that control is achieved.[34]

In the context of Third World labor policies, control is given new meaning: The labor relations of export processing have been established by government laws that translate into absolute control. The potential leverage of labor power via unionization has been eliminated by extramarket forces, such as strict labor laws.

Repression of Labor

A large number of Third World countries adopting export-processing strategies have enacted repressive labor laws. It has been frequently noted that there is a "correlation between export-oriented industry and labor-repressive policies."[35] Among them, the Philippines and South Korea have employed the most draconian, militaristic measures to "discipline" their workforce.[36]

In the Philippines under Marcos, a "presidential decree" banned all strikes in the export-processing industries. In 1982, several weeks after a general strike in Bataan, the largest EPZ in the Philippines, 200 labor organizers were arrested.[37] In an attempt to institutionalize labor conflict, the Philippine government developed a quasi-corporatist association, the Trade Union Congress of the Philippines (TUCP). The two major goals of the TUCP were to "gain greater control over the labor force" and to "purge labor unions of militant forces."[38] In addition, the Marcos government developed a labor code that allowed employers to "black list any worker who posed a serious threat. Thousands of trade unionists were placed on such lists during this period.[39]

After fourteen years of dictatorship, Marcos was overthrown in 1986, and Corazon Aquino emerged as the new leader of the country. However, Aquino inherited a vastly strengthened state apparatus and a stagnant economy. The repressive apparatuses of the state have not been eliminated. Moreover, Aquino was compelled to follow the economic policies of the Marcos administration (i.e., export-oriented development, World Bank austerity measures, and so on). Just six months after the "February Revolution," Aquino ordered a crackdown on illegal strikes and sent a directive to Augusto Sanchez, minister of labor and employment, to become more aggressive in dealing with strikes.[40] The Philippines Department of Labor and Employment has broken many strikes in the export-processing zones. In 1989, the workers went on strike to protest the dismissal of thirty union officers. In response, the police and armed security guards dispersed the workers violently: Twenty-two workers were seriously injured, three were declared missing and three female strikers were beaten.[41] In an attempt to maintain "global competitiveness" in the face of strong rivals (Taiwan, Hong Kong, and Korea) as well as the emerging ones (Thailand, Indonesia, and China), Philippine managers have pushed for low wages and high productivity, and have continued to suppress strikes and work stoppages.[42]

The Ramos government greatly expanded the number of export-processing zones from nineteen to more than thirty-five in 1996–1997. Employment in these zones has doubled to 218,000 in less than three years.[43] The U.S. Department of Labor recently concluded that in 1998, inspectors found 50 percent of the export-processing factories in the Philippines violated labor and safety standards.[44] This report concluded that although the Philippine constitution and labor code protect the right of workers to form trade unions, in practice, however, "complex legal requirements for registration and union elections impede union formation.[45] In addition, women workers in the export-processing industry face "discrimination and sexual harassment as a form of labor control."[46] Thus, the repression of labor in the Philippines continues unabated to this day, as the government continues to provide greater incentives and a favorable investment climate for the transnational corporations in the export-processing industries.

Similarly, in South Korea, the government has taken numerous measures to suppress labor unions and strikes. After General Chun Doo Hwan took power, a "purification program" was undertaken to ban all national trade unions and make strikes illegal. The right to form unions and bargain collectively in the EPZs were restricted in South Korea until the December 1987 election of General Roh Tae Woo. When these legal restrictions were eliminated in 1987, South Korea's EPZs became an active center of union organizing efforts and strikes. Thus in 1988 and 1989, there were more than 11,000 strikes.[47] In response, the state has attempted to control this growing labor militancy. By August 1989, strikes were banned in the EPZs with the directive that corporations in these zones are "public interest companies."[48] The government of President Roh Tae Woo began a new and "more aggressive antilabor campaign."[49] Force was used to end a 109-day strike of 5,000 workers. More than 14,000 combat police were used to break the strike. Hundreds of workers were arrested in 1989. Again, in 1990, more than 10,000 riot police were deployed in Ulsan to break a strike. Between 1990 and 1991, 848 union members were imprisoned.[50]

Historically, Korean police have used beatings and torture to control workers during labor conflicts. In the export processing zones, police have conducted daily briefings with the representatives of management to identify workers with pro-union sympathies. During labor strikes or demonstrations, the police either act as the agent of management to beat the workers or stand by and watch while the workers are brutalized. Korean-style swat teams called *baikgoldan* (white skull squadron) use intimidation and violence against workers to maintain control over labor.[51]

In comparison with South Korea and the Philippines, government labor policies in Mexico are not as severe. However, the major structural barrier to worker autonomy and political power is corrupt union leadership. In the border industries, transnationals have established a "cooperative relationship" with union leaders. The type of cooperative relationship between labor leaders and managers is not comparable with the typical corporatist tripartite association of labor, capital, and the state. Rather, the labor–business alliance is one in which union leadership represents business instead of rank-and-file interests. In labor grievances, for example, the arbitrator is the Conciliation and Arbitration Board (CAB), which is a business-supported labor union.[52] The official trade unions in Mexico, such as the Confederacion de Trabajadores de Mexico (CTM), "act more as a junior partner in the ruling coalition in Mexico, than an independent labor movement."[53] Moreover, these unions are "almost entirely male dominated, even where they operate in plants in which 80 percent or 90 percent of the workforce are women."[54]

A recent human rights report concluded that *maquiladora* managers have traditionally hired women based on women's "willingness to comply with monotonous, repetitive, and highly exhausting work assignments and have argued women's docility discourages organizing efforts by union leaders."[55] This report continued that "two decades after the first studies on women's work in the *maquiladoras,* little has changed about manager's motivations for hiring female workers."[56] Currently, one of the major issues that has emerged is pregnancy-based sex discrimination in Mexico's *maquiladora* sector. In an attempt to "avoid paying maternity leave and the costs of unproductive workers, companies are requiring *maquiladora* workers to take monthly pregnancy checks."[57] Although *maquiladora* workers have the legal right to organize, only "10–20 percent belong to unions compared with 90 percent of the workers in similar non-*maquiladora* industries."[58] A recent *Human Rights Watch* report concluded:

> U.S. corporations were originally drawn to Mexico's maquiladora (export-processing) sector because it was cheaper to manufacture in Mexico than to manufacture in the United States—Mexican wages were low and independent unions were few. In fact, an abundant supply of labor, low wages, high productivity rates, and reportedly weak federal labor protection are still among the incentives the government still offers to multinational companies to move portions of their production to Mexico.[59]

U.S. Embassy officials in Mexico City recently pointed out that "the Mexican government has had a great desire to attract and keep foreign investment, and this desire prevents Mexico from pushing corporations regarding labor standards."[60]

Repressive labor laws in the Third World provide an incentive for transnationals to target countries that guarantee political stability and a "disciplined" labor force. Repressive legal structures in general do not tell us specifically why women have been selectively recruited. However, if we assume that repressive government policies affect a population differentially, we may have the answer as to why women workers are preferred.

Even though the bargaining power of Third World unions is severely restricted by government controls, the likelihood of organization is further reduced by employing a segment of the international pool that exhibits a pattern of nonunionization. Women workers meet this criterion. Third World working women are recruited not only because they are the lowest paid segments of the population, but also because they are the most "unprotected."[61]

A concomitant factor that reinforces the low level of union membership among women is the cultural tradition of patriarchy.[62] In the Philippines, for example, "because of the traditional oppression of women, the predominant female character [of the labor force in export processing] has made union organizing—already difficult under martial law conditions—even more difficult."[63] In 1979, females constituted only 26.8 percent of the 50,000 trade union members.[64] The Mexican machismo cultural tradition and many corrupt, male-dominated trade unions have similarly limited the union participation of *maquiladora* women. In addition, the high unemployment rates in Mexico may further reduce the potential for collective action. Because 55 to 60 percent of all *maquiladora* female employees provide the sole source of family income, the importance of their employment places women workers in a precarious position, and hence, mitigates against strikes and walkouts.[65] Moreover, the instability of *maquiladora* employment further places women in a difficult situation, since the turnover rate is extremely high: Although the average length of employment in the electronics industry is three to four years, the average annual rate of turnover in electronics is 25 to 33 percent of the labor force.[66]

The significance of the low levels of union participation among women export-manufacturing workers is that managerial hegemony is further intensified. In the absence of any countervailing worker power, the patriarchal, bureaucratic, and political dimensions of control are heightened, and worker autonomy under these conditions is severely limited. Nevertheless, women workers in EPZs have put up a determined struggle against transnational capital and state repression, and are fighting back more and more.

Women Workers Fight Back

In Mexico, *maquiladora* workers have made a number of attempts to resist managerial control. In the mid-1970s, assembly workers in Mexicali and Nuevo Laredo went on strike against poor working conditions and "sold-out union bosses."[67] Women in the *maquiladora* industry have played a pivotal role in these labor struggles.[68] Since then, workers have attempted to improve *maquiladora* working conditions through a variety of grassroots organizations. The patterns of "personalism" within the Mexican unions and corruption that has been endemic in the Confederation de Trabajadores Mexicanos or Mexican Worker's Confederation (CTM) have been compelling forces for workers to unionize outside these corrupt organizations.[69] For more than fifty years, Mexico's labor movement has been a "model of subordination to the government and the ruling Institutional Revolutionary Party (PRI)."[70] Members of the dominant labor federation, the CTM has been an automatic dues-paying member of the PRI. "Despite corrupt, nepotistic leaders who run the unions like fiefdoms," the independent labor movement has been growing.[71]

Two of the major independent unions are the National Workers Union (UNT) and the Authentic Labor Front (FAT). Rank-and-file organizing efforts have led to increased activism among a growing number of women workers in *maquiladora* industries all along the United States–Mexican border and led to another wave of strikes in the early 1990s. In January 1992, U.S.-owned *maquiladora* plants in Matamoros, Mexico, were hit with a wave of strikes once again. Thousands of workers, many of them women, walked out in protest of low wages and poor working conditions. Workers at the Deltronicos, Grupo

Nova, and Trico plants rallied in front of the shut-down factories and waved red and black strike flags to make their demands known. In addition, women are understanding the importance of international labor organizations to contest global capitalist exploitation. Women in Mexico, for example, have formed cross-national labor organizations such as the Mujer a Mujer. In 1998, a ten-union, trinational (the United States, Mexico, and Canada) alliance called the Dana Workers alliance was formed. The ten unions in the alliance—the United Electrical Workers (UE), the Teamsters, Union of Needletrade Industrial and Textile Workers (UNITE), the United Paperworkers, the U.S. and Canadian United Steelworkers, the United Autoworkers (UAW), the Canadian Autoworkers (CAW), the Machinists (IAM), and Mexico's FAT—are unifying to develop an international labor organization.[72]

In the Philippines, too, there has been an upsurge in women's political activity culminating in the militant women's organization General Assembly Binding Women for Reforms, Integrity, Equality, Leadership and Action (GABRIELA). Filipino working women have become increasingly aware of their exploitation, and a GABRIELA spokesperson at a recent women's rally in the Philippines concluded that "the struggle for the freedom of all women is inseparable from the struggle of the working classes and from the global struggles of peoples of the world over fighting racism and imperialism."[73]

In South Korea, women workers in the export-processing industries have been among the most militant and organized groups. The Bando Fashions labor struggle in 1974 was led by a strong core of thirty women organizers. More than 1,000 women participated in a militant sit-in strike to protest "company control of their union, and to win better wages and end the violent treatment of workers by management."[74] In the late 1980s, during the period of militant labor insurgency, women workers at the Masan Free Export Zone organized more than 100 factories and formed the "Ma-Chang" Labor Alliance, and as male workers began to become more militant, "they found they were standing on the shoulders of women workers" who had been struggling for more than a decade.[75] Through such resistance, women workers are increasingly becoming an active part of the broader protracted working-class struggle against international capital and repressive client states throughout the Third World.

CONCLUSION

The above account has provided an analysis of the economic and political basis of the "new" international sexual division of labor. It has shown that the structural features of world capitalist accumulation has generated a need for sources of cheap labor. The historical pattern of the flow of foreign capital in and out of countries in the quest for low-wage and unorganized labor illustrates a pattern of investments into those countries where labor is cheap and repressed. When the internal contradictions of profit maximization and the concomitant exploitation of cheap labor foster labor militancy and resistance to this exploitation, there is a shift in investment to regions where labor is cheaper and more compliant. This pattern is illustrated, for example, by the shifting of the labor-intensive operations of the microelectronics industry from the Silicon Valley in California to South Korea during periods of increasing labor repression. And when South Korea was beset by labor militancy that raised labor costs, the transnationals shifted investments to Mexico, where the cost of labor was lower.[76] However, given the structural constraints of world capitalist accumulation, the physiognomy of labor and the type of production process has taken a variable form.

Export processing was adopted as a viable temporary solution to the crisis of capitalism—a reduction in production costs to maximize profit. Because Third World wages are significantly lower than those in the advanced capitalist countries, the transnationals have shifted their production sites to Third World countries. Although foreign labor could expand the labor pool and provide greater selectivity, women are specifically preferred not only because they are cheaper but because of their perceived docility.

While the genesis of export processing may be attributed to the structural exigencies of world capitalist accumulation, the selective recruitment of women workers involves the intentionality of capitalists within the framework of capitalist relations of production.

The mobility of capital not only allows transnationals to transcend national boundaries, but it permits corporations to select peripheral states that have the political machinery and institutional arrangements that would mitigate against the countervailing powers of labor organizations. Women in Mexico, the Philippines, and South Korea have been differentially affected by these repressive policies. The interaction of the political, cultural, social, and organizational dimensions of control makes them more vulnerable to exploitation.

Third World working women are in the forefront of the new international division of labor because of their subordinate position in the international labor market and in the political sphere. They will continue to be used as a primary resource as long as they meet the criteria of cheapness and docility. However, to counter their exploitation and repression, working women in the Third World are becoming more active, and are fighting back; they are becoming part of a global working-class struggle against transnational capital.[77]

NOTES

1. Richard Edwards et al., *Labor Market Segmentation* (New York: D. C. Heath, 1975), 21.

2. David Gordon, Richard Edwards, and Michael Reich developed the theory of labor market segmentation in *Segmented Workers, Divided Workers: The Historical Transformation of Labor in the United States* (New York: Cambridge University Press, 1982). Chris Tilly and Charles Tilly have recently expanded this analysis in *Work under Capitalism* (Boulder, Colo.: Westview Press, 1998). For a detailed analysis of the application of Marx's original theory of surplus value to the concept of superexploitation, see Victor Perlo, *Super Profits and Crises: Modern U.S. Capitalism* (New York: International Publishers, 1988), 35–54, 85–114; see also Peter Knapp and Alan Spector, *Crisis and Change: Basic Questions of Marxist Sociology* (Chicago: Nelson-Hall, 1991), 108–10.

3. James Petras, *Class, State and Power in the Third World* (London: Zed Press, 1981), 123; Kathryn Ward, ed., *Women Workers and Global Restructuring* (Ithaca, N.Y.: Cornell University Press, 1990), 2.

4. Helen I. Safa, "Runaway Shops and Female Employment: The Search for Cheap Labor," in *Women's Work,* ed. Eleanor Leacock and Helen I. Safa (South Headley, Mass.: Bergin and Garvey, 1986), 68; Karen J. Hossfeld, "'Their Logic against Them': Contradictions in Sex, Race, and Class in Silicon Valley," in *Women Workers and Global Restructuring,* ed. Kathryn Ward, 152.

5. Folker Frobel, Jurgen Heinrichs, and Otto Kreye, *The New International Division of Labor* (Cambridge: Cambridge University Press, 1980), 29; Maria Patricia Fernandez-Kelly, "The 'Maquila' Women," *NACLA Report of the Americas* 14, no. 5 (1980), 14–19; Safa, "Runaway Shops and Female Employment"; Marlene Dixon, Suzanne Jonas, and Ed McCaughan, "Reindustrialization and the Transnational Labor Force in the United States Today," in *The New Nomads: From Immigrant Labor to Transnational Working Class,* ed. Marlene Dixon and Suzanne Jonas (San Francisco: Synthesis, 1982), 101–04; Michael Van Waas, "Multinational Corporations and the Politics of Labor Supply," *The Insurgent Sociologist* 11, no. 3 (1982), 49; Robert T. Snow, "The New International Division of Labor and the U.S. Work Force: The Case of the Electronics Industry," in *Women, Men and the International Division of Labor,* ed. June Nash and Maria Patricia Fernandez-Kelly (Albany: State University of New York Press, 1983), 39.

6. International Labor Organization (ILO), *Export Processing in Historical Perspective,* www.ilo.org.

7. Harry Browne, Beth Simms, and Tom Barry, *For Richer, for Poorer: Shaping U.S.–Mexican Integration* (Albuquerque, N.M.: Inter-Hemispheric Resource and Education Center, 1994); Teresa Rendon and Carlos Salas, "The Workforce of the 1990s," *NACLA Report of the Americas* 30, no. 3 (1997), 21–27.

8. ILO, *Export Processing Zones,* 4.

9. U.S. Department of Labor, "Workers Rights," 6; Linda Lim, *Women Workers in Multinational Enterprises in Developing Countries* (Geneva: International Labour Office, 1985).

10. International Labor Organization, *Women's Employment in EPZs,* www.ilo.org.

11. Dixon, Jonas, and McCaughan, "Reindustrialization," 101.

12. Tiano, "Maquiladora Women," 195.

13. U.S. Department of Labor, "Workers Rights," 6; George E. Ogle, *South Korea: Dissent within the Economic Miracle* (London: Zed Books, 1990), 48–49.

14. U.S. Department of Labor, "Workers Rights," 6.

15. Mary Soledad Perpinan, "Philippine Women and Transnational Corporations," in Daniel Schirmer and Stephen R. Shalom, *The Philippines Reader: A History of Colonialism, Neocolonialism, Dictatorship, and Resistance* (Boston, Mass.: South End Press, 1987), 234, 240.

16. *The Economist* (16 September 1989), 82.

17. Jorge Carrillo V, "The Apparel Maquiladora Industry at the Mexican Border," in *Global Production: The Apparel Industry in the Pacific Rim,* ed. Edna Bonacich et al. (Philadelphia: Temple University Press, 1994), 217.

18. Human Rights Watch, *Mexico: A Job or Your Rights: Continued Sex Discrimination in Mexico's Maquila Sector* 10, no. 1B (New York: Human Rights Watch, 1998); Browne, Simms, and Barry, *For Richer, for Poorer.*

19. Human Rights Watch, *Mexico: A Job or Your Rights;* Browne et al., *For Richer, for Poorer.*

20. Judith Ann Warner, "The Sociological Impact of the Maquiladoras," in *The Maquiladora Industry: Economic Solution or Problem?* ed. Khosrow Fatemi (New York: Praeger, 1990), 187–88.

21. Leslie Sklair, *Assembly for Development: The Maquila Industry in Mexico and the United States* (Boston: Unwin Hyman, 1989), 177.

22. Fernandez-Kelly, "Mexican Border Industrialization," 215; Tiano, "Maquiladora Women," 204.

23. Human Rights Watch, *Mexico: A Job or Your Rights,* 14.

24. See Alice H. Amsden, *Asia's Next Giant: South Korea and Late Industrialization* (New York: Oxford University Press, 1989), 203–04.

25. Walden Bello and Stephanie Rosenfeld, *Dragons in Distress: Asia's Miracle Economies in Crisis* (San Francisco: The Institute for Food and Development Policy, 1990), 26.

26. Bello and Rosenfeld, *Dragons and Distress,* 26.

27. Waas, "Multinational Corporations," 50.

28. Diane Elison and Ruth Pearson, "Nimble Fingers Make Cheap Workers: An Analysis of Workers in Employment in Third World Export Processing," *Feminist Review,* 33 (1981), 89; Waas, "Multinational Corporations," 50.

29. Elison and Pearson, "Nimble Fingers," 89; Waas, "Multinational Corporations," 50; June Nash, "The Impact of the Changing International Division of Labor on Different Sectors of the Labor Force," in *Women, Men, and the International Division of Labor,* ed. Nash and Fernandez-Kelly, x.

30. Nash, "The Impact of the Changing International Division of Labor," 31.

31. U.S. Department of Labor, "Workers Rights," 5.

32. Waas, "Multinational Corporations," 50.

33. Harry Braverman, *Labor and Monopoly Capital* (New York: Monthly Review Press, 1974).

34. Braverman, *Labor and Monopoly Capital;* Dixon et al., "Reindustrialization," 101–03.

35. Bonacich et al., eds., *Global Production: The Apparel Industry in the Pacific Rim,* 370.

36. Enloe, "Women Textile Workers," 410.

37. D. Easter and M. Easter, "Women Fight Back: South Korea and the Philippines," *Multinational Monitor* 4, no. 8 (1983), 12.

38. Walden Bello, David Kinley, and Elaine Elison, *Development Debacle: The World Bank and the Philippines* (San Francisco: Institute for Food and Development Policy, 1982), 142.

39. Bello et al., *Development Debacle,* 143.

40. *Asian Labour Review* 3, no. 4 (November 1986), 33.

41. Rosalina Pineda Ofreneo, "The Philippine Garment Industry," in *Global Production,* ed. Bonacich et al., 174.

42. Ofreneo, "The Philippine Garment Industry," 173.

43. U.S. Department of Labor, Bureau of International Labor Affairs, *Foreign Labor Trends: Philippines,* 1997–1998 (Washington, D.C.: Government Printing Office, 1998).

44. U.S. Department of Labor, *Foreign Labor Trends,* 13.

45. U.S. Department of Labor, *Foreign Labor Trends,* 13.

46. Ofreneo, "The Philippine Garment Industry," in *Global Production,* ed. Bonacich et al., 173.

47. International Labour Organization, *Yearbook of Labour Statistics* (Geneva: ILO, 1990), 1027.

48. U.S. Department of Labor, "Workers Rights," 7.

49. Martin Hart-Landsberg, *The Rush to Development: Economic Change and Political Struggle in South Korea* (New York: Monthly Review Press, 1993), 279.

50. Hart-Landsberg, *The Rush to Development,* 279.

51. George E. Ogle, *South Korea: Dissent within the Economic Miracle* (London: Zed Books, 1990), 60.

52. Waas, "Multinational Corporations," 57.

53. Sklair, *Assembly for Development,* 174.

54. Sklair, *Assembly for Development,* 174.

55. Human Rights Watch, *Mexico: A Job or Your Rights,* 13.

56. Human Rights Watch, *Mexico: A Job or Your Rights,* 13.

57. Human Rights Watch, *Mexico: A Job or Your Rights,* 13; Human Rights Watch, *Mexico: Labor Rights and NAFTA* 8, no. 8B (New York: Human Rights Watch, 1996).

58. U.S. Department of Labor, "Workers Rights," 7.

59. Human Rights Watch, *Mexico: A Job or Your Rights,* 10.

60. Human Rights Watch, *Mexico: A Job or Your Rights,* 10.

61. Nash, "The International Division of Labor," 11.

62. Beverly Lindsay, *Comparative Studies of Third World Women: The Impact of Race, Sex, and Class* (New York: Praeger, 1980), 39–42; Beneria and Sen, "Accumulation, Reproduction and Women's Role in Economic Development," 285; I. Schuster, "Research on Women in Development," *Journal of Development Studies* 18, no. 4 (1982), 513.

63. Bello, Kinley, and Elison, *Development Debacle,* 144.

64. Easter and Easter, "Women Fight Back," 13.

65. Pedro Vuskovic, "Economic Internationalism, Neoliberalism and Unemployment in Latin America," in *The New Nomads,* ed. Dixon and Jonas, 85–86; Waas, "Multinational Corporations," 51.

66. Waas, "Multinational Corporations," 50.

67. Waas, "Multinational Corporations," 56.

68. Sklair, *Assembly for Development,* 175.

69. Warner, "The Sociological Impact of the Maquiladoras," 194.

70. David Barkin, Irene Ortiz, and Fred Rosen, "Globalization and Resistance: The Remaking of Mexico," *NACLA* 30, no. 4 (1997), 17.

71. Barkin, Ortiz, and Rosen, "Globalization and Resistance," 17.

72. Fred Rosen, "The Underside of NAFTA: A Budding Cross-Border Resistance," *NACLA* 32, no. 4 (1999), 37; Carlos A. Heredia, "Downward Mobility: Mexican Workers after NAFTA," *NACLA* 30, no. 3 (1996), 34.

73. Brenda J. Stoltzfus, "A Woman's Place Is in the Struggle," in Schirmer and Shalom (eds.) *The Philippines Reader,* 311.

74. Landsberg, *The Rush to Development: Economic Change and Political Struggle in South Korea,* 209.

75. Ogle, *South Korea,* 141, 86.

76. Hossfeld, "'Their Logic against Them,'" 152; Bello and Rosenfeld, *Dragons in Distress.*

77. See Ofelia Gomez de Estrada and Rhoda Reddock, "New Trends in Internationalization of Production: Implications for Female Workers," in *International Labour and the Third World: The Making of the New Working Class,* ed. Rosalind E. Boyd, Robin Cohen, and Peter Gutkind (Brookfield, Vt.: Gower, 1987), 157; Easter and Easter, "Women Fight Back."

9

Dynamics of Globalization: Transnational Capital and the International Labor Movement

Cyrus Bina and Chuck Davis

The development of capitalism during the past two centuries has provided the preconditions for the collective organization of workers, and the structures of labor organizations have evolved accordingly to meet the capitalist challenge. Capitalist competition and accumulation have continuously pitted worker against worker, attempting to drive wages, conditions of work, and the quality of life to the lowest possible level. In combating the extraction of absolute and relative surplus value, workers have always conducted an economic and, in many cases, a political struggle to regulate and improve the terms and conditions under which they are obliged to dispose of their labor power. What is significant is that the expression of trade union unity, by transcending competition in the market for labor power, in itself potentially threatens the stability of capitalism by blocking capital's desire to minimize costs of production and, above all, to solidify the grounds for further control. This is particularly true today. "Workers of the World Unite" is becoming increasingly relevant and applicable as capital transcends the boundaries of nation-states.[1]

The transnationalization of capitalist relations of production (i.e., the emergence of a global tendency to real subsumption of labor under capital—production of relative surplus value), brings the common interests of workers in different countries into sharper focus in the minds of workers themselves and elevates the potential for labor solidarity to an international level. It brings workers in different nations into a new integrated relationship. To the extent that workers can confront transnational capital with their own international organizations, they can mitigate the effects of capital mobility.

For capital to become a de facto global entity, there has to be a global circuit in all its forms that would, in turn, unify the spheres of production and circulation: commodity capital, money capital, and productive capital. This has been historically accomplished through the internationalization of all three circuits of capital and thus has fulfilled the completion of the globalization of capital in all its social forms. In this manner, the transnationalization of productive capital presupposes the transnationalization of commodity and finance capitals. This has resulted in the unfolding of such colossal and integrated entities known as transnational corporations, which operate throughout the world. Having direct control over many different labor processes around the globe, transnational capital, in conjunction with all its circuits, exploits labor power worldwide. Here, global capital can be seen as an organic supranational socioeconomic entity that intimately corresponds to the structure of global social relations. In this context, the most appropriate unit of analysis, therefore, is none other than global capitalist relations. Thus, if capital is a global entity, so must be labor's strategy for revitalization.[2]

This chapter attempts to present a theoretical framework for the study of the labor process in contemporary capitalism and provides an analysis of the contradictions of this process at the global level. It also discusses the nature of transnational capital, the cheapening of labor power, deskilling, and new skill formation,[3] spatial mobility, gender and the transnational labor process, and the roots of working-class unity. The chapter concludes with some observations on the current problems and the potential revitalization of the U.S. labor movement in the context of the transnational economy, and suggests that at the stage of transnational social relations (i.e., the global integration of capital), labor organizations must play a central role to enhance the capacity of the working class and to transform capitalist social relations throughout the world.

CHEAPENING OF LABOR POWER:
SKILLING AND DESKILLING, AND SPATIAL MOBILITY

The proliferation of capitalist relations of production and its impact on generating labor processes that are conducive to the development of capitalism beyond the boundaries of nation-states is today a fact of life within the global economy. As a result, it becomes necessary to understand the specific mechanisms through which the unfolding of the above process takes shape. It is also imperative to investigate the consequences of such a process and its future direction in the world economy.

To be able to unravel the transnational character of the labor process, one has to grasp (1) the transformation of work itself in the advanced capitalist countries, and (2) the emerging global integration of capitalism, having to do directly with the spread of capitalist social relations into the former colonies, semicolonies, and less-developed countries, especially during the second half of the twentieth century. Finally, since the 1970s, at the present stage of global capitalism, the centerpiece of global accumulation is the unifying control of the emerging transnational labor processes that collectively represent the social character of global capital. Here, the resultant transnational labor process is, *prima facie*, a point of departure for the transnationalization of capital in general.

Since the beginning of the twentieth century, a series of remarkable organizational and technological transformations have revolutionized the very foundation of the labor process in the advanced capitalist countries, especially in the United States. These have included the application of Taylorism, which came to further intensify and regulate the real subsumption of labor under capital and which prepared the labor process for a radical transformation toward a continuous system of large-scale mass production.[4]

Based on recent advances in the field of computer technology, applications such as robotics, numerical control (NC), and computer-aided design (CAD), in conjunction with the telecommunications revolution, have found their way into the current production processes. These technologies conferred a new meaning to the deskilling and new skill formation of labor and granted a new outlook to the spatial control of capital over the entire global labor process.

As Harley Shaiken, a leading authority on the application of technology, elucidates, "Once the machining knowledge is embodied in the numerical control program, it becomes possible to transfer production from a struck plant to shops that are still working, regardless of whether they are across the street or halfway around the world."[5] Here, scientific management flourished through the intense application of science and technology for the sake of strengthening the control of constant capital over its variable counterpart.

The consequence has been the continuous and progressive devaluation of labor power everywhere.[6] The continuous deskilling and reskilling of labor in the advanced capitalist countries and the development of capitalism in the Third World are, *pari passu*, the precondition of globalization of the labor process. In this manner, the process of deskilling, rationalization, and reskilling in the advanced capitalist countries, having taken several decades to develop, find their way into the readily transformed structure of many Third World economies. Such developments are now ready to be transmitted and internalized transnationally. This, in turn, corresponds to a series of technological underpinnings that acquire a global character.

Universal deskilling and reskilling, aside from their hegemonic appeal, allow for coexistence of the highest level of technology and the lowest possible labor cost, including the training cost of labor, especially in the case of Third World workers whose industrial training is rather slight. Thus, the intense deskilling and reskilling of labor in the advanced capitalist countries over several decades suddenly find their cumulative application within the countries of the Third World rapidly. As a result, the rising complexity of technology in the production process does not pose a physical limit to raising the level of exploitation of the working classes globally.

A parallel with the above historical dynamics is the unfolding material conditions that surround the participation of women in the global economy. In the Third World, where abject poverty and massive unemployment are the rule, unbounded flexibility and extraordinary discipline are the *sine qua non* of the labor process. Here, the majority of the female labor force had worked in domestic production and agriculture. Given the accelerated pace of transnational investment since the early 1970s, women's labor has increasingly shifted toward the manufacturing sector, especially in the so-called newly industrializing countries (NICs) where the role of the export sector is significant.[7]

In addition to their role as an inexpensive source of labor power, it has been argued by some that employment of women by transnational capital may have also been motivated by (1) women's alleged characteristics of greater discipline in following orders and their display of work habits that generally imply docility, (2) women's possession of skills that are normally attributed to their gender socialization (e.g., "nimble fingers" and the ability to work with delicate objects), and (3) women's condition as a flexible source of labor supply, especially where it comes to the acceptance of temporary assignments, unstable work, and flexible hours, associated with subcontracting in most export processing zones.[8] Yet, it is necessary to note that the physical characteristics attributed to women participating in the labor force obtain no meaning without their particular socialization into the capitalist labor process itself.

THE ROOTS OF WORKING-CLASS UNITY

Today, the continuing globalization of the labor process has, in a contradictory manner, provided the material conditions for the unity of the working class across the seemingly insurmountable boundaries of nation-states. The fundamental basis of this contradictory process is the global accumulation of capital in the presence of divided global social space among nation-states and the objective conditions for working-class unity—based on local struggles that can no longer remain isolated from either the existing social movements or the global center stage. The analogue of all this is the emergence of a historical stage whose transforming capacity goes well beyond the simple export of capital or the transfer of technology from one nation to another. In fact, at the current stage of global transformation, the significance of the above symptomatic activities cannot be adequately understood except through the manifold character of transnational capital beyond the isolated interests and beyond the nation-state.

Given the last three decades of changes in the global economy, the de facto global character of capital has already transcended the framework of national boundaries, despite its historical origin and early embryonic affinity. Here came the mastery of an integrated global territory for reproduction of social relations. This was also a familiar socioeconomic terrain that was long known to the pioneer of labor internationalism, the International Working Men's Association (the First International).[9] The primary issue facing labor, therefore, is how to avoid the trap of nationalism and thus become a formidable force in the struggle against capital transnationally.

In his inaugural address to the International Working Men's Association nearly 150 years ago, Karl Marx wondered, "If the emancipation of the working classes requires their fraternal concurrence, how are they to fulfill that great mission with a foreign policy in pursuit of criminal designs, playing upon national prejudices, and squandering in piratical wars the people's blood and treasure?"[10] Marx tried to respond to this by assigning a specific responsibility to the trade unions of his time:

> Apart from their original purpose, [the trade unions] must now learn to act deliberately as organizing centers of the working class in the broad interest of its *complete emancipation*. They must aid every social and political movement tending in that direction. . . . They must look carefully after the interests of the worst paid trade, such as agricultural laborers, rendered powerless by the exceptional circumstances . . . far from being narrow and selfish, [they must] aim at the emancipation of the downtrodden millions.[11]

The struggles between labor and capital in the Third World, in many instances, are similar to the ones waged during the early development of the advanced capitalist countries. These struggles are primarily political in nature. The workers in the Third World, even in their daily and immediate struggles, must confront the state as their ultimate adversary. For instance, the small-scale, confined appearance of an export processing zone, or a discrete structure of an export-platform business, can hardly misdirect the attention of workers from *political* issues surrounding the workplace. Thus, in such an environment, any economic issue would immediately become *political*, and any local issue would directly become a *global* one. Here, direct confrontation of workers with the state is at the same time a struggle against capital in general and, by implication, a struggle against the hegemony of transnational capital.

In the advanced capitalist countries, such as the United States, the working class (organized and unorganized alike) has already lost substantial ground during the last three decades. Recently, however, there have been indications of labor's resurgence.

The economic gains of the past have disappeared through constant global restructuring, ceaseless deskilling and reskilling of the workforce, the exploding ranks of the working poor, the universal outbreaks of plant closings, and the growth in the size of the reserve armies of unemployed.[12] Having experienced that all these ills arise from the contradictions of the capitalist system itself, workers in the United States (and, more and more, in other advanced capitalist countries) are increasingly coming to realize that their struggle must be against capital in general, particularly transnational capital. Here, the objective conditions present in the global economy provide the basis for working-class unity throughout the world. In other words, the working classes of both the Third World and the advanced capitalist countries are in the same boat, albeit on different decks, moving in the same direction. Thus, a growing number of workers and their organizations are coming to realize that they must free themselves from the shackles of national chauvinism, the narrow limits of economism, and, above all, racism and sexism, to confront transnational capital as a powerful and unified force.

LABOR INTERNATIONALISM AND LABOR ARISTOCRACY

Since the nineteenth century, segments of the U.S. labor movement have supported strongly the need for international labor solidarity to confront the various stages of the internationalization of capital. From the beginning, left-wing Socialist, Communist, and anarcho-syndicalist sections of the working class have battled with the class collaborationists over the control of the labor movement and the meaning of international labor solidarity. More than a century-long struggle continues between those elements in the U.S. labor movement that have traditionally pursued strength through increasing international working-class unity, and those who have consistently tied their future to the fortunes of national capital and its global expansion.[13]

Seeing itself as part of some all-embracing national interest, the American Federation of Labor (AFL) had asserted historically an identity of common global interest with U.S. capital. Recognizing the unique position of the United States after World War II, the AFL tied labor's fate to U.S. capital's growing global hegemony.[14] The national labor federation embraced the doctrine of *Pax Americana*. This doctrine is composed of many subdoctrines, the most significant of which is the cold war "axiom" since World War II. This axiom ramifies a complex triad of containments whose singular ambition has been to preserve U.S. global hegemony, by all means. The first two containments were intended for the former Soviet Union and the Third World. This was motivated by the U.S. postwar position against Soviet ideology and the independent nationalist movements around the world.

The third containment has been a domestic one. It was designed to circumvent democratic freedoms domestically and to crush the spirit of resistance in every facet of life in the United States. McCarthyism is only one of many examples in this tragedy. This, in part, had two important social ramifications for the U.S. labor movement: (1) it broke the back of the most militant segment of organized labor and purged the movement of the best sons and daughters of the working class; and (2) it systematically submitted the workers to a complex set of legitimizing norms, imposed by the ideology of the ruling class, thus openly stigmatizing, penalizing, and, ultimately, terrorizing those who dared to depart from it.[15]

The AFL perceived U.S. labor's well-being as part and parcel of U.S. capital's well-being. This led the AFL (and later the AFL-CIO) to adopt a foreign policy of labor imperialism.[16] In the post–World War II era, labor imperialism has involved an explicit alliance with U.S. capital and the state. This was a specific manifestation of labor aristocracy beyond the boundaries of a nation-state, since the nature of its involvement in both international labor organizations and the internal affairs of unions of other nations had been guided by the priorities of U.S. foreign policy.[17]

Embracing a virulent anticommunism, which saw the world divided into East versus West, the AFL-CIO in Europe, Africa, Asia, and Latin America, in the name of U.S. global hegemony, undermined and weakened in a variety of ways the organizational capacity of the international labor movement. It did so by establishing dual unionism—dividing labor movements along Cold War lines by developing procapitalist, anti-Communist union structures sympathetic to U.S. capital and subservient to U.S. foreign policy—and by participating with the U.S. government in overt and covert political and military interventions with the purpose of overthrowing democratic, prolabor governments considered too leftist.[18] Labor's involvement in the Cold War on behalf of U.S. capital was made possible by the purges of the left-led unions and leftists within the labor movement. As Mike Davis notes, "By accepting the discipline of the Cold War mobilization, the unions and their liberal allies surrendered independence of action and ratified the subordination of social welfare to global anticommunism."[19]

Capital, which had become increasingly internationalized in the post–World War II period through the control of new geoeconomic space and intensification of the realm of competition beyond the nation-state and by weakening international labor solidarity through its divide-and-conquer strategy, was able to prevent labor from defending itself on an international basis. Prior to its change in leadership in the 1990s, the AFL-CIO had compromised the organizational capacity of the working class both domestically and internationally in exchange for perceived further material benefits.[20]

With the new phase of transnationalization of capital beginning in the early 1970s, and accelerating rapidly in the 1970s and 1980s, the U.S. economy started its secular, and possibly irreversible, hegemonic decline in the global economy. This marked the onset of the stage of transnational global relations reflecting the global integration of capitalist production.

The growing significance of transnational corporations illustrated this development. This was tantamount to the undermining of the international system of nation-states and the status of its post–World War II hegemon, the United States.

By the early 1970s, capital accumulation had become truly global. The internationalization of capital brought on a restructuring of industrial production that shifted the concentration of basic industry from its previous centers to new locations throughout the world. Transnational corporations abandoned the United States as a principal production location, resulting in "captive imports," runaway shops, and outsourcing. The expansion of the U.S.-based transnationals was now linked to the relative decline of domestic manufacturing. This investment strategy obviously has had a negative impact on U.S. workers and has contributed significantly to the decline in their standard of living during the past three decades.[21]

The decline of U.S. global hegemony during this stage of the internationalization of capitalist relations of production has, in the meantime, led to a growing divergence between the material interests of labor and capital. The once-shared interest in the global domination of U.S. capital is now seen by many as its opposite: a source of job loss, demands for concessions, and union busting. The economic conditions for post–World War II accommodation with capital are long over. In the absence of global labor solidarity, transnational corporations have shown their willingness to play one group of workers against another, driving down the labor and living standards of the international working class to the lowest possible levels.

The global integration of capitalist production undermined the material conditions that supported AFL-CIO's traditionally nationalist, class-collaborationist posture. The discrepancy between the material foundation of the transnationalization of capitalist relations and the historical record of continuing working-class nationalism (for instance, in the United States) may be interpreted as an indicator of the contradictory balance of class forces, the backwardness of the labor movement, and anachronistic nature of nationalism. More specifically, the absence of international labor solidarity can be viewed as an opportunity on the part of capital to prevent what would be eventually realized in connection with the development of material basis and organizational capacity for working-class consciousness at the global level.

Global capital has been striving ceaselessly to extract additional surplus value by lowering the standard of living of the working class worldwide. However, this decline in living standards is forcing unions to respond to capital and the state in fundamentally new ways, thus creating a significant opportunity and sizeable constituency both for revitalization of the labor movement and formation of a broad-based political movement at home and abroad. The transnationalization of capitalist relations and reorganization of global capitalism provide the material conditions for overcoming class collaboration and national chauvinism, because the labor movement can no longer survive and function without class struggle within an internationalist perspective. This realization is being played out in an ideological struggle within the U.S. labor movement between accommodation and confrontation with transnational capital.[22] This struggle over orientation is visible in the debates within the labor movement over issues of international trade and investment, as the recent battle in Seattle (1999) and its sequel in Washington, D.C. (2000) have clearly shown.

TRADE LIBERALIZATION, REGIONAL INTEGRATION, AND THEIR IMPACT ON LABOR

The global restructuring of capitalism through the adoption of free trade, neoliberalism, monetarism, deregulation, and privatization policies of governments throughout the capitalist world during the 1980s and 1990s coincided with further global integration of capital and the transnationalization of capitalist relations of production. Given the accelerated integration of national economies, with respect to production, finance, and trade, the adoption of aforementioned policies has been almost a universal response both in advanced and Third World capitalist nations.

Labor has weakened considerably because of globalization. As individual capitals move to restore profitability, capital as a whole manifests its very fundamental characteristic through competition for global labor power. Capital launched a series of offensives explicitly designed to weaken or destroy the development of the labor movement internationally, and to force its capitulation to transnational capital. For instance, an important move was to create a global pool of surplus labor and the corresponding reserve army of unemployed beyond national boundaries. Falling real wages; rising unemployment; increasing poverty and income inequality across the board; deteriorating living and working conditions; and increasing violations of worker, human, and civil rights are common problems shared by workers throughout both the Third World and the advanced capitalist countries. This shows that, when it comes to harm, capital is universally dispassionate.

Global capital is attempting to use international organizations and trade agreements, such as the World Trade Organization (WTO), formerly known as the General Agreement on Tariffs and Trade (GATT), and the North American Free Trade Agreement (NAFTA), to preempt democratic self-government at local, national, regional, and international levels. Global capital and its representatives follow a golden rule by which any attempt by democratic institutions to impose restrictions on transnational corporations should be outlawed by international agreements. If there is to be any regulation, it should be in the interests of global capital.[23]

NAFTA formalized and accelerated the process of transnationalization of capital and the global integration of production and exchange that began in Mexico and many other countries more than thirty years ago. U.S.-based transnational corporations began to construct their own integrated production systems (including the export processing zones) to transfer much of the previously U.S.-based production activities to Mexico. The intermediate goods and final products produced in the *maquiladoras* would then flow back as imports into the United States.

Limitations on foreign investment have been practically eliminated by dismantling restrictions on foreign ownership, and reducing remaining tariffs and import barriers. This export growth strategy has proved to be an utter disaster for Mexico; it has failed to fuel national growth or to improve the overall debt situation. According to the logic of transnational capital, however, one cannot expect other than such results. For the Mexican working class, it has meant increasing poverty and polarization, declining living and working conditions, and intensified state repression of workers' rights.[24]

Trade liberalization within the stage of transnationalization of capital means the further undermining of working and living conditions of labor everywhere. With the global integration of the labor process, trade unions are quickly realizing that solidarity across borders is an essential step for defending the most tangible interests of their members. Today, workers are discovering that defensive strategies intended for protecting the interests of local workers cannot be effective except through internationally based alliances. The globalization of working-class unity, therefore, is necessary to confront the globalization of capital.[25]

STRATEGIC CONSIDERATIONS FOR LABOR

Capitalism's success in overcoming barriers to accumulation through trade liberalization and economic integration has increased the costs significantly for labor to pursue a strategy of nationalism. Continued reliance on nationalism will only further cripple the labor movement in the face of global capital's offensive.[26] Transnationalization of capital has gone too far for protectionism to save domestic jobs. Nationalistic confrontation with the global character of capitalist competition will only continue to demand greater concessions from workers.[27]

The struggle for labor internationalism is necessary to break down the divisiveness of nationalism and build solidarity with workers' struggles throughout the world. As Primitivo Rodriquez has so eloquently stated:

Some trade union leaders in the more developed countries seem to be opposing free trade talks out of an outmoded belief that preventing a free trade agreement will save their members' jobs. But blocking such an agreement won't erase the increasing integration among the American economies.

Rather, we should look at the free trade agreement debate as an opportunity to develop a vision and an agenda which responds from a people's perspective. . . . What's promising is that today's transnational exchange may lead to the dismantling of barriers imposed by narrow and fragmented interests based on nationalistic perspectives that are increasingly ineffective in enhancing rights and a better life.[28]

Although denying free trade access to domestic markets to nations who violate internationally recognized worker rights has been inconsistently and rarely enforced and is, at the same time, protectionist, there is a growing consensus within the labor movement that recognition and struggle for international labor standards as a condition of trade are a political act that has the potential to enhance the organizational capacity of the working class internationally and, thereby, provide legitimacy for international solidarity.

The concern for internationally recognized labor rights goes beneath the level of trade and calls attention to the very global relations of capital. Global integration of the labor process is, at the same time, integration of the social relations of capital worldwide, which is providing workers with the opportunity to build international solidarity. Workers are increasingly recognizing and acting on the notion that "an injury to one [anywhere in the world] is an injury to all." Thus, as William Tabb points out, "making the linkage between labor repression in the developing nations . . . and the decline of U.S. labor standards represents growth in class awareness and is a major milestone in the decline of U.S. exceptionalism."[29]

Labor unions are finding trade union unity essential in their efforts to defend the interests of their members, and are jointly demanding the enforcement of international labor standards. Ending violations of worker rights is increasingly being seen as mutually beneficial and as a direct challenge to the prerogatives of global capital.

Although enforcement of such labor standards are unlikely, their importance for labor lies in using them along with other measures as a focus for domestic and international political actions in the process of developing international labor solidarity and working-class consciousness. In the struggle to protect their wages and working conditions, workers are building new and using pre-existing transnational structures to confront global capital. The task of establishing effective international activity is an extremely difficult one—a task which often seems impossible, given the contradictions between and within national labor movements.[30]

The objective conditions for international working-class solidarity are stronger today than ever before. Plans for international cooperation and mutual aid in support of organizing the unorganized, collective bargaining, strikes, and so forth, in both the Third World and the advanced capitalist countries, reflect the increasingly transnational character of capitalist relations of production. Economic integration has provided the context for international solidarity networks of workers within the same corporations, industries, and geographic region. By working for the same transnational corporation, workers are recognizing that "they have more in common with each other than with their respective national capitals."[31] Rather than just lamenting job loss to Mexico as a result of trade liberalization, unions are making united working-class action a living reality. For example, the United Auto Workers (UAW) Council of Ford Workers, which represents Canadian, U.S., and Mexican workers, has proclaimed "the time has come to prevent Ford from pitting worker against worker, plant against plant, nation against nation."[32] Also, the Cuautitlan Ford workers' democratic union movement in Mexico pledged to resist Canadian and U.S. transferred work if Canadian and U.S. workers assist them in gaining wage and benefit increases, and in building democratic unions.

In late 1991, trade union leaders from the Americas met to assess the economic and social effects of free trade in the Western Hemisphere. Shirley Carr, president of the CLC, prophetically summed up the situation as follows: "Either we sit back and let capital divide us one against the other or we try and find ways to cooperate and develop common strategies to tackle the challenges. There is no question that international capital is on the march in this hemisphere and these forces are driving the restructuring of our societies."[33]

A new strategy for labor is emerging in response to transnationalization of capital. This strategy is to establish a "new popular internationalism" which can combine the strengths of class politics and popular social movements—a new kind of international working-class solidarity that incorporates many forms of struggle and organization as has been exhibited recently in Seattle. The growing response to such development is transnational cooperation and coalition building among labor, political, environmental, women's, human rights, social justice, and other groups. The goal is to wrestle political and economic control from transnational capital at both the domestic and international arenas.

CONCLUSION

Considering capital as a social relation, not a fetishized object of exchange, we have argued that essentially any contemporary labor process would exhibit two broadly recognized historical tendencies: (1) a progressive deskilling and reskilling of labor power through the everlasting subjugation of living labor by machinery, thus raising the rate of exploitation, and (2) a global victory of capital over the remaining vestiges of old and disintegrating modes of production, beyond the boundary of the nation-state.

Hand in hand with the above tendencies is the spatial mobility of capital based on the global victory of the capitalist mode of production. The result has been the formation of an integrated network of transnationalized labor processes. This global process of socialization of production, in turn, demands an all-embracing and unified action on the part of labor. The concept of international solidarity is indeed a minimal platform upon which labor can stand, especially in view of today's world in which the very existence of labor is threatened, both in the advanced capitalist nations and their counterparts in the Third World.

The issue of trade liberalization and its formalization in free trade agreements within the context of capitalist relations of production has accelerated the development of global trade unionism, and has begun to legitimate a popular progressive internationalism. Many labor unions in the Third World and in advanced capitalist countries are beginning to view themselves as part of a broader process of economic and political transformation. They see their problems as rooted in the nature of world capitalism and are struggling to find fundamental solutions.

A new labor movement is emerging internationally where unions (1) are becoming more autonomous in relation to their respective nation-states; (2) are becoming increasingly committed to organizing the unorganized (including the traditionally underrepresented); (3) are encouraging rather than impeding rank-and-file involvement in their organizations; (4) are reaching out and building alliances with other groups; (5) are more committed to global agendas; and (6) through a more class-oriented politics are more pledged to democratizing societies.

The final act is yet to be written. The new labor movement worldwide is divided between reformism, which desires to obtain the best deal possible for workers from a regulated transnational capital, and a more confrontational approach that seeks remedies that go beyond the status quo. The outcome of the process now unfolding on a global scale will be in good part determined by the struggle over leadership of the labor movement itself.

NOTES

1. The theoretical arguments advanced in this chapter are adapted from our "Wage Labor and Global Capital: Global Competition and Universalization of the Labor Movement," in *Beyond Survival: Wage Labor in the Late Twentieth Century,* ed. Cyrus Bina, Laurie Clements, and Chuck Davis (New York: M.E. Sharpe, 1996). The literature on the globalization of capital is vast. At the same time, there are several strands within this literature, from viewing the global transformation along the neo-Smithian division of labor, to the Monthly Review School of Monopoly Capitalism, to the classical Marxian Social Relations School. This chapter follows Marx's lead, in the latter framework, to explain the emergence of global labor processes that are

currently proliferating, albeit unevenly, beyond the boundaries of nation-states. See Cyrus Bina, "Globalization: The Epochal Imperatives and Developmental Tendencies," in *Political Economy of Globalization,* ed. D. Gupta (Boston, Mass.: Gluwer Academic Press, 1997), 41–58; Cyrus Bina and Behzad Yaghmaian, "Post-War Global Accumulation and the Transnationalization of Capital," *Capital & Class,* no. 43 (Spring 1991), 107–30; Sol Picciotto, "The Internationalization of the State," *Capital & Class,* no. 43 (Spring 1991), 43–63; Berch Berberoglu, *The Internationalization of Capital* (New York: Praeger Publishers, 1987); Jerry Lembcke, *Capitalist Development and Class Capacities: Marxist Theory and Union Organization* (Westport, Conn.: Greenwood Press, 1988); James Cypher, "The Internationalization of Capital and the Transformation of Social Formations: A Critique of the Monthly Review School," *Review of Radical Political Economics* 11, no. 4 (1979); Rhys Jenkins, *Transnational Corporations and Uneven Development* (New York: Methuen, 1987); William K. Tabb, "Capital Mobility, the Restructuring of Production, and the Politics of Labor," in *Instability and Change in the World Economy,* ed. Arthur MacEwan and William K. Tabb (New York: Monthly Review Press, 1989); John Willoughby, *Capitalist Imperialism, Crisis and State* (New York: Harwood Press, 1986); Robert Brenner, "The Origins of Capitalist Development: A Critique of Neo-Smithian Marxism," *New Left Review,* no. 104 (July–August 1977), 25–92; Cyrus Bina and Chuck Davis, "The Transnationalization of Capital and the Decline of the U.S. Labor Movement" (paper presented at the annual meeting of the Allied Social Science Associations in Washington, D.C., December 28–30, 1990). For a systematic treatment of the issue of international trade, see Anwar Shaikh, "Foreign Trade and the Law of Value I–II," *Science and Society* (Fall 1979 and Spring 1980).

2. See Tabb, "Capital Mobility, the Restructuring of Production, and the Politics of Labor," 259–78. Unfortunately, Tabb offers no specific theoretical framework concerning the transnationalization of the labor process. In this essay, the author's position is one of international solidarity.

3. Contrary to the neo-Marxian notion of deskilling, à la Braverman, we contend that the labor process in capitalism proper, involves intense deskilling as well as reskilling of labor according to the hegemonic direction of capital. See Cyrus Bina and Chuck Davis, "Globalization, Technology, and Skill Formation in Capitalism," in *Political Economy and Contemporary Capitalism: Radical Perspectives on Economic Theory and Policy,* ed. Ron Baiman et al. (New York: M. E. Sharpe, 2000).

4. See Frederick W. Taylor, *Scientific Management* (New York: Harper, 1947).

5. Harley Shaiken, *Work Transformed: Automation and Labor in the Computer Age* (Lexington, Mass.: Lexington Books, 1986), 260.

6. Harry Braverman, *Labor and Monopoly Capital: The Degradation of Work in the Twentieth Century* (New York: Monthly Review Press, 1974). Here, Braverman defines *deskilling* in terms of (1) the disassociation of the labor process from the skills of the workers, (2) the separation of conception from execution, and (3) monopoly over knowledge to control each step of the labor process and its mode of execution. Although these and many other points in the above volume present new insights in the analysis of the labor process, we believe that Braverman's failure to incorporate the historical importance of class struggle diminishes his work. Deskilling is only half the story. The transformation of the labor process involves simultaneously the deskilling *and* reskilling of labor along with the real subordination of labor by capital.

7. Lourdes Beneria, "Gender and the Global Economy," in MacEwan and Tabb, *Instability and Change in the World Economy*, 246–47.

8. Beneria, "Gender and the Global Economy," 250–51. Also see Diane Elson and Ruth Pearson, "Nimble Fingers Make Cheap Workers: An Analysis of Workers in Employment in Third World Export Processing," *Feminist Review* 33 (1981).

9. See L. E. Mins, ed., *Founding of the First International: A Documentary Record* (New York: International Publishers, 1937).

10. Mins, ed., *Founding of the First International*, 38.

11. Karl Marx, "Trades' Unions, Their Past, Present and Future," in *Theories of the Labor Movement*, ed. Simeon Larson and Bruce Nissen (Detroit: Wayne State University Press, 1987), 36–37 [emphasis in original].

12. For extensive data and analysis of these and other related domestic consequences of the globalization process, see Berch Berberoglu, *The Legacy of Empire: Economic Decline and Class Polarization in the United States* (New York: Praeger, 1992), chaps. 4 and 5.

13. See Lembcke, *Capitalist Development and Class Capacities*.

14. Stanley Aronowitz, *Working Class Hero: A New Strategy for Labor* (New York: Adama Books, 1983).

15. See Noam Chomsky, *Necessary Illusions: Thought Control in Democratic Societies* (Boston: South End Press, 1989).

16. Jack Scott, *Yankee Unions, Go Home! How the AFL Helped the U.S. Build an Empire in Latin America* (Vancouver: New Star Books, 1978), 9–14, 201–38.

17. Kim Moody, *An Injury to All: The Decline of American Unionism* (London: Verso, 1988). See also Sheila Cohr's review of Moody's book, titled: "Us and Them: Business Unionism in America and Some Implications for the U.K.," *Capital and Class*, no. 45 (Autumn 1991), 95–127.

18. Scott, *Yankee Unions, Go Home!* chaps. 15–19.

19. Mike Davis, *Prisoners of the American Dream: Politics and Economy in the History of the U.S. Working Class* (London: Verso, 1986), 96.

20. Carolyn Howe, "The Politics of Class Compromise in an International Context: Considerations for a New Strategy for Labor," *Review of Radical Political Economics* 18, no. 3 (1986), 1–22.

21. See Berberoglu, *The Legacy of Empire*, chaps. 4 and 5.

22. Berberoglu, *The Legacy of Empire*, chaps. 4 and 5; Tabb, "Capital Mobility."

23. Jeremy Brecher and Tim Costello, *Global Village vs. Global Pillage: A One-World Strategy for Labor* (Washington, D.C.: International Labor Rights Education and Research Fund, 1991).

24. Jack Sheinkman, "Preface: Worker Rights in Central America," in *Worker Rights in the New World Order* (New York: The National Labor Committee in Support of Democracy and Human Rights in El Salvador, 1991).

25. John Willoughby, "The Promise and Pitfalls of Protectionist Politics," in *The Imperiled Economy*, ed. Robert Cherry et al., Book I (New York: Union for Radical Political Economics, 1987), 215–23.

26. David McNally, "Beyond Nationalism, beyond Protectionism: Labor and the Canada–U.S. Free Trade Agreement," *Capital & Class*, no. 43 (Spring 1991), 233–52.

27. McNally, "Beyond Nationalism, beyond Protectionism," 233–52.

28. Quoted in Brecher and Costello, *Global Village vs. Global Pillage*, 33–34.

29. Tabb, "Capital Mobility, the Restructuring of Production, and the Politics of Labor," 268.

30. See "Solidarity across Borders: U.S. Labor in a Global Economy," *Labor Research Review* 8, no. 1 (1989).

31. Howe, "The Politics of Class Compromise in an International Context," 18.

32. Elaine Burns, "Free Trade Era Looms over Mexico," *Guardian,* 8 January 1991, 16.

33. Quoted in *The Union Advocate,* 5 August 1991.

10

Globalization of Capital and Class Struggle

Walda Katz-Fishman, Jerome Scott, and Ife Modupe

As we enter the twenty-first century, it is becoming increasingly clear that contemporary advanced capitalism has for quite some time been operating on a global level. The current stage of advanced capitalism—characterized by globalization and high technology—is not only fostering the superexploitation of the working class throughout the world, which has served as a significant source of superprofits for the capitalists, but is also eliminating much of the domestic industrial and service sector labor force from the production process and driving down the quality of work (e.g., wages, job security, working conditions) for the jobs that remain. This reality, coupled with the ending of reform policies and the spread of neoliberalism across the globe, is setting the stage for renewed class struggles and working-class resistance throughout the world.[1]

The globalization of capital (relocation of production to low-wage areas of the less-developed world) *and* the technological revolution (high-tech computer automation, robotics, etc.) in the labor process, leading to the elimination of many domestic manufacturing and service jobs, are the dual dynamics in the global restructuring of the division of labor and the labor process under late capitalism. Both contribute to the growing domestic economic crisis, class polarization, and class struggle.

This chapter provides a brief analysis of the globalization of capital and the changing role of labor in the production process, and outlines the nature and forms of the class struggle on the shop floor and in the larger society on a global level.

GLOBALIZATION OF CAPITAL AND THE
SUPEREXPLOITATION OF LABOR ON A WORLD SCALE

Today, transnational capital, through its worldwide expansion and restructuring of the international division of labor, has elevated the exploitation of wage labor to the global level.[2] Increasingly in the postwar period, transnational capital has moved manufacturing production to low-wage areas of the Third World where cheaper labor, and especially women workers, continue to be exploited at extremely high rates. To facilitate this process, significant export processing zones (EPZs) were created, particularly in the Pacific Rim and in Central and South America, to extract the most profits through the superexploitation of labor.[3]

During the 1990s, a number of international legislative bodies and agreements were created to promote "free-trade" ideology and practice by reducing, and in many cases eliminating, trade barriers. The North American Free Trade Agreement (NAFTA) and the World Trade Organization (WTO) have in this context played a central role in undermining unionization efforts and suppressing workers' wages by allowing companies to relocate jobs around the world. Such institutions and arrangements independently and collectively promote the exploitation of labor on a world scale. They accomplish this in large part by empowering transnational corporations with the ability to shape and implement policies in their own countries and other countries, regardless of human and environmental costs, so that their profit-driven interests are fulfilled.[4]

For global corporations, NAFTA has facilitated the transfer of production to profit-enhancing locations like Mexico, where wages are much lower, there is little or no independent union activity, and few if any worker benefits and environmental protections exist. Since NAFTA's implementation, the percentage of U.S. companies following through on threats to relocate production in response to unionization drives have tripled.[5] In all, more than 200,000 U.S. jobs have been lost since the implementation of NAFTA in 1993—and this does not include jobs lost in related businesses.[6] NAFTA has especially accelerated the transfer of production to the U.S.–Mexican border where *maquiladora* workers earn as little as $1.51 per hour.[7]

The WTO, established in 1995 by the Uruguay Round of GATT, expands the scope of GATT from the reduction of tariffs in the trade of goods to the reduction of all trade barriers for not only goods, but also for services and intellectual property.[8] The danger of WTO, as a global political body, lies in its promotion of free trade at all costs, including and especially the manner in which its policies compromise fundamental human and worker rights.[9] The WTO can rule that national (state, regional, and local) laws conflict with the maximization of free trade and corporate profit, even if those laws are designed to protect the environment, the health of the population, and the survivability of domestic business and/or workers' rights. Additionally, the WTO can impose penalties on nations considered to be in violation of its rules. A country found in violation of the "principles of free trade" can choose to change its law to conform with WTO requirements, pay permanent compensation to the affected country, or face non-negotiated trade sanctions.[10] In this way, the WTO cripples national sovereignty and, by extension, the ability of nations to protect their economies, environment, and the rights of their citizens from the onslaught of global corporate interests.

THE CHANGING ROLE OF
LABOR IN LATE CAPITALIST PRODUCTION

The historic and ongoing transfer of the manufacturing process to cheap labor areas overseas has resulted in a shift in the U.S. labor force structure from manufacturing to the service sector where wages are much lower.[11] Today, even service sector jobs are being globalized and computerized, and full-time workers are replaced by temporary and part-time workers who have few if any benefits. The accompanying rise in overall unemployment and underemployment, and the growing glut of labor have served to erode further the position of labor in its struggles for higher wages and benefits. Workers, now an abundant commodity, compete in a global labor market and are exploited through much lower wages, with the lowest paid workers acting as a drag on the price of higher priced labor.

While the superexploitation of a growing segment of the working class around the world continues to expand as the globalization of production spreads and deepens worldwide, another significant process at work that drives down wages and increases profits is the growth in technology and automation—a process that is also creating a major problem for the continued employment of human labor.

Machine-based factory production, which has historically enhanced the productivity of human labor, is rapidly being replaced by a new computer-automated high-tech production system—computer-run machines, robotics, and all forms of automation in the production process.[12] This type of production, although it may at first appear as a quantitative advance within the era of machine-based production, is in fact a qualitatively new type of productive force.[13] The application of computer technologies to production does not simply augment the productive capacity of human labor power; rather, it increasingly displaces human labor from the production process. Thus, under advanced capitalism, production itself is increasingly becoming a process requiring less and less human labor.[14]

Application of Technologies to the Labor Process

The development of technology and its application within the capitalist production process challenges the very foundations of capitalist social relations. The development of capitalist society has demanded the ever-expanding application of machine technology to the production process to enhance the production and distribution of goods in emerging domestic and international markets. The continuous application of advanced technologies at the point of production has simultaneously enhanced labor productivity, while further degrading the role of human labor in production. This degradation begins as human beings are transformed into wage laborers in a profit-driven economy, whereby their labor-power becomes a commodity to be sold for a wage, which is then used to purchase items for survival.

With high-tech production, labor is increasingly superfluous; unemployment increases, and the value of employed labor is driven down; purchasing power declines, and capital cannot sell the glut of commodities being produced. Working people, as consumers, constitute two-thirds of the market for the sale of commodities. Enhanced productivity, coupled with the increasing degradation of labor, fuel the economic crisis because of a decline in consumption, while an abundance of commodities is produced and enters the market. The key to capitalist development is the production and sale of commodities for profit in an expanding market. When the glut of commodities produced can no longer circulate for profit in the market, a serious economic crisis ensues.[15]

During the era of capitalist expansion, the capitalists sought to maximize their profits by driving down the cost of production. They accomplished this in large measure by driving down wages, the largest component of the cost of production. Keeping down the wage component of the cost of production has depended, in part, on the capitalists' ability to stifle union development and to deny to the workers the weapon of organizing in their fight for higher wages and safer workplaces.

The institutional denial of workers' right to organize can best be understood within the historical context of slave labor in the southern plantation economy, and the political and economic struggles that ensued during the Civil War and Reconstruction eras. With the defeat of Reconstruction, the political and economic system in the South, as with the earlier slave system, undercut the position of labor throughout the country (and increasingly throughout the world).[16] The southern states, through "states' rights" and the enactment of Jim Crow constitutions in the 1890s and early 1900s, followed by passage of "right-to-work" laws in the 1940s and 1950s, blocked aggressive unionization of labor on a national basis.[17] An ample supply of nonunion, cheaper labor was used time and again as a threat and as a reality to break strikes and to break the unity of workers in their struggle for organization and higher wages. In the North, in Appalachia, and in the West, the bosses employed the Pinkerton guards, the national guard, state troopers, and other forms of state repression to fight the unions.

The development of a distinct northern and southern labor market, breaking the unity of labor nationwide, was further fragmented by significant internal divisions within labor in the North. Immigrant labor from Europe and later black labor from the South were used to drive down the value of labor throughout the country. By the turn of the century and the advent of modern imperialism, the superexploitation of colonial and later neocolonial labor set the material basis for the conservatism of a skilled section of the U.S. working class. The incorporation of low-paid women workers into the labor force during and after World War II also helped keep wages down.[18]

The inability of unions to exert influence over the labor process in recent decades is a product of the decline in union membership in the postwar period to the present. Union membership went from an all-time high of 30 percent, or 15 million workers in 1955, to 20 percent, or 17.7 million workers in 1983, to its all-time low of 14 percent, or 16 million workers in 1997.[19]

In the last two decades of the twentieth century, the accelerated globalization of capital has set the basis for changes in state policy from the earlier reform era expansion of the social safety net to the emergence of neoliberalism and reactionary politics. The international financial structure of the Bretton Woods institutions of 1944 (International Monetary Fund, World Bank, and General Agreement on Tariffs and Trade) has been undergoing a similar transformation. Neoliberalism at the national and global level promotes "free markets," privatization, downsizing, deregulation, and other policies that speed up the decline in workers' quality of life and right to organize, as well as environmental standards. Specific policies such as the 1993 signing of the North American Free Trade Agreement (NAFTA), the 1994 formation of the World Trade Organization (WTO), and the 1996 passage of the Personal Responsibility and Work Opportunity Reconciliation Act, eliminating "welfare as we know it," have brought home to U.S. workers these new realities.

Today in the United States, wage labor in the South, of all colors and nationalities and both women and men, is paid less than its counterparts in the rest of the country. Throughout the United States, African American workers are paid less and have higher unemployment rates than other workers. All workers of color, generally, are paid less and are more often unemployed than white workers. Among workers of all colors, regions, and nationalities, women workers in the South are the most superexploited workers in the United States.[20]

From the air traffic controllers' strike in the early 1980s to the lockout of the paper workers' union at the end of the decade to the continual refusal of southern employers to negotiate contracts with workers who have voted in unions (e.g., the catfish workers in the Mississippi Delta and the textile workers in the black belt of Georgia), the state has openly attacked unions or used its power in support of capital over labor.

Throughout the era of capitalist development, from the invention of the steam engine to the present, the continuous introduction of advanced technology was labor-enhancing. It rendered human labor power more and more productive. Workers were needed to run the machines, which made them more productive. Despite their falling wages, they were still able to afford the necessities of life and thus maintain the market. The labor-enhancing technology of the past period, however, is more and more being replaced by the labor-eliminating technology of the current period. The fluctuations in poverty and cyclical unemployment of the earlier period are increasingly giving way to the polarization of wealth and poverty, and growing permanent unemployment of the present period.[21] Thus, the expansion and maintenance of the market of the previous period have turned into the contraction and decline of the market of the current period.

THE CAPITALIST CRISIS AND ITS
IMPACT ON THE WORKING CLASS

Today's economic crisis is devastating for the working class. Millions of workers are unemployed, and millions more are working part-time because full-time jobs are not available. Many workers who are employed are paid lower and lower wages, and have lost benefits once taken for granted.[22] Workers' standard of living is rapidly declining, and their children are now the age group most threatened by poverty.[23] Education, housing, food, health care, the environment, and the services and infrastructure of working-class communities are deteriorating daily—all this in a world that has developed the capacity to produce enough goods and services so that no human being needs to be in want.[24] Ironically, there is not only an abundance of goods, but there is a glut that is unsold, unused, and often destroyed while millions of working people are unable to afford the basic necessities of life.

This overproduction of commodities and the blockage of their circulation to people who need them means that even the capitalists are experiencing the effects of the crisis. As the economic expansion of the postwar period came to a close in the mid-1970s, the contraction of the past twenty-five years evolved into a full-blown crisis of immense proportions.[25] In the 1980s and 1990s, financial, manufacturing, and service sector corporations were restructured. Through bankruptcies, mergers, and acquisitions, the smallest and weakest corporations were eliminated, further concentrating capital into bigger and more powerful global corporations. U.S. workers ultimately paid for these through government (tax-dollar financed) bailouts and guarantees. A third of the nation's savings and loan institutions went under, with an estimated cost to the taxpayers of $500 billion. Failures in the banking industry followed; with FDIC bailouts in 1991 alone costing $64 billion.[26]

The financial crisis spread to the insurance industry, forcing the Pension Benefit Guarantee Corporation (PBGC), the federal agency that insures the pensions of 40 million workers, into the red by $2 billion to cover huge shortfalls as high as $40 billion because of failures and underfunding by major corporations, like Chrysler for $3.3 billion, Bethlehem Steel for $1.3 billion, and General Motors for $7.2 billion.[27]

Debt and bankruptcies, personal and corporate, continue to soar. In 1991 a record 810,000 Americans filed for bankruptcy; this figure had increased to 1.2 million in 1997.[28] While business bankruptcies decreased slightly from 64,688 in 1990 to 53,993 in 1997, business failures increased over the same period—from 60,747 in 1990 to 83,384 in 1997.[29] Failures were up in every region of the country and in every major industry sector except mining, and the size of failed businesses is growing larger.[30] Total household debt grew from $1.4 trillion in 1980 to $3.7 trillion in 1990 to $5.8 trillion in 1997, of which $1.2 trillion is consumer debt. The average household debt during this same year was $57,000.

Throughout the era of capitalist development, the capitalists sought to maximize their profits by driving down the cost of production. They accomplished this in large part by driving down wages, the largest component of the cost of production. During the postwar economic expansion from 1947 to 1973, hourly wages for nonsupervisory and production workers increased from $7.12 to $12.72; however, between 1973 and 1995, they declined from $12.72 to $11.46—a drop of 10 percent.[31]

The purchasing power of the hourly minimum wage fell dramatically between 1968 and 1997. Adjusted for inflation and reported in constant 1997 dollars, the value of the minimum wage increased from $4.96 in 1950 to $7.36 in 1968, but plummeted to $5.15 in 1997.[32] Thus, despite the corporate and media hype about how "well" the economy is doing, low-wage workers in the late 1990s were substantially worse off than they were thirty years earlier. Because of the prevalence of low-wage work, nearly 30 percent of full-time workers were earning poverty-level wages in 1995, up from 23.5 percent in 1973.[33] Unlike workers' wages, however, CEO salaries have increased from 42 times the average factory worker's pay in 1980, to 85 times in 1990, to 419 times in 1998.[34]

The polarization between wealth and poverty is increasing rapidly. In 1976, the wealthiest 1 percent of Americans held 19 percent of the wealth, and the wealthiest 10 percent held 49 percent, leaving 51 percent for the bottom 90 percent of the population. By 1997, the wealthiest 1 percent had doubled its total share of wealth to 40 percent, and the wealthiest 10 percent had increased its total share of the wealth to 73 percent, leaving the bottom 90 percent a mere 27 percent.[35]

In 1992, the official unemployment rate was more than 7 percent, with nearly 10 million workers out of work; for African Americans, the rate was 14 percent. Moreover, another million workers were listed as discouraged, having stopped looking for work. Also, more than 7 million workers were working part-time and wanted full-time work, but were unable to find it.[36] The unemployment rate dropped to 6 percent in 1994, decreased again to just under 5 percent in 1997, and fell to 4.3 percent in 1999.[37] However, several millions of unemployed workers and several millions more of under-employed workers continued to suffer the ill effects of poverty and destitution throughout the decade of the 1990s.

If the 7 million workers counted as "officially" unemployed in 1997 are combined with the 4.6 million "discouraged workers" (i.e., workers not "officially" in the labor force because they do not have a job and are not actively looking for work) who later said they do want a job, then a total of 11.6 million workers were looking for work, and the unemployment rate was in fact 6.8 percent (of the 16–64 age group). By 1999, these figures were slightly lower at 5.75 million "officially" unemployed and 4.1 million who said they wanted a job but couldn't find one—a total of 9.85 million workers, or 5.6 percent (of the 16–64 age group) who are actually unemployed.[38]

Despite the lower unemployment rate in the late 1990s, having a job has not assured that workers are able to go much beyond meeting their basic needs. Fewer people have the money to buy the growing volume of goods that are produced; food is grown and harvested but cannot be sold. As a result, many go hungry; houses and apartments are built but remain empty because many workers cannot afford the rent or mortgage payments; millions of women, men, and children are in the streets or near homelessness; hospitals and doctors' offices close or turn away those who are ill, because they cannot afford to pay insurance and/or medical expenses. Although the gross national product continues to increase, the unsold goods and services translate into a glut—an overproduction—of things that cannot be sold in the market because the workers who are unemployed, in poverty, or paid less and less cannot afford to buy them.

Such are the consequences of the process of capitalist development, as the fundamental contradiction between advances in the productive forces and capitalist social relations within which they develop intensifies on a world scale. Thus, the stage is set for the political struggle necessary to resolve this contradiction.

CLASS STRUGGLE AND SOCIAL TRANSFORMATION

The dire conditions that labor faces in the United States today call forth and make possible the potential for much needed social transformation. Throughout human history, every society has been organized around its tools, labor power, and the production process. Capitalist organization of society based on private ownership of the productive forces and distribution of the necessities of life through capitalist relations of production and exchange is no longer viable. Today, technological expansion in the productive forces is the material foundation of the economic, social, and political changes that are taking place in society around the world. Capitalist relations of production and exchange have, as a result, moved from contradiction to antagonism in an openly political way. Social transformation is the process of the developing class struggle that will and must bring the social relations of production and organization of society into line with the advanced productive forces.[39]

Class Struggle at the Point of Production

There is increasing evidence of renewed working-class struggles in the United States. Organizing efforts are expanding across the country, and rank-and-file workers' movements are springing up in a number of major industries. During the past two decades, workers across the United States have engaged in numerous strikes, walkouts, and other forms of protest. The period from the late 1970s onward saw intensified rank-and-file struggles in confronting the power of capital at the point of production. An increasing number of workers at the grassroots level have taken the initiative to exert their collective strength and fight back to protect their hard-won rights.

In 1978, more than 160,000 coal miners went on strike, which lasted several months; the strike ended only when the government intervened with the full force of the Taft-Hartley Act. In 1979, more than 35,000 International Harvester workers walked out of their jobs, striking the company for five and a half months. In early 1980, more than 60,000 oil and petrochemical workers went on strike against Gulf, Texaco, Cities Service, and other big oil companies. In March 1981, about 170,000 miners belonging to the United Mine Workers of America (UMWA) went on strike once again, and in September, nearly 400,000 workers gathered in Washington, D.C., on Solidarity Day, one of the largest protest demonstrations in U.S. history.[40]

With the onset of the recession in 1982, early in the year, more than 30,000 demonstrators, including many trade unionists and unemployed workers, marched in New York City against Reagan administration policies. In August 1983, more than 700,000 workers went out on strike against American Telephone & Telegraph (AT&T) and paralyzed the phone system nationwide. Just one week after the AT&T strike, 40,000 Western Electric workers walked out in support of the striking AT&T workers on the picket lines.[41]

In April 1985, more than 150,000 people, including a large contingent of workers, marched nationwide for jobs, peace, and justice. In October 1986, some 30,000 longshoremen went on strike in ports from Maine to Virginia along the eastern coastline of the United States. In April 1987, more than 45,000 workers took part in an antiwar march of 150,000 in Washington, D.C., protesting against U.S. intervention in Central America and demanding that plant closings and layoffs, as well as the rollback in wages and benefits, be stopped. In May, thousands of meat-packing workers went on strike at the John Morrell plant in Sioux Falls, South Dakota. Later, in August, several thousand union members and their supporters from neighboring states converged on the city in a militant demonstration of support for the striking meat packers.[42]

In January 1988, all commercial shipping in every port in Oregon and Washington came to a standstill as thousands of Northwest longshore workers went out on strike on the West Coast. In March 1989, more than 8,000 machinists went on strike against Eastern Airlines, which turned into one of the longest strikes in U.S. history; in April, thousands of Pittston miners in Virginia went on strike and stood firm in their stand against the coal companies. Also, Solidarity Day II on Labor Day 1991, brought thousands of workers from organized labor, joined by the unemployed, the homeless, students, environmentalists, and others, to Washington, D.C., to express their dissatisfaction with government and corporate policies.[43]

Since the early 1990s, workers at three plants in Decatur, Illinois—Caterpillar, Bridgestone/Firestone, and A. E. Staley Manufacturing—have been engaged in struggles around employer demands for concessions.[44] Workers at Caterpillar, one of the worlds largest manufacturers of earth moving equipment, attempted to resist the company's efforts to enhance competitiveness on a global market by organizing a number of strikes between 1991 and 1995.[45] In 1996, workers' efforts at Bridgestone/Firestone were met with success when management agreed to reinstate the locked out workers, provide partial back-pay, and increase their wages.[46] Similar struggles to protect hard-won benefits of workers in various other industries in the United States have led to greater mobilization of labor and have effected positive change. In 1997, United Parcel Service (UPS) workers led a successful campaign for the creation of more full-time jobs, raises for full-time and part-time workers, and the prohibition of using subcontractors without agreement from local unions.[47]

In June 1999, Union of Needle Trades, Industrial and Textile Employees (UNITE)—the 1995 merger of International Ladies Garment Workers Union (ILGWU) and Amalgamated Clothing and Textile Workers Union (ACTWU)—declared a victory in organizing the Fieldcrest Cannon plant's 5,200 workers.[48] In November, Pollowtex Corp, parent company of Fieldcrest Cannon Inc., withdrew its legal challenges to the June election.[49] This represents a big victory for labor, particularly given the company's history of hostility to the labor.

According to the Bureau of Labor Statistics, there were eight work stoppages in 1998 involving more than 5,000 workers each. Strikers represented such companies as Kaiser Permanente, General Motors, Bell Atlantic, Consolidated Rail Company, US West Corporation, Southern New England Telecommunication Company, and Northwest Airlines. Together, these strikes involved a total of 1,687,600 workers and 4,173,600 estimated days idle.[50]

Throughout the United States, workers who have been displaced at the point of production and who have lost their jobs in the service sector are becoming part of the growing army of the permanently unemployed, underemployed, and part-time/contingent workforce. Working-class women and men employed in low-wage, contract jobs, are beginning to organize in large numbers. As their struggles mature, these unemployed and underemployed workers, as well as those fighting on the shop floor and in the service and public sectors, are increasingly confronting the repressive arm of the capitalist state. From these struggles will emerge the further development of class consciousness that will lead the working class to take political action to protect and advance its class interests.

Class Struggle and Political Action

The social and political changes developing in the United States today are a historical outcome of the process of transformation that U.S. society is undergoing as productive technologies further advance, and as capitalism further globalizes and evolves along its contradictory path.

Although the social struggle is scattered, disorganized, and isolated, a class-conscious working class is emerging across the country. The development of class consciousness among a growing number of working class people and their organizations is setting the stage for the emergence of an independent political organization of the working class that will play an active role in political battles that are part and parcel of the continuing class struggle between labor and capital at various levels of life under capitalism.

Working people are engaging in struggles linking workplace and community around broad issues of social and economic justice. Over 10,000 religious and community leaders recently rallied in Washington, D.C., around expanding the living wage campaigns to raise wages above the poverty level and improve the plight of the working poor in cities, counties, and states throughout the United States.[51]

Using the economic human rights articles of the United Nations' 1948 Declaration of Human Rights, activists in the United States and throughout the world have been building the economic and human rights movement. The Kensington Welfare Rights Union (KWRU), an organization of poor and homeless women, men, and children from various races from Kensington, Pennsylvania, struggling to end poverty, are part of this growing international struggle for economic human rights. Efforts culminated in the "March of the Americas" in October 1999, a thirty-day walk from Washington, D.C., to the United Nations in New York. Members of several organizations met with the Office of the High Commissioner on Human Rights to report U.S. human rights violations—which include the denial of such basic human rights as adequate housing, food, education, health care, and jobs at living wages, to millions of women, men, and children in the United States.[52]

In the United States and around the world, activists from women's organizations, trade unions and workers' organizations, poor people's organizations, environmental organizations, farm organizations, student and youth organizations, and other nongovernmental organizations (NGOs) mobilized to challenge the neoliberal policies of the Millennium Round of the WTO Ministerial (successor to GATT). Many of the same "Internet guerrillas" who helped defeat the Multilateral Agreement on Investment (MAI) were part of the global mobilization in Seattle from November 30 to December 3, 1999. More than 50,000 activists, including 20,000 trade unionists, participated in teach-ins, protest rallies, marches, and direct action to voice their opposition to the WTO and its global corporate agenda that puts maximization of profit before labor and human rights and the environment. On November 30, massive street demonstrations shut down the opening ceremonies of the WTO Ministerial. The Seattle police met the protesters with violence—tear gas, pepper spray, rubber bullets, and almost 600 arrested and jailed.[53] Late in the day on December 3, the WTO Ministerial talks ended in failure, with not even a joint statement. Seattle represents an important beginning in building a global movement from the bottom-up to transform capitalist globalization from the top-down. A similar protest at the International Monetary Fund (IMF) and World Bank meetings in Washington, D.C., in April 2000 has further reinforced the determination of the movement for change in confronting global capitalism as we enter the twenty-first century.

As the objective conditions for the transformation of capitalism ripen, and as the subjective factors facilitating the development of class consciousness take root among an increasing number of working-class women and men of all racial/ethnic groups in the United States, the articulation of the interests of the working class through its own independent organizations will become more and more a reality. Through this process, the objectives of the global working-class struggle will become clarified and a shared vision of society will be developed—control over the labor process and the products of our labor, transformation of work relations, restructuring of relations of production at the societal level, the abolition of private ownership of the major means of production, and the development of an inclusive structure of governance. The abolition of the control and exploitation of labor depends on the outcome of the struggle between labor and capital in holding on to or capturing the reign of state power, a struggle that at root is a *polit-*

ical struggle. Thus, as its protection of property rights over workers' human rights increasingly reveals the class nature of the capitalist state, these struggles will more and more take on a *political* character—one that will point to the necessity for the revolutionary transformation of capitalist society by the working class.

CONCLUSION

We have shown in this chapter that there has occurred a major change in the production process and the labor force structure in the United States and around the world over the past several decades, such that traditional machine-based factory production, which constituted the basis of U.S. manufacturing industry for more than a century, has given way to computer-automated mass production. This development—coupled with the internationalization of U.S. capital since World War II in search of cheap labor and a more favorable investment climate overseas, and the implementation of neoliberal policies, including the elimination of welfare—has effected a shift toward low-paid service occupations and has led to increased unemployment and underemployment among a growing segment of the U.S. working class, a situation that has become a permanent fixture of contemporary U.S. capitalism.

The resulting decline in purchasing power and standard of living of workers in the United States who are now consuming less and less of the goods produced in a shrinking market has plunged the U.S. economy into a structural crisis that has ushered in a period of decline and decay for large segments of the U.S. working class, and even for those sectors of the economy that have gone through major restructuring through bankruptcies and mergers, including real estate, banking, insurance, auto, and manufacturing and retail/sales sectors in general. The stock market boom in the late 1990s masks the bankruptcies and debt at all levels that continue to soar, as well as the deeper structural crises of the capitalist market. The U.S. and global polarization of wealth and poverty expresses the growing economic instability and crises that are affecting a great majority of the people in the United States who are increasingly becoming conscious of their class interests and are beginning to take political action to reverse the current situation.

Class consciousness and class struggles are beginning to develop and are becoming widespread at the shop-floor level and beyond in an increasing number of industries and communities throughout the United States. Working people are winning union campaigns, are increasingly participating in economic human rights movements and living wage campaigns, and are challenging global neoliberal policies of the WTO, and the international financial architecture of the Bretton Woods institutions.

As the economy sinks further into crisis, causing many more human casualties, an emerging class-conscious working class leadership will come to play a pivotal role in building a new movement that is visionary, strategic, and capable of fundamentally transforming the structures of today's global high-tech capitalism. Such a movement must fundamentally transform society so that the control and exploitation of labor for private profit will become a thing of the past, and the abundance of goods and services that exist today will benefit all working-class people around the world.

NOTES

1. See Ellen Meiksins Wood, Peter Meiksins, and Michael Yates, eds., *Rising from the Ashes? Labor in the Age of "Global" Capitalism* (New York: Monthly Review Press, 1998).

2. See Howard M. Wachtel, *The Money Mandarins: The Making of a Supranational Economic Order* (New York: Pantheon Books, 1986). See also Edna Bonacich, Lucie Cheng, Norma Chinchilla, Nora Hamilton, and Paul Ong, eds., *Global Production: The Apparel Industry in the Pacific Rim* (Philadelphia: Temple University Press, 1994).

3. See Bruno Amoroso, *On Globalization: Capitalism in the 21st Century* (New York: St. Martin's Press, 1998).

4. Leslie Sklair, *Sociology of the Global System* (Baltimore: The Johns Hopkins University Press, 1991).

5. K. Bonfenbrenner, "Final Report: The Effects of Plant Closing or Threat of Plant Closing on the Right of Workers to Organize," submitted to the Labor Secretariat of North American Commission for Labor Cooperation (30 September 1996). Bonfenbrenner's work was cited in Public Citizen Global Trade Watch's "School of Real Life Results: Report Card." See www.citizen.org.

6. Brian Burgoon, "Job-Destroying Villain: Is It NAFTA or the Mexican Currency Crisis?" in *Real World International: 4th ed.,* ed. M. Breslow, D. Levy, A. Scher (Somerville, Mass.: Dollars and Sense, 1997).

7. U.S. Bureau of Labor Statistics, Division of Foreign Labor Statistics, "Comparative Hourly Compensation Costs for Production Workers in Manufacturing Industries, Selected Countries: 1997."

8. Public Citizen Global Trade Watch, *A Citizen's Guide to the World Trade Organization* (Washington, D.C.: Inkworks, 1999).

9. Marc Breslow, "Why Free Trade Fails: The Dangers of GATT, NAFTA, and the WTO," in *Real World International,* ed. Breslow et al.

10. Public Citizen Global Trade Watch, *A Citizen's Guide to the World Trade Organization.*

11. In *The Great American Job Machine,* Barry Bluestone and Bennett Harrison reported that in the late 1970s and early 1980s when jobs were eliminated in manufacturing, workers—mostly white men in unionized jobs—who found jobs in the service sector were paid about one-fourth of their previous wages. See Barry Bluestone and Bennett Harrison, *The Great American Job Machine: The Proliferation of Low Wage Employment in the U.S. Economy* (Washington, D.C.: U.S. Congress, Joint Economic Committee, 1986), 1–7.

12. Barry Bluestone and Bennett Harrison, *The Deindustrialization of America: Plant Closings, Community Abandonment, and the Dismantling of Basic Industry* (New York: Basic Books, 1982); Jeremy Rifkin, *The End of Work* (New York: G. P. Putnam's Sons Pub., 1995); Jim Davis, "Globalization and the Technological Transformation of Capitalism," *Race & Class* 40 nos. 2–3 (October 1998–March 1999); Stanley Aronowitz and William DiFazio, *The Jobless Future: Sci-Tech and the Dogma of Work* (Minneapolis: University of Minnesota Press, 1994).

13. J. Francis Reintjes, *Numerical Control: Making a New Technology* (New York: Oxford University Press, 1991); Davis, "Globalization and the Technological Transformation of Capitalism."

14. David E. Noble, *Forces of Production: A Social History of Industrial Automation* (New York: Oxford University Press, 1984); Rifkin, *The End of Work.*

15. David Harvey, *The Limits to Capital* (Chicago: University of Chicago Press, 1982).

16. See, for example, John Keller, *Power in America: The Southern Question and the Control of Labor* (Chicago: Vanguard Press, 1983).

17. Union membership in right-to-work states declined from 34,193,000 in 1983 to 20,607,000 in 1997—a drop of 13,586,000. Similarly, union membership in states where there existed no right-to-work laws dropped from 142,961,000 in 1983 to 140,492,000 in 1997—a difference of 2,469,000, according to the U.S. Bureau of the Census, 1998.

18. James Geschwender, "Race, Ethnicity, and Class," in *Recapturing Marxism,* in R. Levine and J. Lembcke (New York: Praeger, 1987), 136–60.

19. U.S. Bureau of the Census, *Statistical Abstract of the United States, 1998* (Washington, D.C.: Government Printing Office, 1998), 443.

20. *Statistical Abstract, 1991,* 415.

21. Walda Katz-Fishman and Ralph C. Gomes, "A Critique of *The Truly Disadvantaged,*" *Journal of Sociology and Social Welfare* 16, no. 4 (1989), 77–98.

22. Frances Fox Piven and Richard Cloward, *The New Class War* (New York: Pantheon Books, 1982).

23. Children's Defense Fund, *The State of America's Children* (Washington, D.C.: CDF, 1991); *Statistical Abstract, 1991,* 463.

24. F. Block, R. Cloward, B. Ehrenreich, and F. Piven, *The Mean Season: The Attack on the Welfare State* (New York: Pantheon Books, 1987).

25. Berch Berberoglu, *The Legacy of Empire: Economic Decline and Class Polarization in the United States* (New York: Praeger Publishers, 1992).

26. David Skidmore, "Bank, S&L Failures Declined in '91, but Analysts Expect a New Upswing," *The Washington Post,* 2 January 1992, D13.

27. Marc Levinson, "Retire or Bust," *Newsweek,* 25 November 1991, 50, 52.

28. *Statistical Abstract, 1998,* 555.

29. *Statistical Abstract, 1998,* 554.

30. John Berry, "Recession Deeper in First Quarter," *Washington Post,* 27 April 1991, A1.

31. Edith Rasell, Barry Bluestone, and Lawrence Mishel, *The Prosperity Gap: A Chartbook of American Living Standards* (Washington, D.C.: Economic Policy Institute, 1997), 13.

32. *Statistical Abstract, 1998,* 443.

33. Rasell, Bluestone, and Mishel, *The Prosperity Gap,* 21.

34. *Business Week,* "Executive Pay," 19 April 1999, 72–73.

35. Wolff, *Top Heavy,* 1996, 78–96.

36. U.S. Bureau of Labor Statistics, *Employment and Earnings* (January 1992), 12

37. John Berry, "Jobless Numbers That Set Off Bells," *The Washington Post,* 28 September 1999, E1.

38. Berry, "Jobless Numbers That Set Off Bells," E1.

39. Walda Katz-Fishman et al., "African American Politics in an Era of Capitalist Economic Contraction," in *From Exclusion to Inclusion,* ed. R. Gomes and L. Williams (New York: Greenwood Press, 1992), 85–96.

40. Berberoglu, *The Legacy of Empire,* chap 7.

41. Berberoglu, *The Legacy of Empire,* chap 7.

42. Berberoglu, *The Legacy of Empire,* chap 7.

43. Berberoglu, *The Legacy of Empire,* chap 7.

44. Jeremy Brecher, *Strike!* (Boston: South End Press, 1997).

45. Brecher, *Strike!*

46. Brecher, *Strike!*

47. Brecher, *Strike!*

48. David Firestone, "In Huge Win for Labor in South, Textile Workers Appear to Approve Unionization," www.sweatshopwatch.org/swatch/headlines/1999/unite_jun99.html, 1999.

49. Frank Swoboda, "A Union-Shy Firm Throws in the Towel," *The Washington Post,* 11 November 1999, E1.

50. U.S. Bureau of Labor Statistics, http://stats.bls.gov/news.release/wkstp.t02.htm.

51. Michael Fletcher, "Religious Leaders Push 'Living Wage' as Issue in Election," *The Washington Post,* 31 October 1999, A10.

52. See www.libertynet.org/kwru/ehur/moa/moaccll.html.

53. Robert Kaiser and John Burgess, "A Seattle Primer: How Not to Hold WTO Talks," *The Washington Post* (December 12, 1999), A40.

Bibliography

Adler, Marina. "Gender Differences in Job Autonomy: The Consequences of Occupational Segregation and Authority Position." *The Sociological Quarterly* 34 (1993).

Adler, Paul. "Tools for Resistance: Workers Can Make Automation Their Ally." *Dollars and Sense* (October 1984).

Aglietta, Michel. *A Theory of Capitalist Regulation: The U.S. Experience.* London: New Left Books, 1979.

————. *Regulation and the Crisis of Capitalism.* New York: Monthly Review Press, 1982a.

————. "World Capitalism in the 1980s." *New Left Review* (November–December 1982b).

Altshuler, Alan, et al. *The Future of the Automobile.* Cambridge, Mass.: MIT Press, 1984.

Amin, Ash. *Post-Fordism: A Reader.* Oxford: Blackwell, 1994.

Amin, A., and K. Robins. "The Reemergence of Regional Economies? The Mythical Geography of Flexible Accumulation." *Environment and Planning D: Society and Space*, vol. 8, 1990.

Amoroso, Bruno. *On Globalization: Capitalism in the 21st Century.* London: Macmillan Press Ltd., 1998.

Aronowitz, Stanley. *False Promises: The Shaping of American Working-Class Consciousness.* New York: McGraw-Hill, 1973.

————. *Working Class Hero: A New Strategy for Labor.* New York: Adama Books, 1983.

Aronowitz, Stanley, and William DiFazio. *The Jobless Future: Sci-Tech and the Dogma of Work.* Minneapolis: University of Minnesota Press, 1994.

Baker, Elizabeth Faulkner. *Technology and Women's Work.* New York: Columbia University Press, 1964.

Baran, Paul, and Paul M. Sweezy. *Monopoly Capital.* New York: Monthly Review Press, 1966.

Baron, James N., and William T. Bielby. "The Organization of Work in a Segmented Economy." *American Sociological Review* 49 (1984).

Beechey, Veronica, and Tessa Perkins. *A Matter of Hours: Women, Part-Time Work, and the Labor Market.* Minneapolis: University of Minnesota Press, 1987.

Belous, Richard. *The Contingent Economy: The Growth of the Temporary, Part-Time and Subcontracted Workforce.* Washington, D.C.: National Planning Association, 1989.

Beneria, Lourdes. "Gender and the Global Economy." In *Instability and Change in the World Economy,* ed. Arthur MacEwan and William K. Tabb. New York: Monthly Review Press, 1989.

Bensman, David, and R. Lynch. *Rusted Dreams: Hard Times in a Steel Community.* New York: McGraw-Hill, 1987.

Berberoglu, Berch. *The Internationalization of Capital: Imperialism and Capitalist Development on a World Scale.* New York: Praeger Publishers, 1987.

———. *The Political Economy of Development.* Albany: State University of New York Press, 1992a.

———. *The Legacy of Empire: Economic Decline and Class Polarization in the United States.* New York: Praeger Publishers, 1992b.

———. *Class Structure and Social Transformation.* Westport, Conn.: Praeger Publishers, 1994.

Berman, Daniel M. *Death on the Job: Occupational Health and Safety Struggles in the United States.* New York: Monthly Review Press, 1978.

Bernardi, Gigi M., and Charles M. Geisler. *The Social Consequences and Challenges of New Agricultural Technologies.* Boulder, Colo.: Westview Press, 1984.

Bina, Cyrus, and Chuck Davis. "Wage Labor and Global Capital: Global Competition and the Universalization of the Labor Movement." In *Beyond Survival: Wage Labor in the Late Twentieth Century,* ed. Cyrus Bina et. al. Armonk, N.Y.: M. E. Sharpe, 1996.

———. "Globalization, Technology, and Skill Formation in Capitalism." In *Political Economy and Contemporary Capitalism: Radical Perspectives on Economic Theory and Policy,* ed. Ron Baiman et al. New York: M. E. Sharpe, 2000.

Bina, Cyrus, and Behzad Yaghmaian. "Post-War Global Accumulation and the Transnationalization of Capital." *Capital & Class,* no. 43 (Spring 1991).

Black, Stanley W., ed. *Globalization, Technological Change, and Labor Markets.* Boston: Kluwer, 1998.

Blau, Francine D. "Women in the Labor Force: An Overview." In *Women: A Feminist Perspective,* ed. Joe Freeman. Palo Alto, Calif.: Mayfield, 1984.

Bluestone, Barry, and Bennett Harrison. *The Deindustrialization of America.* New York: Basic Books, 1982.

Bonacich, Edna, et al., eds. *Global Production: The Apparel Industry in the Pacific Rim.* Philadelphia: Temple University Press, 1994.

Borrego, John, et al., eds. *Capital, the State, and Late Industrialization.* Boulder, Colo.: Westview Press, 1996.

Bowles, Gladys K. "The Current Situation of the Hired Farm Labor Force." In *Farm Labor in the United States,* ed. E. E. Bishop. New York: Columbia University Press, 1967.

Bowles, Samuel, and Richard Edwards. *Understanding Capitalism.* New York: Harper & Row, 1985.

Boyd, Monica. "Feminizing Paid Work." *Current Sociology* 45 (1997).
Boyer, Robert. *Labor Flexibility in Europe*. Oxford: Oxford University Press, 1987.
———. "Regulation." In *The New Palgrave: Marxian Economics,* ed. John Eatwell, Murray Milgate, and Peter Newman. London: Macmillan, 1990a.
———. *The Regulation School: A Critical Introduction*. New York: Columbia University Press, 1990b.
Braverman, Harry. *Labor and Monopoly Capital: The Degradation of Work in the Twentieth Century*. New York: Monthly Review Press, 1974.
Brecher, Jeremy. *Strike!* Greenwich, Conn.: Fawcet, 1972.
Brecher, Jeremy, and Tim Costello. *Global Village or Global Pillage: Economic Reconstruction from the Bottom Up*. Cambridge, Mass.: South End Press, 1998.
Brenner, Robert. "The Origins of Capitalist Development: A Critique of Neo-Smithian Marxism." *New Left Review*, no. 104 (July–August 1977).
Bridges, William P. "The Sexual Segregation of Occupations: Theories of Labor Stratification in Industry." *American Journal of Sociology,* 88 (1982).
Brogan, Timothy W. *Staffing Services Annual Update*. Alexandria, Va.: National Association of Temporary and Staffing Services, 1999.
Brown, Jonathan C., ed. *Workers' Control in Latin America, 1930–1979*. Chapel Hill: University of North Carolina Press, 1997.
Bryan, Dick. "The Internationalization of Capital and Marxian Value Theory." *Cambridge Journal of Economics* 19 (1995a).
———. *The Chase Across the Globe: International Accumulation and the Contradictions for Nation States*. Boulder, Colo.: Westview Press, 1995b.
Burawoy, Michael. 1979. "Toward a Marxist Theory of the Labor Process: Braverman and Beyond." *Politics and Society* 8, Nos. 3-4.
Burawoy, Michael. *Manufacturing Consent: Changes in the Labor Process under Monopoly Capitalism*. Chicago: University of Chicago Press, 1979.
———. "Between the Labor Process and the State: The Changing Face of Factory Regimes under Advanced Capitalism." *American Sociological Review* 48, no. 3. (1983).
Cappelli, Peter, ed. *Airline Labor Relations in the Global Era: The New Frontier*. Ithaca, N.Y.: ILR Press, 1995.
Chan, Sucheng. *This Bittersweet Soil: The Chinese in California Agriculture, 1860–1910*. Berkeley: University of California Press, 1989.
Charles, Ruth A. *Immigrant Women's Lives: Weaving Garment Work and Legislative Policy*. New York: Garland Publishing, 1999.
Clark, Charles S. "Contingent Work Force." *CQ Researcher* (24 October 1997).
Clark, Gordon L., and Won Bae Kim, eds. *Asian NIEs and the Global Economy: Industrial Restructuring and Corporate Strategy in the 1990s*. Baltimore: Johns Hopkins University Press, 1995.
Clawson, Dan. *Bureaucracy and the Labor Process*. New York: Monthly Review Press, 1980.
Clawson, Patrick. "The Internationalization of Capital and Capital Accumulation in Iran and Iraq." *The Insurgent Sociologist* 7, no. 2 (1977).
Clement, Andrew. "Office Automation and the Technical Control of Information Workers." In *The Political Economy of Information,* ed. Vincent Mosco and Janet Wasko. Madison: University of Wisconsin Press, 1988.

Cockcroft, James D. *Outlaws in the Promised Land: Mexican Immigrant Workers and America's Future.* New York: Grove Press, 1986.

Cohr, Sheila. "Us and Them: Business Unionism in America and Some Implications for the U.K." *Capital and Class,* no. 45 (Autumn 1991).

Collins, Susan M., ed. *Imports, Exports, and the American Worker.* Washington, D.C.: Brookings Institution Press, 1998.

Copley, Frank B. *Frederick W. Taylor: Father of Scientific Management.* 2 vols. New York: Harper and Brothers, 1923.

Coriat, B. "The Restructuring of the Assembly Line: A New Economy of Time and Control." *Capital and Class* 11 (1980).

Craypo, Charles, and Bruce Nissen, eds. *Grand Designs: The Impact of Corporate Strategies on Workers, Unions, and Communities.* Ithaca, N.Y.: ILR Press, 1993.

Cypher, James. "The Internationalization of Capital and the Transformation of Social Formations: A Critique of the Monthly Review School." *Review of Radical Political Economics* 11, no. 4 (1979).

Davis, Mike. *Prisoners of the American Dream: Politics and Economy in the History of the U.S. Working Class.* London: Verso, 1986.

De Vroey, Michel. "A Regulation Approach Interpretation of Contemporary Crisis." *Capital and Class* 23 (1984).

Dicken, Peter. *Global Shift: The Internationalization of Economic Activity.* New York: The Guilford Press, 1992.

Dixon, Marlene, et al. "Reindustrialization and the Transnational Labor Force in the United States Today." In *The New Nomads: From Immigrant Labor to Transnational Working Class,* ed. Marlene Dixon and Suzanne Jonas. San Francisco: Synthesis, 1982.

Dohse, K., U. Jurgens, and T. Malsch. "From Fordism to Toyotism? The Social Organization of the Labor Process in the Japanese Automobile Industry." *Politics and Society* 14, no. 2 (1985).

Dunne, John G. *Delano, the Story of the California Grape Strike.* New York: Farrar, Straus & Giroux, 1967.

Edwards, Richard. "Social Relations of Production at the Point of Production." *Insurgent Sociologist* 8, nos. 2–3 (1978).

———. *Contested Terrain: The Transformation of the Workplace in the Twentieth Century.* New York: Basic Books, 1979.

Edwards, Richard, et al. *Labor Market Segmentation.* New York: D. C. Heath, 1975.

Elger, Tony. "Braverman, Capital Accumulation and Deskilling." In *The Degradation of Work?* ed. Stephen Wood. London: Hutchinson, 1982.

Elison, Diane, and Ruth Pearson. "Nimble Fingers Make Cheap Workers: An Analysis of Workers in Employment in Third World Export Processing." *Feminist Review* 33 (1981).

Eviota, Elizabeth U. *The Political Economy of Gender: Women and the Sexual Division of Labour in the Philippines.* London: Zed Books, 1992.

Forman, Michael. *Nationalism and the International Labor Movement: The Idea of the Nation in Socialist and Anarchist Theory.* University Park: Pennsylvania State University Press, 1998.

Fantasia, Rick. *Cultures of Solidarity: Consciousness, Action, and Contemporary American Workers.* Berkeley: University of California Press, 1988.

Ford, Henry. *My Life and My Work.* London: Heinemann, 1923.

Foster, John. *Class Struggle and the Industrial Revolution*. New York: St. Martin's Press, 1974.

Foster, John Bellamy, and Henryk Szlajfer, eds. *The Faltering Economy: The Problem of Accumulation under Monopoly Capitalism*. New York: Monthly Review Press, 1984.

Foster, J., and C. Woolfson. "Post-Fordism and Business Unionism." *New Left Review*, no. 174 (1989).

Friedland, William, and Dorothy Nelkin. *Migrant Workers in America's Northeast*. New York: Holt, Rinehart and Winston, 1971.

Friedland, William, Amy Barton, and Robert Thomas. *Manufacturing Green Gold: Capital, Labor, and Technology in the Lettuce Industry*. Cambridge: Cambridge University Press, 1981.

Freidman, Andrew L. *Industry and Labor: Class Struggle at Work and Monopoly Capitalism*. London: Macmillan, 1977.

Frobel, Folker, Jurgen Heinrichs, and Otto Kreye. *The New International Division of Labor*. Cambridge: Cambridge University Press, 1980.

Fuentes, Annette, and Barbara Ehrenreich. *Women in the Global Factory*. Boston: South End Press, 1983.

———. "New Factory Girls." *Multinational Monitor* 4, no. 8 (1983).

Garlarza, Ernesto. *Merchants of Labor: The Mexican Bracero Story, an Account of the Managed Migration of Mexican Farm Workers in California*. Santa Barbara, Calif.: McNally and Lofton, 1964.

Garson, Barbara. *All the Livelong Day: The Meaning and Demeaning of Routine Work*. New York: Doubleday, 1975.

Gartman, David. "Basic and Surplus Control in Capitalist Machinery." *Research in Political Economy* 5 (1982).

———. *Auto Slavery: The Labor Process in the American Automobile Industry*. New Brunswick, N.J.: Rutgers University Press, 1986.

Georgakas, Dan, and Marvin Surkin. *Detroit: I Do Mind Dying*. New York: St. Martin's Press, 1975.

Geschwender, James. *Class, Race, and Worker Insurgency*. Cambridge: Cambridge University Press, 1977.

Ginzberg, Eli. *The Changing U.S. Labor Market*. Boulder, Colo.: Westview Press, 1994.

Glenn, Evelyn Nakano, and Roslyn L. Feldberg. "Degraded and Deskilled: The Prolatarianization of Clerical Work." *Social Problems* 25 (1977).

Gordon, David, R. Edwards, and M. Reich. *Segmented Work, Divided Workers*. Cambridge: Cambridge University Press, 1982.

Green, J. *The World of the Worker: Labor in Twentieth Century America*. New York: Hill and Wang, 1980.

Greenaway, David. "Trade Related Investment Measures and Development Strategies." *Kyklos* 45 (1992).

Gregory, James. *American Exodus: The Dust Bowl Migrations and Okie Culture in California*. New York: Oxford University Press, 1989.

Guarasci, R., and G. Peck. "Work, Class, and Society: Recent Developments and New Directions in Labor Process Theory." *Review of Radical Political Economics* (1987).

Gutman, Herbert. *Work, Culture, and Society in Industrializing America*. New York: Alfred A. Knopf, 1976.

Hakken, David. "Studying New Technology after Braverman: An Anthropological Review." *Anthropology of Work Newsletter* 1, no. 1 (1988).

Halperin, Martin. *UAW Politics in the Cold War Era.* Albany: State University of New York Press, 1988.

Hartman, Heidi. "Capitalism, Patriarchy and Job Segregation by Sex." *Signs* 1 (1976).

Harvey, David. *The Condition of Postmodernity.* Cambridge: Blackwell, 1991.

Hayes, Dennis. *Behind the Silicon Curtain.* Boston: South End Press, 1989.

Heckscher, C. "Worker Participation and Management Control." *Journal of Social Reconstruction* 3, no. 1 (1980).

Helleiner, Gerald K. *Trade Policy and Industrialization in Turbulent Times.* London: Routledge, 1994.

Helleiner, G. K., and R. Lavergne. "Intra-Firm Trade and the Industrial Exports of the United States." *Oxford Bulletin of Economics and Statistics* 41 (1979).

Henson, Kevin D. *Just a Temp.* Philadelphia, Pa.: Temple University Press, 1996.

Herman, A. "Conceptualizing Control: Domination and Hegemony in the Capitalist Labor Process." *The Insurgent Sociologist* 11, no. 3 (1982).

Hesse-Biber, Sharlene, and Gregg Lee Carter. *Working Women in America. Split Dreams.* New York: Oxford University Press, 2000.

Hill, Stephen. *Competition and Control at Work: The New Industrial Sociology.* Cambridge, Mass.: MIT Press, 1981.

Hipple, Steven. "Contingent Work: Results from the Second Survey." *Monthly Labor Review* (November 1998): 22–35.

Hodson, Randy, and Teresa A. Sullivan. *The Social Organization of Work,* 2nd ed. Belmont, Calif.: Wadsworth Publishing Company, 1995.

Holloway, John. "Transnational Capital and the National State." *Capital and Class* 52 (1994).

Holloway, John, and Sol Picciotto. "Introduction: Towards a Materialist Theory of the State." In *State and Capital: A Marxist Debate,* ed. John Holloway and Sol Picciotto. London: Edward Arnold, 1977.

Hossfeld, Karen J. "'Their Logic Against Them': Contradictions in Sex, Race, and Class in Silicon Valley." In *Women Workers and Global Restructuring,* ed. Kathryn Ward. Ithaca, N.Y.: Cornell University Press, 1990.

Howe, Carolyn. "The Politics of Class Compromise in an International Context: Considerations for a New Strategy for Labor." *Review of Radical Political Economics* 18, no. 3 (1986).

Hudson, Yeager, ed. *Globalism and the Obsolescence of the State.* Lewiston, N.Y.: Edwin Mellen Press, 1999.

Hunnius, Gerry, et al., eds. *Workers' Control: A Reader on Labor and Social Change.* New York: Vintage Books, 1973.

Jacobs, Jerry, and Sue T. Lin. "Trends in Occupational and Industrial Sex Segregation in 56 Countries, 1960–1980." in *Gender Inequality at Work,* ed. J. A. Jacobs. Thousand Oaks, Calif.: Sage, 1995.

Jacoby, Sanford M. *The Workers of Nations: Industrial Relations in a Global Economy.* New York: Oxford University Press, 1995.

Jenkins, Rhys. *Transnational Corporations and Uneven Development.* New York: Methuen, 1987.

Jessop, Bob. "Neo-Conservative Regimes and the Transition to Post-Fordism: The Case of Great Britain and West Germany." In *Modern Capitalism and Spatial*

Development: Accumulation, Regulation, and Crisis Theory, ed. M. Gottdiener. New York: St. Martin's Press, 1988.

——. "Regulation Theory, Post-Fordism and the State: More than a Reply to Werner Bonefeld." In *Post-Fordism and Social Form: A Marxist Debate on the Post-Fordist State,* ed. Werner Bonefeld and John Holloway, London: Macmillan, 1991.

——. "Post-Fordism and the State." In *Post-Fordism: A Reader,* ed. Ash Amin, Oxford: Backwell, 1994.

Johnson, Barbara. *Working Whenever You Want.* Upper Saddle River, N.J.: Prentice Hall, 1983.

Julius, DeAnne. *Global Companies and Public Policy: The Growing Challenge of Foreign Direct Investment.* London: Pinter, 1990.

Kahne, Hilda. *Reconceiving Part-Time Work: New Perspectives for Older Workers and Women.* Atlantic Highlands, N.J.: Rowman & Littlefield, 1985.

Kalleberg, Arne L., and Ivar Berg. *Work and Industry: Structures, Markets and Processes.* New York: Plenum Press, 1987.

Kalleberg, Arne L., et al. *Nonstandard Work, Substandard Jobs.* Washington, D.C.: Economic Policy Institute, 1997.

Kanter, Rosabeth Moss. *Men and Women of the Corporation.* New York: Basic Books, 1977.

Kapstein, Ethan B. *Sharing the Wealth: Workers and the World Economy.* New York: W. W. Norton, 1999.

Katz, Harry C. *Shifting Gears: Changing Labor Relations in the U.S. Automobile Industry.* Cambridge, Mass.: MIT Press, 1985.

Katz-Fishman, Walda, et al. "African American Politics in an Era of Capitalist Economic Contraction." In *From Exclusion to Inclusion,* ed. R. Gomes and L. Williams, New York: Greenwood Press, 1992.

Keeran, Roger. *The Communist Party and the Auto Workers' Unions.* Bloomington, Ind.: Indiana University Press, 1980.

Keller, John. *Power in America: The Southern Question and the Control of Labor.* Chicago: Vanguard Press, 1983.

Kennedy, Martin, and Richard Florida. "Beyond Mass Production: Production and the Labor Process in Japan." *Politics and Society* 16 (1988).

Kim, Sueng-Kyung. *Class Struggle or Family Struggle?: The Lives of Women Factory Workers in South Korea.* Cambridge: Cambridge University Press, 1997.

Kimeldorf, Howard. *Reds or Rackets? The Making of Radical and Conservative Unions on the Waterfront.* Berkeley: University of California Press, 1988.

Kitano, Harry, and Roger Daniels. *Asian Americans: Emerging Minorities.* Upper Saddle River, N.J.: Prentice Hall, 1988.

Krugman, Paul. *Geography and Trade.* Cambridge: MIT Press, 1991.

Leggett, John C. *Mining the Fields: Farm Workers Fight Back.* Highland Park, N.J.: The Raritan Institute, 1991.

Lembcke, Jerry, and W. Tattam. *One Union in Wood: A Political History of the International Woodworkers of America.* New York: International Publishers, 1984.

Lembcke, Jerry. *Capitalist Development and Class Capacities: Marxist Theory and Union Organization.* Westport, Conn.: Greenwood Press, 1988.

Levenstein, Harvey. *Communism, Anticommunism, and the CIO.* Westport, Conn.: Greenwood Press, 1981.

Levine, Marvin J. *Worker Rights and Labor Standards in Asia's Four New Tigers: A Comparative Perspective.* New York: Plenum Press, 1997.

Levine, Rhonda. *Class Struggle and the New Deal: Industrial Labor, Industrial Capital, and the State.* Lawrence: University Press of Kansas, 1988.

Lingenfelter, Richard E. *The Hardrock Miners: A History of the Mining Labor Movement in the American West, 1863–1893.* Berkeley: University of California Press, 1974.

Lipietz, Alain. "Towards Global Fordism." *New Left Review,* no. 132 (1982).

———. "New Tendencies in International Division of Labor: Regime of Accumulation and Mode of Regulation." In *Production, Work, Territory: The Geographical Anatomy of Industrial Capitalism,* ed. A. Scott and M. Stroper, London: Allen & Unwin, 1986a.

———. "Beyond the Crisis: The Exhaustion of the Regime of Accumulation. A 'Regulation School' Perspective on Some French Empirical Works." *Review of Radical Political Economics* 18, nos. 1 and 2 (1986b).

———. *Mirage and Miracles: The Crisis of Global Fordism.* London: Verso, 1987.

———. "Post-Fordism and Democracy." In *Post-Fordism: A Reader,* ed. Ash Amin, Oxford: Blackwell, 1994.

Littler, Craig R. *The Development of the Labour Process in Capitalist Societies.* London: Heinemann Educational, 1982.

Lynd, Alice, and Staughton Lynd. *Rank and File.* Boston: Beacon Press, 1973.

Lynd, Staughton. "Workers' Control in a Time of Diminished Workers' Rights." *Radical America* 10, no. 5 (September–October 1976).

MacEwan, Arthur, and Bill Tabb, eds. *Instability and Change in the World Economy.* New York: Monthly Review Press, 1989.

Mandel, Ernest. *Late Capitalism.* London: Verso, 1975.

Marglin, Stephen. "What Do Bosses Do? The Origins and Functions of Hierarchy in Capitalist Production." *Review of Radical Political Economics* 6 (Summer 1974).

Marx, Karl. *Capital.* 3 vols. New York: International Publishers, 1967.

———. *Grundrisse.* New York: Vintage, 1973.

———. "Trades' Unions, Their Past, Present and Future." In *Theories of the Labor Movement,* ed. Simeon Larson and Bruce Nissen. Detroit, Mich.: Wayne State University Press, 1987.

McCulloch, R. "Investment Policies in GATT." *The World Economy* 13, no. 4 (1990).

McGuire, Gart M., and Barbara Reskin. "Authority Hierarchy at Work: The Impact of Race and Sex." *Gender and Society* 7 (1993).

McMichael, Philip, and David Myhre. "Global Regulation vs. the Nation State: Agro-Food Systems and the New Politics of Capital." *Review of Radical Political Economic* 22, no. 1 (1990).

McNally, David. "Beyond Nationalism, beyond Protectionism: Labor and the Canada–U.S. Free Trade Agreement." *Capital and Class,* no. 43 (Spring 1991).

———. "Globalization on Trial: Crisis and Class Struggle in East Asia." In *Rising from the Ashes? Labor in the Age of "Global" Capitalism,* ed. Ellen Meiksins Wood et al. New York: Monthly Review Press, 1988.

McWilliams, Carey. *Factories in the Field.* Santa Barbara, Calif., and Salt Lake City, Utah: Peregrine Publishers, 1971.

Meier, August, and Elliot Rudwick. *Black Detroit and the Rise of the UAW.* New York: Oxford University Press, 1979.

Meiksins Wood, Ellen, et al., eds. *Rising from the Ashes? Labor in the Age of "Global" Capitalism.* New York: Monthly Review Press, 1998.

Meyer III, Stephen. *The Five Dollar Day: Labor Management and Social Control in the Ford Motor Company, 1908–1921.* Albany: State University of New York Press, 1981.

Miles, Marina. *Patriarchy and Accumulation on a World Scale: Women in the International Division of Labor.* London: Zed Books, 1990.

Milkman, Ruth. *Gender at Work.* Urbana: University of Illinois Press, 1987.

——. *Farewell to the Factory: Auto Workers in the Late Twentieth Century.* Berkeley: University of California Press, 1997.

Mines, Richard, and Philip L. Martin. *A Profile of California Farm Workers.* Berkeley, Calif.: The Giannini Foundation of Agricultural Economics, University of California, Berkeley, 1986.

Mins, L. E. *Founding of the First International: A Documentary Record.* New York: International Publishers, 1937.

Montgomery, David. "Workers' Control of Machine Production in the Nineteenth Century." *Labor History* 17, no. 4 (1976).

Moody, Kim. *An Injury to All: The Decline of American Unionism.* London: Verso, 1988.

——. *Workers in a Lean World: Unions in the International Economy.* London: Verso, 1997.

Moore, Truman. *The Slaves We Rent.* New York: Random House, 1965.

——. *Workers' Control in America.* Cambridge: Cambridge University Press, 1979.

——. *The Fall of the House of Labor.* Cambridge: Cambridge University Press, 1987.

Murray, Robin. "The Internationalization of Capital and the Nation State." *New Left Review* 67 (May–June 1971).

Nash, June. "The Impact of the Changing International Division of Labor on Different Sectors of the Labor Force." In *Women, Men, and the International Division of Labor,* ed. June Nash and Maria Patricia Fernandez-Kelly. Albany: State University of New York, 1983.

Nelkin, Dorothy. *On the Season: Aspects of the Migrant Labor System.* Ithaca, N.Y.: New York School of Industrial and Labor Relations, 1970.

Nevins, Allan, and Frank Hill. *Ford: The Times, the Man, the Company.* New York: Scribner's, 1954.

Nichols, Theo, and Huw Beynon. *Living with Capitalism: Class Relations and the Modern Factory.* London: Routledge and Kegan Paul, 1977.

Nissen, Bruce, ed. *Which Direction for Organized Labor? Essays on Organizing, Outreach, and Internal Transformations.* Detroit: Wayne State University Press, 1999.

Noble, David F. *Forces of Production: A Social History of Industrial Automation.* New York: Oxford University Press, 1984.

O'Connor, James. "Productive vs. Unproductive Labor." *Politics and Society* 5, no. 3 (1975).

Padfield, Harland, and William E. Martin. *Farmers, Workers and Machines.* Tucson, Ariz.: University of Arizona Press, 1965.

Palmer, Brian. "Class, Conception and Conflict: The Thrust for Efficiency, Managerial Views of Labor and the Working Class Rebellion, 1903–22." *Review of Radical Political Economics* 7, no. 2 (1975.)

Parker, Robert E. *Flesh Peddlers and Warm Bodies: The Temporary Help Industry and Its Workers.* New Brunswick, N.J.: Rutgers University Press, 1994.

Parker, Mike. "Industrial Relations Myth and Shop-Floor Reality: The 'Team Concept' in the Auto Industry." In *Industrial Democracy in America,* ed. Nelson Lichtenstein and Howell John Harris. New York: Cambridge University Press, 1993.

Paus, Eva. "Economic Growth through Neoliberal Restructuring? Insights from the Chilean Experience." *The Journal of Developing Areas* 28 (1994).

Peet, Richard, ed. *International Capitalism and Industrial Restructuring.* Boston: Allen & Unwin, 1987.

Perelman, Michael. *Class Warfare in the Information Age.* New York: St. Martin's Press, 1998.

Peterson, Joyce Shaw. *American Automobile Workers, 1900–1933.* Albany: State University of New York Press, 1987.

Pfeffer, Richard M. *Working for Capitalism.* New York: Columbia University Press, 1979.

Phillips, Brian. *Global Production and Domestic Decay: Plant Closings in the U.S.* New York: Garland Publishing, 1998.

Picciotto, Sol. "The Internationalization of the State." *Review of Radical Political Economics* 22, no. 1 (1990).

Piven, Frances Fox, and Richard Cloward. *The New Class War.* New York: Pantheon Books, 1982.

Polloix, Christian. "The Internationalization of Capital and the Circuit of Social Capital." In *International Firms and Modern Imperialism,* ed. Hugo Radice. Harmondsworth: Penguin, 1975.

———. "The Self-Expansion of Capital on a World Scale." *Review of Radical Political Economics* 9 (1977).

Prechel, Harland. "Steel and the State: Industry Politics and Business Policy Formation, 1940–1989." *American Sociological Review* 55, no. 5 (October 1990).

Rasell, Edie, and Eileen Appelbaum. "Nonstandard Work Arrangements: A Challenge for Workers and Labor Unions." *Social Policy* 28, no. 2 (1997).

Remy, Dorothy, and Larry Sawers. "Women's Power in the Workplace." In *Social Power and Influence of Women,* ed. Liesa Stamm and Carol D. Ryff. Boulder, Colo.: Westview Press, 1984.

Reskin, Barbara. "Sex Segregation in the Workplace." *Annual Review of Sociology* 19 (1993).

Rifkin, Jeremy. *The End of Work.* New York: G. P. Putman's Sons, 1995.

Roman, Richard, and Edur Velasco Arregui. "Worker Insurgency, Rural Revolt, and the Crisis of the Mexican Regime." In *Rising from the Ashes? Labor in the Age of "Global" Capitalism,* ed. Ellen Meiksins Wood et al. New York: Monthly Review Press, 1988.

Roobeek, Annemieke. "The Crisis of Fordism and the Rise of a New Technological Paradigm." *Futures* 19 (April 1987).

Roos, Patricia. "Sexual Stratification in the Workplace: Male-Female Differences in Economic Returns to Occupation." *Social Science Research* 10 (1981).

Ross, Robert, and Kent C. Trachte. *Global Capitalism: The New Leviathan.* Albany: State University of New York Press, 1990.

Ruccio, David. "Fordism on a World Scale: The International Dimension of Regulation." *Review of Radical Political Economics* 21, no. 4 (1989).

Sabel, Charles. *Work and Politics: The Division of Labor in Industry.* Cambridge: Cambridge University Press, 1982.

Safa, Helen I. "Runaway Shops and Female Employment: The Search for Cheap Labor." In *Women's Work,* ed. Eleanor Leacock and Helen I. Safa. South Headley, Mass.: Bergin and Garvey, 1986.

Sattel, Jack. "The Degradation of Labor in the 20th Century: Harry Braverman's Sociology of Work." *The Insurgent Sociologist* 8, no. 1 (1978).

Sayer, A. "New Developments in Manufacturing: The Just in Time System." *Capital and Class* 30 (1985).

Scott, Jack. *Yankee Unions, Go Home! How the AFL Helped the U.S. Build an Empire in Latin America.* Vancouver: New Star Books, 1978.

Shaiken, Harley. *Work Transformed: Automation and Labor in the Computer Age.* Lexington, Mass.: Lexington Books, 1986.

Sheinkman, Jack. "Worker Rights in Central America." Preface to *Worker Rights in the New World Order.* New York: The National Labor Committee in Support of Democracy and Human Rights in El Salvador, 1991.

Sirianni, C. *Workers' Control and Socialist Democracy: The Soviet Experience.* London: Verso Books, 1982.

Sklair, Leslie. *Assembly for Development: The Maquila Industry in Mexico and the United States.* Boston: Unwin Hyman, 1989.

——. *Sociology of the Global System.* Baltimore: The Johns Hopkins University Press, 1991.

Smith, Tony. "Flexible Production and the Capital/Wage Labor Relation in Manufacturing." *Capital and Class* 53 (1994).

Snow, Robert T. "The New International Division of Labor and the U.S. Work Force: The Case of the Electronics Industry." In *Women, Men and the International Division of Labor,* ed. June Nash and Maria Patricia Fernandez-Kelly. Albany: State University of New York Press, 1983.

Stalker, Peter. *Workers without Frontiers: The Impact of Globalization on International Migration.* Boulder, Colo.: Lynne Rienner Publishers, 2000.

Stein, Walter J. *California and the Dust Bowl Migration.* Westport, Conn.: Greenwood Press, 1973.

Stone, Katherine. "The Origins of Job Structures in the Steel Industry." *Review of Radical Political Economics* 6, no. 2 (1974).

Storper, Michael, and R. Walker. *The Capitalist Imperative: Territory, Technology, and Industrial Growth.* New York: Basil Blackwell, 1989.

Sullivan, Teresa. *Marginal Workers, Marginal Jobs.* Austin: University of Texas Press, 1979.

Sweezy, Paul M. *The Theory of Capitalist Development.* New York: Monthly Review Press, 1942.

Szymanski, Albert. "Braverman as a Neo-Luddite?" *Insurgent Sociologist* 8, no. 1 (Winter 1978).

——. *Class Structure.* New York: Praeger, 1983.

Tabb, William K. "Capital Mobility: The Restructuring of Production, and the Politics of Labor." In *Instability and Change in the World Economy,* ed. Arthur MacEwan and William K. Tabb. New York: Monthly Review Press, 1989.

Taylor, Frederick Winslow. *Scientific Management.* New York: Harper, 1947.

Terkel, Studs. *Working*. New York: Random House, 1972.

Theriault, Reg. *How to Tell when You're Tired: A Brief Examination of Work*. New York: W. W. Norton, 1995.

Thomas, Robert J. "The Social Organization of Industrial Agriculture." *The Insurgent Sociologist* (Winter 1981).

———. "Citizenship and Gender in Work Organization: Some Considerations for Theories of the Labor Process." *American Journal of Sociology* (Supplement) 88 (1982).

Thompson, E. P. *The Making of the English Working Class*. New York: Pantheon, 1963.

———. "Time, Work Discipline, and Industrial Capitalism." *Past and Present* 38 (1967).

Tillman, Ray M., and Michael S. Cummings, eds. *The Transformation of U.S. Unions: Voices, Visions, and Strategies from the Grassroots*. Boulder, Colo.: Lynne Rienner Publishers, 1999.

Tilly, Chris. *Half a Job*. Philadelphia, Pa.: Temple University Press, 1996.

Twiss, Brian C., ed. *The Managerial Implication of Microelectronics*. London: Macmillan, 1981.

Visvanathan, Nalini, et al., eds. *The Women, Gender, and Development Reader*. London: Zed Books, 1997.

Waas, Michael Van. "Multinational Corporations and the Politics of Labor Supply." *The Insurgent Sociologist* 11, no. 3 (1982).

Wachtel, Howard M. *The Money Mandarins: The Making of a Supranational Economic Order*. New York: Pantheon Books, 1986.

Ward, Kathryn, ed. *Women Workers and Global Restructuring*. Ithaca, N.Y.: Cornell University Press, 1990.

Warren, Bill. "The Internationalization of Capital and the Nation State: A Comment." *New Left Review*, no. 68 (July–August 1971).

———. "Imperialism and Capitalist Industrialization." *New Left Review*, no. 81 (September–October 1973).

———. *Imperialism: Pioneer of Capitalism*. London: Verso, 1980.

Wasser, Steven A. "Economics of the Temporary Help Services Industry." *Contemporary Times* 3, no. 9 (1984).

Waterman, Peter. *Globalization, Social Movements, and the New Internationalisms*. London: Mansell, 1998.

Webber, Michael John. *The Golden Age Illusion: Rethinking Postwar Capitalism*. New York: Guilford Press, 1996.

Weeks, John. "Epochs of Capitalism and the Progressiveness of Capital's Expansion." *Science and Society* 49, no. 4 (1985).

Wells, Miriam J. *Strawberry Fields: Politics, Class, and Work in California Agriculture*. Ithaca, N.Y.: Cornell University Press, 1996.

Western, Bruce. *Between Class and Market: Postwar Unionization in the Capitalist Democracies*. Princeton, N.J.: Princeton University Press, 1997.

Wilk, V., and D. M. Hancock. "Farmworker Occupational Health and Safety in the 1990s." *New Solutions* 1 (Spring 1991).

Wilkinson, Alec. *Big Sugar: Seasons in the Cane Fields of Florida*. New York: Vintage Books, 1989.

Willoughby, John. *Capitalist Imperialism, Crisis and State.* New York: Harwood Press, 1986.

———. "The Promise and Pitfalls of Protectionist Politics." In *The Imperiled Economy,* book 1, ed. Robert Cherry et al., New York: Union for Radical Political Economics, 1987.

Wolf, Wendy C., and Neil D. Fligstein. "Sex and Authority in the Work Place: The Causes of Sexual Inequality." *American Sociological Review* 44 (1979).

Wood, Stephen, ed. *The Degradation of Work? Skill, Deskilling, and the Labor Process.* London: Hutchinson and Company, 1982.

———. *The Transformation of Work?* London: Unwin Hyman, 1989.

Wright, Dale. *They Harvest Despair: The Migrant Farm Workers.* Boston: Beacon Press, 1965.

Yaghmaian, Behzad. "Development Theories and Development Strategies: An Alternative Theoretical Framework." *Review of Radical Political Economics* 22, nos. 2–3 (1990).

Zimbalist, Andrew. "The Limits of Work Humanization." *Review of Radical Political Economics* 7, no. 2 (1975).

———. *Case Studies on the Labor Process.* New York: Monthly Review Press, 1979.

Zupnick, Elliot. *Visions and Revisions: The United States in the Global Economy.* Boulder, Colo.: Westview Press, 1999.

Index

About the Contributors

Marina A. Adler is associate professor of sociology at the University of Maryland, Baltimore County. She received her Ph.D. from the University of Maryland, College Park, in 1990. She has published articles in *The Sociological Quarterly, Critical Sociology,* and *Journal of Marriage and the Family.* Her areas of specialization include gender, race, and class inequality, the welfare state and social policy, and work and family issues. She is a member of Sociologists for Women in Society (SWS).

Cyrus Bina is associate professor of economics and management at the University of Minnesota, Morris Campus. He received his Ph.D. in economics from The American University in 1982. He is the author and editor of several books, including *The Economics of the Oil Crisis* and *Beyond Survival: Wage Labor in the Late Twentieth Century,* as well as many articles on globalization, technology, and skill formation in advanced capitalist society. He has served as editor of the *Journal of Economic Democracy* and the *Review of Radical Political Economics.*

Chuck Davis is director of labor relations for the Minnesota Nurses Association. He received his Ph.D. in economics from The American University in Washington, D.C., in 1986. He is co-editor of *Beyond Survival: Wage Labor in the Late Twentieth Century.* His areas of specialization include labor studies, the labor process and globalization, and collective bargaining in the United States. He is former vice president of the University and College Labor Education Association and is currently a member of Workers' Education Local #189, CWA.

Julia D. Fox is assistant professor of sociology at Marshall University in Huntington, W.Va. She received her Ph.D. from the University of Oregon in 1993. She is the author of a number of articles on transnational corporations, university–corporate connections, and corporate greenwashing and the environmental movement. Her areas of research interest include comparative political economy, class analysis, and labor, with a focus on women workers in the global economy.

David Gartman is professor of sociology at the University of South Alabama. He received his Ph.D. from the University of California at San Diego in 1980. He is the author of *Auto Slavery: The Labor Process in the American Automobile Industry* and *Auto Opium: A Social History of American Automobile Design*. He is working on a book on the influence of auto design on modern and postmodern architecture.

Walda Katz-Fishman is professor of sociology at Howard University. She received her Ph.D. from Wayne State University in Detroit in 1978. She is a past president of the Association for Humanist Sociology, and past editor of *Humanity & Society*. She has published numerous articles in *Humanity & Society, Sociological Forum, Critical Sociology*, and other journals. Her areas of specialization include social theory and race, class, and gender inequality.

John C. Leggett is professor of sociology at Rutgers University. He received his Ph.D. from the University of Michigan in 1962. He is the author and editor of numerous books and articles, including *Class, Race, and Labor; Race, Class, and Political Consciousness; Taking State Power; Mining the Fields: Farm Workers Fight Back;* and *The American Working Class*. He is one of the founders of Students for a Democratic Society and UC Berkeley's Free Speech Movement.

Jerry Lembcke is associate professor of sociology at Holy Cross College in Worcester, Massachusetts. He received his Ph.D. from the University of Oregon in 1978. He is the author of several books, including *One Union in Wood* and *Capitalist Development and Class Capacities*, and numerous articles on labor and class analysis. His areas of interest include political economy, class structure, labor studies, and other related fields.

Ife Modupe is a Ph.D. candidate in sociology at Howard University in Washington, D.C. She received her master's degree in sociology from the University of Toledo in 1995. Her areas of research interest include race, class, and gender relations and urban sociology. Her research work centers on the shifting role of black women's labor in the process of production.

Robert E. Parker is associate professor of sociology at the University of Nevada, Las Vegas. He received his Ph.D. in sociology from the University of Texas at Austin in 1986. He is the author of *Flesh Peddlers and Warm Bodies: The Temporary Help Industry and Its Workers* and co-author (with Joe R. Feagin) of *Building American Cities*, as well as the author of numerous articles and chapters in urban sociology, the sociology of work, and race relations.

Harland Prechel is associate professor of sociology at Texas A&M University. He is the author of *Big Business and the State: Historical Transitions and Corporate Transformation, 1880s–1990s* and *Corporate and Class Restructuring* (forthcoming), and has published numerous articles in scholarly journals. In addition to his research on corporate restructuring and corporate political behavior, he has conducted research on inequality in the global economy in the 1990s.

Jerome Scott is director of Project South in Atlanta, Georgia. He is a labor and community organizer and educator, and was a founding member of the League of Revolutionary Black Workers in Detroit in the late 1960s. He has contributed articles to *Race, Class, and Urban Change, Sociological Forum, Humanity & Society*, and other publications. He is affiliated with several nonprofit grassroots organizations in the South.

Behzad Yaghmaian is professor of economics at Ramapo College of New Jersey. He received his Ph.D. in economics from Fordham University in 1985. He has published articles in *Science and Society, The International Journal of Applied Economics, World Development*, and other journals. His areas of research interest include international political economy, globalization, Third World development, and the political economy of the World Bank, the IMF, and other international financial institutions.

About the Editor

Berch Berberoglu is professor of sociology and director of the Institute for International Studies at the University of Nevada, Reno, where he has taught for the past twenty-four years. He received his Ph.D. from the University of Oregon in 1977. He is the author and editor of eighteen books, including *The Internationalization of Capital: Imperialism and Capitalist Development on a World Scale; The Political Economy of Development; The Legacy of Empire: Economic Decline and Class Polarization in the United States;* and *Class Structure and Social Transformation,* as well as many articles published in various professional journals. His areas of research and scholarly interest include international political economy, labor studies, class analysis, the state, social movements, and revolution.

331
Lab

Labor and capital in
the age of
globalization.

DATE			
10/17/05			

BAKER & TAYLOR